How You Can Preach Salvation

DAG HEWARD-MILLS

Parchment House

Unless otherwise stated, all Scripture quotations are taken from the King James Version of the Bible.

HOW YOU CAN PREACH SALVATION

First Edition published 2017 by Parchment House
2nd Printing 2018

Find out more about Dag Heward-Mills at:

ᵣHealing Jesus Campaign
Email: evangelist@daghewardmills.org
Website: www.daghewardmills.org
Facebook: Dag Heward-Mills
Twitter: @EvangelistDag

ISBN: 978-1-68398-195-4

Contents

SECTION 1: THE PURE MESSAGE OF SALVATION

SECTION 2: SALVATION AND THE LOVE OF GOD

SECTION 3: SALVATION AND THE BLOOD OF JESUS

SECTION 4: SALVATION, JUDGMENT AND HELL

SECTION 5: SALVATION AND VARIOUS INDIVIDUALS

SECTION 6: SALVATION AND THE GREAT INVITATION

SECTION 7: SALVATION AND CHOICES

SECTION 8: SALVATION AND THE NEW LIFE

SECTION 9: SALVATION AND JESUS CHRIST

SECTION 13: SALVATION FROM THE OLD TESTAMENT

SECTION 1:

THE PURE MESSAGE OF SALVATION

SECTION 1:

The Pure Message of Salvation

Receiving the end of your faith, even THE SALVATION OF YOUR SOULS. OF WHICH SALVATION THE PROPHETS HAVE ENQUIRED and searched diligently, who prophesied of the grace that should come unto you: searching what, or what manner of time the Spirit of Christ which was in them did signify, when it testified beforehand the sufferings of Christ, and the glory that should follow.

1 Peter 1:9-11

Did you know that the prophets of old inquired and searched to find out more about this *great salvation* that was to be revealed to mankind? No one could fathom the depth of God's love and kindness towards His creation. No one knew how this salvation would come to men. Peter described it this way, "Of which salvation the prophets have enquired and searched diligently, who prophesied of the grace *that should come* unto you: searching what, or what manner of time the Spirit of Christ which was in them did signify, when it testified beforehand the sufferings of Christ, and the glory that should follow" (1 Peter 1:10-11).

1

If the prophets of old searched out to discover and understand our wonderful salvation, should the study of our salvation not be a major topic of our own journey?

Salvation is a miracle!

Salvation is the greatest transformative miracle of the Holy Spirit!

Salvation is the mighty Hand of God at work!

Salvation is the unbelievable mercy of God in action!

Demons cannot believe the salvation available to human beings. Satan is filled with even more anger and hatred when people are saved from his captivity and domination. Satan is filled with wicked jealousy when he sees that human beings are saved from hell.

How shall we escape, if we neglect so GREAT SALVATION; which at the first began to be spoken by the Lord, and was confirmed unto us by them that heard him;

Hebrews 2:3

It is this "great salvation" that I am seeking to share about in this book. This book will help anyone who wants to understand our great salvation and share the gospel of Jesus Christ. It will help evangelists to learn many different ways to preach the gospel of salvation. It will help crusaders to fearlessly preach the power-packed gospel of salvation.

I have been accused of preaching "basics". To describe the preaching of the "great salvation" in a derogatory way is to reveal the unfortunate and embarrassing confusion that is in your soul. To imply that someone preaches "great salvation" because he does not have revelation of the Holy Spirit is to reveal that you are spiritually empty! We are not called to preach new, current and modern messages, but to preach the Word of God. What is

2

more current, what is more relevant and what is more important than the "great salvation" that Jesus purchased for us with His blood?

Christians do not understand our "great salvation" because they are not taught pure salvation teachings. Pastors cannot preach the gospel because they lack the ability to expound on the profound statements of Jesus Christ. How many pastors can speak for one hour on a profound statement like, *"Come unto me all ye that labour and are heavy laden and I will give you rest"?*

Teaching the Word of God in church is quite different from preaching the pure message of our "great salvation". Many Christians understand the principles of prosperity much more than they understand the principles of salvation. Many believers are good at preaching the principles of prosperity but not so many can preach about *"pure salvation"*.

It is my prayer that through this book you will understand our "great salvation" better and become an effective salvation gospel preacher both in the church and outside the church.

Are you faithful with the glorious gospel?

According to THE GLORIOUS GOSPEL of the blessed God, which was committed to my trust. And I thank Christ Jesus our Lord, who hath enabled me, for that HE COUNTED ME FAITHFUL, putting me into the ministry;

1 Timothy 1:11-12

To be faithful means to be constant, to be loyal, to be the same and not to change. Are you *faithful* with the message of our "great salvation"? Have you been *constant* with the message of "great salvation"? Or have you changed the incomparable message of "great salvation" into a message of financial prosperity?

Are you *faithful* with the glorious gospel or have you swerved into vain jangling? Jesus was counting on your faithfulness that is why He blessed you with this commission. Many pastors are not faithful with the glorious gospel of our "great salvation". The message of prosperity is a good message, but cannot be compared with the message of our salvation.

Jesus Christ did not die on the cross to make people rich! He came to this world to save us from our sins! "And she shall bring forth a son, and thou shalt call his name Jesus: for *he shall save his people from their sins*" (Matthew 1:21).

Jesus' mission on this earth was to destroy the works of the devil and save us from our sins. No matter how you spin the Bible around, you cannot change the pivotal message of the Bible. You cannot change the message of salvation into a message of "How to Become Rich"!

I believe in prosperity and it is because of that prosperity that you are enjoying this book today. However, the fact that prosperity is true does not make it the central theme of the Bible or the central message of Jesus Christ!

Stop over-magnifying the fact of God's prosperity!

Stop taking the message of prosperity out of context!

Stop misleading the church and giving the wrong impression about Christianity!

Stop peddling the false "gospel of riches"!

You are misleading the whole church into the way of error when you over-emphasize riches and prosperity and take it out of proportion.

It is amazing that Apostle Paul warned the church to be careful of this exact error.

But THEY THAT WILL BE RICH fall into temptation and a snare, and into many foolish and hurtful lusts, which drown men in destruction and perdition. For the love of money is the root of all evil: which while

4

some coveted after, they have ERRED FROM THE FAITH, and pierced themselves through with many sorrows.

1 Timothy 6:9-10

One day, I attended an open-air crusade organised by a great man of God. This man of God was well known for his wonderful "financial" ministry. This man of God was obviously led by the Lord to reach out to the lost souls and to win more people to Christ.

On the first day of this crusade, an invited evangelist preached the gospel and won lots of souls to the Lord. On the second, third and fourth days however, the pastor who organised the crusade took to the stage and preached the Word. To my amazement, he preached about financial prosperity for the next three days. I sat in amazement as the crowd received a secular motivational message instead of a pure "great salvation" message. This pastor obviously had many wonderful messages on financial prosperity. Somehow, he was unable to break away from those messages of financial prosperity even at an open-air soul-winning crusade.

He simply did not know how to preach about our "great salvation". Of course, there were many people there who congratulated him for his financial message at the crusade. People may congratulate you but do not forget that it is the Lord's approval that you really need!

How Many Sermons Can You Get Out of John 3:16?

Some years ago, I read about how the famed evangelist D. L. Moody learnt how to preach effectively. He met Henry Moorhouse who promised to come to America and preach in his church. When he eventually arrived in February 1868, he preached for seven nights from John 3:16. He also counselled D.L. Moody to "Teach what the Bible says and not your own words and show people how much God loves them."

5

This is perhaps the most beautiful, meaningful and important piece of advice any minister could ever receive. Stay with the scripture! Preach the words that are in the Bible! Show people that God loves them! Do not use your own words! Do not use your own knowledge!

All sorts of bondage and captivity have crept into the church because people are deprived of the knowledge of salvation.

Therefore my people are gone into captivity because they have no knowledge:...

Isaiah 5:13

I asked myself if I could preach for seven nights on John 3:16. Preaching about salvation is not as simple as it sounds. We live in a time where pastors rarely preach the "great salvation" gospel of Jesus Christ. Indeed, many of us do not even know how to preach about the "great salvation". The knowledge of "this beautiful salvation" and the different ways to present it is very limited today. Anyone who embarks on the journey of being an evangelist will discover for himself that the "pure salvation" which we rarely preach about is a deep well of revelation.

A Pastor Must Do the Work of An Evangelist

But watch thou in all things, endure afflictions, DO THE WORK OF AN EVANGELIST make full proof of thy ministry.

2 Timothy 4:5

A pastor must do the work of an evangelist because the scriptures say so. To be a good pastor you must somehow get into the work of evangelism.

A pastor must win souls!

A pastor must lead his congregation to win souls!

A pastor must teach about soul winning!

A pastor must teach salvation at crusades!

A pastor must teach salvation at breakfast meetings, concerts and other church outreaches!

A pastor must do the work of an evangelist; otherwise he will never make full proof of his ministry. Most ministers fulfil only a section of their calling. Most of us could have done much more if we were led by the Spirit. Your church would be larger and more effective if you were to do the work of an evangelist. It is time to release yourself from stereotyped pastoring that does not involve evangelism. It is time to stop leaving evangelism to people you consider to be "immature zealots".

You must be an evangelist because that is the only way to be a good shepherd. Read the following passage carefully and see Jesus' description of a good shepherd. Remember that the good shepherd is a good pastor and a winner of souls.

What man of you, having an hundred sheep, if he lose one of them, doth not leave the ninety and nine in the wilderness, and go after that which is lost until he find it? And when he hath found it, he layeth it on his shoulders, rejoicing.

And when he cometh home, he calleth together his friends and neighbours, saying unto them, rejoice with me, for I have found my sheep which was lost.

I say unto you, that likewise joy shall be in heaven over one sinner that repenteth, more than over ninety and nine just persons which need no repentance.

Luke 15:4-7

According to Jesus Christ, to be a good shepherd you must leave the ninety-nine and go looking for the one lost sheep. *A good shepherd looks for the lost sheep, the lost coin and the lost son.*

In the fifteenth chapter of Luke, Jesus Christ teaches about the "good shepherd", the "good woman" and the "good father".

The "good woman" looked for the lost coin and that made her a good woman! (Luke 15:8-10)

The "good father" looked out of the window for his lost son and that made him a good father! (Luke 15:11-32). The "good shepherd" searched for the lost sheep and that made him a good shepherd! (Luke 15:4-7).

These scriptures make it clear that to be a "good shepherd" you must actively seek out the lost. Therefore a good shepherd or a pastor is really an evangelist as well. I did not write the Bible and I am simply quoting from the scripture. These scriptures come from the words of Jesus Himself as well as from the letters of Paul. They clearly reveal God's intention for pastors to fulfil their calling by doing the work of an evangelist.

My own experience as a healing evangelist has proved to me that leaving the ninety-nine sheep and looking for the "lost" *does not diminish the church*. Indeed, the church is stronger and healthier when pastors do the work of an evangelist.

Develop the Ability to Explain Salvation

I once heard a lady describe how she had been saved when she heard Billy Graham preaching on the radio on the topic, "God commended His Love toward us in that while we were yet sinners Christ died for us". I thought to myself, "What a wonderful statement and a wonderful message!" I desired greatly to preach the message of salvation in an equally simple way using the statements of Jesus Christ.

It is time for Christians and preachers to develop the ability to expound on the profound statements of Jesus Christ. Some of these profound statements about Jesus are:

"I am the way, the truth, and the life." (John 14:6)

"There is no salvation in any other name except the name of Jesus." (Acts 4:12)

"I am the bread of life." (John 6:35)

"I am the living water."(John 4:10)

It is time for pastors to teach, illustrate and explain the gospel. The few stories in this book are intended to help the gospel preacher bring alive the gospel of Jesus Christ. Often, the most difficult part of preaching the message of salvation is in finding a way to illustrate the simple truths of the gospel. It is my prayer that this book will help lovers of the gospel message to preach with greater strength and clarity.

Some pastors are power-preaching ministers who cannot deliver a crystal clear message of salvation. Other ministers can preach about the ABC's of the gospel but cannot link it to the power of God. It is time to blend the power of God with the clear knowledge of the gospel of Christ as it is laid out in the Bible.

The gospel messages bring out the message of Jesus Christ as a Healer and a Saviour. Those messages are critical when evangelism is done in hostile regions where other religions dominate. After all, our Jesus is a healing Jesus!

Pastors must also preach these messages of salvation in the church. It has been wrongly assumed that the message of salvation, the message of the cross and the message of the blood of Jesus are well known and understood by all in the church. Amazingly, it is often Christians who are blessed by the message of salvation. When a preacher expounds the message of salvation, Christians respond heartily as they hear their faith being explained. It gives Christians great confidence to hear about their salvation. Christians learn about what they believe as well as *why* they believe what they believe!

I pray that many pastors will begin to teach about salvation again. I pray that through this book we will drive out the canker of "other gospels" that have replaced the teaching of salvation. Today, the gospel of success, the gospel of prosperity, and the gospel of wealth have replaced the simplicity of the gospel of salvation through Jesus Christ.

Salvation can be taught from many different angles. Salvation can be taught using the love of God, the sin of man or the dangers of hell fire. You must endeavour to understand salvation in many different ways. Different kinds of messages on salvation will reaffirm and re-establish the ordinary Christian.

In the next sections of this book, you will understand the message of salvation in different ways.

Indeed, you will discover that "pure salvation" can and must be preached from many different and important angles. Every preacher must be able to preach the gospel in a hundred different ways. Over the last decade, I have been privileged to preach most of these messages on salvation to thousands of eager souls and I pray that you will also preach to thousands in your lifetime.

SECTION 2:

SALVATION AND THE LOVE OF GOD

God Commended His Love

For when we were yet without strength, in due time Christ died for the ungodly. For scarcely for a righteous man will one die: yet peradventure for a good man some would even dare to die.

But **GOD COMMENDETH HIS LOVE** toward us, in that, while we were yet sinners, Christ died for us. Much more then, being now justified by his blood, we shall be saved from wrath through him. For if, when we were enemies, we were reconciled to God by the death of his Son, much more, being reconciled, we shall be saved by his life.

Romans 5:6-10

1. God commended His love toward us when we were helpless and without strength.

Many older women find it difficult to get husbands to marry them. When they were younger and more attractive they did not lack suitors. As the difficulties in life abounded and poverty struck from all angles, these women found it increasingly difficult to get husbands. It is only Jesus who is attracted to people who are not so attractive.

Fear thou not; for I am with thee: be not dismayed; for I am thy God: I will strengthen thee; yea, I WILL HELP thee; yea, I will uphold thee with the right hand of my righteousness.

Isaiah 41:10

2.   **God commended His love toward us when we were ungodly.**

But God, who is rich in mercy, for his great love wherewith he loved us, Even WHEN WE WERE DEAD IN SINS, hath quickened us together with Christ, (by grace ye are saved;) and hath raised us up together, and made us sit together in heavenly places in Christ Jesus:

Ephesians 2:4-6

For CHRIST ALSO HATH ONCE SUFFERED FOR SINS, THE JUST FOR THE UNJUST, that he might bring us to God, being put to death in the flesh, but quickened by the Spirit:

1 Peter 3:18

3.   **God commended His love toward us when we were sinners.**

This is a faithful saying, and worthy of all acceptation, that Christ Jesus came into the world TO SAVE SINNERS; of whom I am chief.

1 Timothy 1:15

For God sent not his Son into the world to condemn the world; but that the world through him might be saved.

John 3:17

The Man Who Loved the Cripple

A beautiful young lady went to play sports and got terribly injured. As a result of the injury she could not walk or move any

13

part of her body from her neck downwards. All the young men who had wanted to marry her changed their minds.

But one day, a Chinese man went up to her and said he wanted to marry her. Everyone was shocked that someone wanted to marry a lady who could not walk or even lift her hand. To everyone's amazement he actually married her; and the next thing we knew, he had had a baby with her.

Most of us would choose someone who looks "nice". As soon as there is something "unpleasant" about somebody, people stop loving the person. In this case, the young man married the young lady even though she did not have the use of her limbs.

That is the kind of love that Jesus has shown us. He loved us and chose us when we were yet dirty, ugly and sinful. Christ has shown us the extreme love that no one else can demonstrate.

4.   God commended His love toward us when we were His enemies.

And, having made peace through the blood of his cross, by him to reconcile all things unto himself; by him, I say, whether they be things in earth, or things in heaven. And YOU, THAT WERE SOMETIME ALIENATED AND ENEMIES IN YOUR MIND BY WICKED WORKS, yet now hath he reconciled

Colossians 1:20-21

5.   God commended His love toward us when we were far away.

But now in Christ Jesus YE WHO SOMETIMES WERE FAR OFF are made nigh by the blood of Christ. For he is our peace, who hath made both one, and hath broken down the middle wall of partition between us; having abolished in his flesh the enmity, even the law of commandments contained in ordinances; for to make in himself of twain one new man, so making peace;

Ephesians 2:13-15

6. **God commended His love toward us when we were thieves. Jesus loved the thief on the cross.**

And one of the malefactors (thieves) which were hanged railed on him, saying, if thou be Christ, save thyself and us.

But the other answering rebuked him, saying, dost not thou fear God, seeing thou art in the same condemnation? And we indeed justly; for we receive the due reward of our deeds: but this man hath done nothing amiss.

And he said unto Jesus, Lord, remember me when thou comest into thy kingdom. And Jesus said unto him, Verily I say unto thee, TODAY SHALT THOU BE WITH ME IN PARADISE.

Luke 23:39-43

7. **God commended His love toward us when we were blasphemers.**

And I thank Christ Jesus our Lord, who hath enabled me, for that he counted me faithful, putting me into the ministry; WHO WAS BEFORE A BLASPHEMER, and a persecutor, and injurious: but I obtained mercy, because I did it ignorantly in unbelief. And the grace of our Lord was exceeding abundant with faith and love which is in Christ Jesus.

1 Timothy 1:12-14

8. **God commended His love toward us when we were poor.**

The Spirit of the Lord is upon me, because he hath anointed me to preach the GOSPEL TO THE POOR; he hath sent me to heal the brokenhearted, to preach deliverance to

15

the captives, and recovering of sight to the blind, to set at liberty them that are bruised,

Luke 4:18

Blessed are the poor in spirit: for theirs is the kingdom of heaven.

Matthew 5:3

9.   God commended His love toward us when we were fornicators.

And the scribes and Pharisees brought unto him a woman taken in adultery; and when they had set her in the midst. They say unto him, Master, this woman was taken in adultery, in the very act. Now Moses in the law commanded us, that such should be stoned: but what sayest thou?

This they said, tempting him, that they might have to accuse him. But Jesus stooped down, and with his finger wrote on the ground, *as though he heard them not.*

So when they continued asking him, he lifted up himself, and said unto them, He that is without sin among you, let him first cast a stone at her. And again he stooped down, and wrote on the ground.

And they which heard it, being convicted by their own conscience, went out one by one, beginning at the eldest, even unto the last: and Jesus was left alone, and the woman standing in the midst.

When Jesus had lifted up himself, and saw none but the woman, he said unto her, Woman, where are those thine accusers? Hath no man condemned thee?

She said, No man, Lord. And Jesus said unto her, neither do I condemn thee: go, and sin no more.

John 8:3-11

10. God commends His love by loving us when we had many problems.

We do not like people with problems, but Jesus likes us with our problems. Many African countries previously did not need visas to visit Europe. As the poverty mounted in the developing world, poor African countries were asked to obtain visas before going. Similarly, poor South American countries were asked to obtain visas to visit the United States of America. You will notice rich countries try to keep out poor people and difficult situations. They try to stay away from people who are heavy laden. But Jesus wants those who are heavy laden with problems to come to Him.

> Come unto me, all YE THAT LABOUR AND ARE HEAVY LADEN, and I will give you rest. Take my yoke upon you, and learn of me; for I am meek and lowly in heart: and ye shall find rest unto your souls. For my yoke is easy, and my burden is light.
>
> Matthew 11:28-30

11. God commends His love by loving us when we were sick.

One day, whilst doing ward rounds in the teaching hospital, I noticed how the doctors passed by and avoided the smelly corner that had patients with long-standing ulcers. Doctors doing ward rounds would often pass by when they got to the section where those patients with smelly sores were. I felt sorry for those old men who seemed to be neglected because their conditions were so chronic and so foul-smelling. Then I thought of Jesus who said we should come to Him with our chronic and foul-smelling problems. People usually do not want to have anything to do with problematic people. Yet Jesus said, "Come to me with all your burdens."

But he was wounded for our transgressions, he was bruised for our iniquities: the chastisement of our peace was upon him; and WITH HIS STRIPES WE ARE HEALED.

Isaiah 53:5

Greater Lov

This is my commandment, that ye love one another, as I have loved you. GREATER LOVE hath no man than this, that a man lay down his life for his friends. Ye are my friends, if ye do whatsoever I command you.

John 15:12-14

1. **God has a special kind of love, which is the greatest kind of love in existence.**

Behold, what MANNER OF LOVE the Father hath bestowed upon us, that we should be called the sons of God: therefore the world knoweth us not, because it knew him not.

1 John 3:1

But God, who is rich in mercy, FOR HIS GREAT LOVE wherewith he loved us, Even when we were dead in sins, hath quickened us together with Christ, (by grace ye are saved;)

Ephesians 2:4-5

we have known and believed THE LOVE THAT GOD HATH TO US. God is love; and he that dwelleth in love dwelleth in God, and God in him. Herein is our love made perfect, that we may have boldness in the day of judgment: because as he is, so are we in this world.

1 John 4:16-17

The LORD hath appeared of old unto me, saying, Yea, I have loved thee with AN EVERLASTING LOVE: therefore with lovingkindness have I drawn thee.

Jeremiah 31:3

The Beloved and The Greater Love

I once knew a young lady who had a "beloved". This beloved young man wanted to marry the young lady but he did not treat her well. He seemed to be torn between his "beloved" and some other girls. Their relationship was tumultuous, to say the least. One day, this young lady finally came home and said, "It's over." She was tearful because her heart was broken by the ended relationship. But I comforted her and told her that God would give her somebody else. I promised her an even better "beloved" and a greater love.

After some months God answered our prayers and a nice young man came out of nowhere and fell in love with her. They seemed to be enjoying their relationship and one day I asked the young lady, "How is your new relationship?"

She smiled and said, "It's far nicer than the first relationship. God has been good to me."

She was experiencing a greater love and a nicer relationship. So I asked her, "Why is this relationship better?"

She said, "I didn't even know I could be this happy. I didn't know there was a much greater love that I could experience."

Indeed, this young lady experienced a greater kind of love. This is how God's love is. It is a far greater kind of love. Behold, what manner of love the Father has bestowed on us!

2. There is "the love of brothers" but the love of Jesus is greater.

Many families have disintegrated despite the fact that they are related. They break up and fight each other time and time again. The love of Jesus must be far greater than the love between brethren.

Seeing ye have purified your souls in obeying the truth through the Spirit unto unfeigned LOVE OF THE BRETHREN, see that ye love one another with a pure heart fervently.

1 Peter 1:22

The Kidney Donation

One day, there was a prayer meeting at which prayers were offered up for a brother who needed a kidney donation. Those present at the meeting declared their love for the sick brother and their desire for him to continue to live through a kidney donation.

However, as the prayer meeting went on, it was realised that no one was prepared to donate their kidney even though that was what they were praying about. Finally, the leader of the prayer meeting decided to allow God to choose whose kidney should be donated. So he took a feather and told the gathering that he was going to throw the feather in the air and whomever it landed on would have to donate his kidney. Everyone agreed to this process of divine selection.

He threw the feather in the air. Up it went and came sailing down, amazingly in the direction of the leader himself. Suddenly, the leader began to shout and blow at the feather to re-direct it, so that it would not come to him. It was evident that no one was prepared to donate his kidney; not even the leader.

It is one thing to say you love someone but it is another thing to have the "greater love" which makes you sacrifice yourself for him.

3. **There is the love of women but the love of Jesus is greater.**

I am distressed for thee, my brother Jonathan: very pleasant hast thou been unto me: THY LOVE TO ME WAS WONDERFUL, PASSING THE LOVE OF WOMEN.

2 Samuel 1:26

AND JACOB LOVED RACHEL; and said, I will serve thee seven years for Rachel thy younger daughter. And Laban said, It is better that I give her to thee, than that I should give her to another man: abide with me. And Jacob served seven years for Rachel; and they seemed unto him but a few days, for the love he had to her.

Genesis 29:18-20

AND THE KING LOVED ESTHER ABOVE ALL THE WOMEN, and she obtained grace and favour in his sight more than all the virgins; so that he set the royal crown upon her head, and made her queen instead of Vashti.

Esther 2:17

The love of women is the love of the female body. With this kind of love a man loves a woman and she gives her body to him. The love for women is short-lived. Most women are unable to keep the attention of a man for very long. I had a friend who had two girlfriends. I asked him how he could have two girlfriends at the same time. Then he answered, "I used to have eight girlfriends when I was in sixth form but now that I am in the university I have only two."

The love of Jesus has lasted throughout the centuries. It has persisted until it reached you and me. The love of Jesus Christ is a far greater kind of love than the love a man can have for a woman.

There are limitations with this "love of women". Even the most passionate couples need counselling shortly after they are married. Many who say "I love you"; "You're my dream"; "I'm so happy I met you" will often say it to another person. Obviously there is something missing from this "love for women".

The Widow and The Greater Love

There was a certain pastor who lived happily with his wife until he died unexpectedly. The wife was heartbroken and she cried continually. Her pastor tried to console her but she could not be comforted. She went to the graveside and wept from morning to evening. She cried, she scratched and she clawed at the grave. She wanted to pull her husband out of the grave.

One day, the pastor had a vision and he was taken to heaven where he saw the husband of this lady. To his amazement, this man was very happy in heaven. The dead man spoke to the pastor and told him that he was very happy to be in heaven. The pastor told him, "Your wife is crying everyday and she cannot be comforted."

Then the dead pastor told him something truly shocking.

He said, "Oh don't worry about my wife. The Lord told me when I got here that she was going to be ok and that He was even going to give her a new husband who would be better than me."

He continued, "Please tell my wife when you go that this is what the Lord said."

"But she won't believe me," the pastor responded.

"Don't worry," the dead pastor said, "I will tell you a secret between her and me. When you tell her she will know that you have spoken to me."

Then the dead husband told him a secret that only he and his wife knew.

After the vision, the pastor called this woman and told her that he had seen her husband and that she was going to have a new husband who would be better than the old one.

She said, "No way, it can never happen. I will never have a new husband and no one could be better than my husband."

Then he told her the secret. She screamed and said, "You had been standing outside our window to listen to our conversation."

It was then that she realised that the pastor had had a real vision.

As time passed by she did marry again; and one day the pastor asked her, "How is your new marriage?"

She smiled sheepishly and said, "Indeed this new husband is far greater than my first husband. I am experiencing a greater love."

This lady experienced a greater love in her second marriage. Indeed, there are lesser and greater loves. Jesus' love is a far greater love than the love of women or the love of the brethren.

4. There is the love for a nation but the love of Jesus is far greater.

Although people love their nations, at certain times, when the country is poor, they claim the citizenship of another country. A lot of Ghanaians and Nigerians have changed their nationalities and are now proud to be British, American, Italians and German citizens. People change their accents and dissociate from their countries at the slightest inconvenience. But Jesus Christ stayed by His cross and died for the whole world. The love of Jesus

Christ is far greater than the love anyone could have for his country.

5. There is the love of a mother for her children, but the love of Jesus is greater.

Mothers can, and do forget their children. Some mothers drop their children on a doorstep and turn away forever. Indeed, the love of a mother is a great thing to behold. But it cannot be compared to the greater love that Jesus exhibited when He gave up His life for the whole world.

Can a woman forget her sucking child, that she should not have compassion on the son of her womb? Yea, they may forget, yet will I not forget thee.

Isaiah 49:15

6. The love of Christ is greater love because He sacrificed Himself for us.

A man will usually give gifts to the one he loves. Jesus' love is greater because He did not give us money, houses or cars as some do to show their love. He laid down his life! He gave His life. He did not get to live to be 70 years. He poured out His blood for us! His blood is His life! He gave us His life by giving His blood.

HEREBY PERCEIVE WE THE LOVE OF GOD, because he laid down his life for us: and we ought to lay down our lives for the brethren.

1 John 3:16

And from Jesus Christ, who is the faithful witness, and the first begotten of the dead, and the prince of the kings of the earth. UNTO HIM THAT LOVED US, and washed us from our sins in his own blood,

Revelation 1:5

The Man in the Deep Freezer

One day a young man met a lady and told her how much he loved her. This young lady was enthralled by the love the young man showered on her and decided to marry him. They got married, moved into their new house and bought furniture, a (chest) deep freezer, a fridge and all the things they needed to make a happy home.

One night they were in bed when armed robbers broke into the house. The husband managed to escape into the living room but did not know where to go next. When he saw the new empty deep freezer, it occurred to him to jump into it and hide there. When the armed robbers could not find him, they beat up his wife and maltreated her. As the wife screamed and called for help the husband was nowhere to be found because he was hiding in the deep freezer. When the armed robbers finally left, he came out of the deep freezer to console his wife. But she would have none of it.

"You don't love me," she said. "If you had loved me you would have come out of the deep freezer to save me."

The husband said, "I love you but not that much."

Then he continued, "Don't you understand? There is nothing much that I could have done. Those guys would have killed me. I would have lost my life trying to save you. I would have been a hero but I would have lost my life."

Later on when the lady went to church, she heard the pastor preaching, "Greater love hath no man than this that a man lay down his life for his friends."

Then she realized that her husband had been unable to lay down his life for her. Even though he did love her to an extent, her husband's love could not be compared with the love that Jesus had for her. Jesus Christ laid down His life for her.

7. You Shall Not Escape If You Neglect Such A Great Love

HOW SHALL WE ESCAPE, if we neglect so great salvation; which at the first began to be spoken by the Lord, and was confirmed unto us by them that heard him;

Hebrews 2:3

The Desperate Young Lady

When I was in university, I knew many beautiful Christian girls. There was this particular Christian girl who was outstandingly beautiful. All the young men wanted to enter in a relationship with her and marry her. She received many letters from many young men. She simply read every letter and made fun of the people who had written to her. She would show the letters to her friends and they would have a good laugh. Eventually, she left the university and fewer and fewer young men showed interest in her. At a point no one proposed to her anymore.

As the years went by, she became desperate and decided to join a church where the pastor did not have a wife. After some time she realised that the pastor was not noticing her so she decided to dance in front of him during the praise and worship time. Somehow, he still did not notice her. Eventually, she decided to go and propose to the pastor herself. Someone who was desired and wanted by everyone had fallen to such a low state.

You see, if you reject great love you will one day regret it. You will live to discover that you cannot escape if you neglect the great love that Jesus offers.

The Grieving Widow

One day, I met a lady whose husband had died. Her husband had been a pastor who had died in his early forties. She told me how her husband loved to reach out and pat her body any time he passed by her.

27

She said, "Anytime he walked past me at home, he would touch me. But I did not like it. I did not appreciate his constant touching."

She proceeded to tell me about how he had been stricken by cancer in the midst of his years. According to her, a time came when he would lie down at home, unable to raise his hands. She would pass by him, as at other times, but this time he could neither raise his hands nor give her one of his cuddles.

She said, "As he lay there dying, I wished so much that he would stretch his hand and touch me."

But it was all over. The love that she rejected and complained about was no longer available.

SALVATION MESSAGE 3:

The Prodigal Son

And he said, a certain man had two sons: And the younger of them said to his father, Father, give me the portion of goods that falleth to me. And he divided unto them his living.

And not many days after the younger son gathered all together, and took his journey into a far country, and there wasted his substance with riotous living.

And when he had spent all, there arose a mighty famine in that land; and he began to be in want.

And he went and joined himself to a citizen of that country; and he sent him into his fields to feed swine. And he would fain have filled his belly with the husks that the swine did eat: and no man gave unto him.

And when he came to himself, he said, How many hired servants of my father's have bread enough and to spare, and I perish with hunger!

I will arise and go to my father, and will say unto him, Father, I have sinned against heaven, and before thee, And am no more worthy to be called thy son: make me as one of thy hired servants.

And he arose, and came to his father. But when he was yet a great way off, his father saw him, and had compassion, and ran, and fell on his neck, and kissed him.

And the son said unto him, Father, I have sinned against heaven, and in thy sight, and am no more worthy to be called thy son.

But the father said to his servants, bring forth the best robe, and put it on him; and put a ring on his hand, and shoes on his feet:

And bring hither the fatted calf, and kill it; and let us eat, and be merry: For this my son was dead, and is alive again; he was lost, and is found. And they began to be merry.

Luke 15:11-24

1. This world contains "two types" of children: obedient children and rebellious children. "A certain man had 'two sons'…" (Luke 15:11).

There is both good and bad in everyone. There are 'two types' of children. Not everybody is all good, and not everybody is all bad. Not everybody is going to heaven and neither is everybody is going to hell. You may be going to hell but do not think that everyone will go to hell with you. Do not think that everyone is going to heaven either, some will go to hell. Everyone will have to choose their final destination for themselves.

2. Rebellious youth turn away from God. "… the younger son gathered all together, and took his journey…" (Luke 15:13)

Many people turn away from God in their youth. It was the younger son and not the older son who took off on a tangent. It was the younger son who proudly asked his father to give him his inheritance whilst he was still alive. Many young people are prone to foolishness and destruction. Some people repent and become wiser as they grow older. Unfortunately, some people persist in the foolishness of their childhood. Others die before they get the chance to mature and repent. That is why it is important for you to remember your Creator when you are young.

REMEMBER NOW THY CREATOR IN THE DAYS OF THY YOUTH, while the evil days come not, nor the years draw nigh, when thou shalt say, I have no pleasure in them;

Ecclesiastes 12:1

Remember not the sins of my youth, nor my transgressions: according to thy mercy remember thou me for thy goodness' sake, O Lord.

Psalm 25:7

Foolishness is bound in the heart of a child; but the rod of correction shall drive it far from him.

Proverbs 22:15

3. **Rebellious men forsake God and embark on self-destructive journeys. "And not many days after the younger son gathered all together, and took his journey ..." (Luke 15:13).**

It does not take a long time for foolish people to embark on self-destructive journeys. It didn't take a long time for the younger son to begin his downward journey to the regions of darkness. There is a way that seems right unto a man but the end of that way is death. What journey of life are you on? Where are you headed? What will be the outcome of your life's journey?

All we like sheep have gone astray; we have turned every one to his own way; and the Lord hath laid on him the iniquity of us all.

Isaiah 53:6

Ah sinful nation, a people laden with iniquity, a seed of evildoers, children that are corrupters: they have forsaken the Lord, they have provoked the Holy One of Israel unto anger, they are gone away backward.

Isaiah 1:4

The man that wandereth out of the way of understanding shall remain in the congregation of the dead.

Proverbs 21:16

4.   People go as far from God as possible when they are filled with the spirit of rebellion. "...and he took his journey into a far country..." (Luke 15:13)

Rebellious people want to go as far from God as they possibly can. They want to be as far from church as possible. They want to be as far from prayer and the Bible as possible.

Thus saith the Lord, What iniquity have your fathers found in me, that they are gone far from me, and have walked after vanity, and are become vain?

Jeremiah 2:5

For, lo, they that are far from thee shall perish: thou hast destroyed all them that go a whoring from thee.

Psalm 73:27

5.   Many People Are Wasting Their Lives. "... and there wasted his substance..." (Luke 15:13).

Some women 'waste' their bodies on men until they are so old-looking that no one is interested in them any longer. Many men also waste their money acquiring unnecessary things.

He also that is slothful in his work is brother to him that is a great waster.

Proverbs 18:9

There is treasure to be desired and oil in the dwelling of the wise; but a foolish man spendeth it up.

Proverbs 21:20

The Boy Who "Drank" the Air Conditioners Away

I heard of a wealthy man who died and left his property to his children. One of his children reminded me of the prodigal son because of the way he wasted his inheritance. His father had left him a large house with many rooms. This young man, who was a great waster, would spend his time 'boozing' at a local drinking bar.

One day, he ran out of money and was unable to pay his bill at the bar. So he came up with an idea to pay his bill by giving the bar man one of the air conditioning units from his father's house. The bar man agreed to defray his bills with the cost of the air conditioner. Naturally, the air conditioner cost more than one drink. So the young man had a huge surplus of money with the bar man.

From then on, he bought drinks and paid for them with the balance due him from the air conditioner. Eventually, when the credit from that air conditioner ran out, he decided to bring yet another air conditioning unit to pay for his drinking bills. The bar man agreed again and this young man completely "drank away" another air conditioner.

Amazingly, this young man brought more air conditioners to the drinking bar until he had "drunk away" all the air conditioners in the house. Indeed, he wasted away his inheritance until there was nothing left. This is the kind of person the prodigal son was.

6.   **Rebellious people, just like everyone, else will encounter crisis and trouble. "...there arose a mighty famine and he began to be in want." (Luke 15:14)**

Rebellious men will encounter the storms of life that everyone on this earth experiences. There are uncontrollable circumstances that no one can control or manage.

Beauty and strength are short-lived. Money makes wings and flies away. Money that is spent on pleasure and loose living eventually runs out. Pretty girls lose their beauty and become sickly after years of fooling around with multiple partners.

Wilt thou set thine eyes upon that which is not? For riches certainly make themselves wings; they fly away as an eagle toward heaven.

Proverbs 23:5

The fining pot is for silver, and the furnace for gold: BUT THE LORD TRIETH THE HEARTS.

Proverbs 17:3

7. Rebellious people do not look to God for solutions to their problems. They look elsewhere. "And he went and joined himself to a citizen of that country..." (Luke 15:15).

Rebellious people try to find their own solutions to their problems. Many people seek solutions through witchcraft and sorcery. Others seek to find love through boyfriends or girlfriends. Others seek refuge in alcohol or drugs. Some rebellious men seek help through work and education. But none of these things can really help. Going back to his father's house was the only proper solution to the young man's problems.

Put not your trust in princes, nor in the son of man, in whom there is no help.

Psalm 146:3

8. No one can help you in this world. "... and no man gave unto him." (Luke 15:16). Men cannot help you. Do not put your trust in man.

Give us help from trouble: for vain is the help of man. Through God we shall do valiantly: for he it is that shall tread down our enemies."

Psalms 108:12-13

It is better to trust in the LORD than to put confidence in princes.

Psalms 118:9

Woe to them that go down to Egypt for help; and stay on horses, and trust in chariots, because they are many; and in horsemen, because they are very strong; but they look not unto the Holy One of Israel, neither seek the Lord!

Isaiah 31:1

9.   When things go from bad to worse it is supposed to turn you towards God. "And when he came to himself, he said…" (Luke 15:17)

Your problems are supposed to bring you towards God.

Then Jonah prayed unto the LORD his God out of the fish's belly,

And said, I CRIED BY REASON OF MINE AFFLICTION unto the LORD, and he heard me; out of the belly of hell cried I, and thou heardest my voice.

For thou hadst cast me into the deep, in the midst of the seas; and the floods compassed me about: all thy billows and thy waves passed over me.

Then I said, I am cast out of thy sight; YET I WILL LOOK AGAIN TOWARD THY HOLY TEMPLE.

Jonah 2:1-4

10.   It is time to repent and turn to God. "I will arise and go to my father, and will say unto him, Father, I have sinned…" (Luke 15:18)

35

You must repent now! Think correctly now! Repentance means turning around and going in the opposite direction. Repentance means to change your mind; repentance means to humble yourself.

> Come, and let us RETURN UNTO THE LORD: for he hath torn, and he will heal us; he hath smitten, and he will bind us up.
>
> After two days will he revive us: in the third day he will raise us up, and we shall live in his sight.
>
> Hosea 6:1-2

SALVATION MESSAGE 4:

God Sent Not His Son to Condemn the World

For God sent not his Son into the world to condemn the world; but that the world through him might be saved.

John 3:17

And the scribes and Pharisees brought unto him a woman taken in adultery; and when they had set her in the midst, They say unto him, Master, this woman was taken in adultery, in the very act. Now Moses in the law commanded us, that such should be stoned: but what sayest thou? This they said, tempting him, that they might have to accuse him. But Jesus stooped down, and with his finger wrote on the ground, as though he heard them not. So when they continued asking him, he lifted up himself, and said unto them, He that is without sin among you, let him first cast a stone at her. And again he stooped down, and wrote on the ground.

And they which heard it, being convicted by their own conscience, went out one by one, beginning at the eldest, even unto the last: and Jesus was left alone, and the woman standing in the midst. When Jesus had lifted up himself, and saw none but the woman, he said unto her, Woman, where are those thine accusers? hath no man condemned thee? She said, No man, Lord. And Jesus said unto her, NEITHER DO I CONDEMN THEE: go, and sin no more.

John 8:3-11

1. God sees our bare naked and ugly sins and yet He loves us.

Just as the Pharisees saw the sins of the woman so clearly, likewise God sees our sins very clearly. When things are seen clearly, it can be very horrifying and frightening and yet God does not condemn us.

The Scene of Sin

I once went to visit somebody. As I knocked on the door there was no response from within; but I was sure this person was in. When I peeped through a crack in the door, I saw two people having sex, in the very act. I was terrified!

Later on in life God showed me that that is what He sees everyday. Our bare and ugly sins are before Him and yet it is a wonder that He does not condemn us.

2. God could have condemned us when He saw our bare and ugly sins.

The Condemned Wife

I knew a man who had a beautiful wife. When he went to work, his beautiful wife would receive her boyfriend into the house and have sex with him. One day, the husband came home unexpectedly. He opened the front door quietly and walked to the bedroom. When he opened the bedroom door, his wife was having sex with somebody else. He was so angry that he called the police, ended the marriage relationship and sacked the lady from his life. When God saw us in our sins He could have sacked us just as this man sacked his wife.

3.   Jesus did not condemn us when He saw our ugly sins.

The Wife Who Was Not Condemned

A certain man married a beautiful lady. Somebody used to visit his wife everyday to give her advice. After some time, the adviser would also have sex with her.

One day, the man discovered his wife having sex with the adviser.

When I heard about this, I was expecting that the husband would condemn his wife and drive her away but he did not. He rather turned to her and said, "I love you and I want you to be my wife. It does not matter what has happened. You are the only wife I want."

This was an amazing show of love to a wife he should have condemned.

This is how Jesus' love is. He sees every thing but He does not condemn us!

4.   We are not condemned because of the blood of Jesus which protects us, covers us and washes away all our sins.

But if we walk in the light, as he is in the light, we have fellowship one with another, and the blood of Jesus Christ his Son cleanseth us from all sin.

1 John 1:7

5.   We must be grateful to Jesus for His great love wherewith He has loved us.

For the love of Christ constraineth us; because we thus judge, that if one died for all, then were all dead: And that

39

he died for all, that they which live should not henceforth live unto themselves, but unto him which died for them, and rose again.

2 Corinthians 5:14-15

The Grateful Soldier

Many years ago there was a man who used to come and visit my father every year with gifts of chicken and eggs. One day, my mother told me why this man was always coming to our house.

There had been a coup d'état in Ghana and a number of soldiers had been arrested as being conspirators of the coup. This man was one of them and he was put on trial with other people. Everybody who was tried was in great danger of being condemned and executed.

My father was a lawyer and decided to defend this particular soldier. He argued and discussed and pleaded with the court and in the end the man was set free. He was not condemned. But indeed he was almost condemned!

This army officer was always grateful to my father for defending him and even after my father died he continued to visit the house with chicken and eggs. He was showing his gratitude for not being condemned.

In the same way, we must show our gratitude to Jesus because it is because of His blood that we are not condemned. We are not condemned because the blood of Jesus has washed away our sins.

6. **God did not send His Son, Jesus, to condemn the world.**

That is why Jesus did not condemn the woman caught in adultery and He is not condemning you today.

The Good Samaritan

And Jesus answering said, A certain man went down from Jerusalem to Jericho, and fell among thieves, which stripped him of his raiment, and wounded him, and departed, leaving him half dead.

And by chance there came down a certain priest that way: and when he saw him, he passed by on the other side.

And likewise a Levite, when he was at the place, came and looked on him, and passed by on the other side.

But a certain Samaritan, as he journeyed, came where he was: and when he saw him, he had compassion on him,

And went to him, and bound up his wounds, pouring in oil and wine, and set him on his own beast, and brought him to an inn, and took care of him.

And on the morrow when he departed, he took out two pence, and gave them to the host, and said unto him, Take care of him; and whatsoever thou spendest more, when I come again, I will repay thee.

Which now of these three, thinkest thou, was neighbour unto him that fell among the thieves? And he said, He that shewed mercy on him. Then said Jesus unto him, Go, and do thou likewise.

Luke 10:30-37

1.   Like the man who journeyed from Jerusalem to Jericho, you are on the journey of life from birth to death.

With most journeys you know the beginning and the end. With the journey of life we do not know when or how it will end.

And this know, that if the goodman of the house had known what hour the thief would come, he would have watched, and not have suffered his house to be broken through. Be ye therefore ready also: for the Son of man cometh at an hour when ye think not.

Luke 12:39-40

For man also knoweth not his time: as the fishes that are taken in an evil net, and as the birds that are caught in the snare; so are the sons of men snared in an evil time, when it falleth suddenly upon them.

Ecclesiastes 9:12

2.   Like the man who journeyed from Jerusalem to Jericho, you are on the journey of life and will experience various problems on that journey.

Man that is born of a woman is of few days, and full of trouble. He cometh forth like a flower, and is cut down: he fleeth also as a shadow, and continueth not.

Job 14:1-2

And Jacob said unto Pharaoh, The days of the years of MY PILGRIMAGE are an hundred and thirty years: few and evil have the days of the years of my life been, and have not attained unto the days of the years of the life of my fathers in the days of their PILGRIMAGE.

Genesis 47:9

3. **Like the man who journeyed from Jerusalem to Jericho, you are on the journey of life and will need the help of God in this life.**

I am the vine, ye are the branches: He that abideth in me, and I in him, the same bringeth forth much fruit: for WITHOUT ME YE CAN DO NOTHING.

John 15:5

I will lift up mine eyes unto the hills, from whence cometh my help. My help cometh from the Lord, which made heaven and earth.

Psalms 121:1-2

4. **Like the man who journeyed from Jerusalem to Jericho, you are on the journey of life that has many troubles. God knows your troubles and has sent help in the form of Jesus Christ.**

For while we were still helpless, at the right time Christ died for the ungodly. For one will hardly die for a righteous man; though perhaps for the good man someone would dare even to die. But God demonstrates His own love toward us, in that, while we were yet sinners, Christ died for us.

Romans 5:6-8 (NASB)

5. **Like the man who journeyed from Jerusalem to Jericho, you are on the journey of life on which you help from need others. The help you need may not come in the way you expect it.**

Sometimes people expect help in a particular way. Naaman, the Syrian, expected Elijah to help him in a particular way but he did not. The help you need may not come in the form of money, medicine, a visa, clothes or even a car, it may come in another way.

And his servants came near, and spake unto him, and said, My father, IF THE PROPHET HAD BID THEE DO SOME GREAT THING, wouldest thou not have done it? how much rather then, when he saith to thee, Wash, and be clean?

2 Kings 5:13

6. **Like the man who journeyed from Jerusalem to Jericho, you are on the journey of life. God has sent someone to pour in the oil. The oil speaks of the Holy Spirit who has been sent to lead you to Jesus Christ. God sends the Holy Spirit to convict you.**

Nevertheless I tell you the truth; it is expedient for you that I go away: for if I go not away, the Comforter will not come unto you; but if I depart, I will send him unto you. And when he is come, he will reprove the world of sin, and of righteousness, and of judgment: Of sin, because they believe not on me; of righteousness, because I go to my Father, and ye see me no more; Of judgment, because the prince of this world is judged.

John 16:7-11

7. **Like the man who journeyed from Jerusalem to Jericho, you are on the journey of life. God has sent someone to pour in the wine. The red wine speaks of the Blood of Jesus Christ that is poured out to cleanse you from your sins.** Receive Jesus Christ today and you will be saved!

But if we walk in the light, as he is in the light, we have fellowship one with another, and THE BLOOD OF JESUS CHRIST his Son cleanseth us from all sin.

1 John 1:7

8.   Like the man who journeyed from Jerusalem to Jericho, you are on the journey of life and only someone who loves you will dare to stop and help you on such a dangerous road. God sent Jesus Christ into this dangerous world because of His great love for you.

Do you think it was soldiers who made Jesus Christ go up on the cross for you? Do you think it was money that motivated Jesus Christ to pour out His love for you? Only the love of God made the Good Samaritan stop his journey and attend to a suffering, wounded and dying man.

The Adopted Korean Baby

I remember a story that was reported in the Korean press. There was an American family that lived happily in the United States of America. One of the children in this family, a young man, had Asian features and it was obvious that he was not an original member of the family.

One day, this young man, who was now in university asked his father, "Daddy, how come I have Asian features but you all don't? How come I am so different? Where did you get me from?"

His father answered, "I have been waiting for you to ask this question. Do you really want to know?"

"Yes I do," he answered and his father proceeded to tell him.

Many years ago, I was a missionary in Korea when war broke out between the north and the south. Your mother and I were fleeing from the communist north to the south. It was a very cold wintry day. When we passed over a bridge your mother asked me to stop the car because she heard a baby crying. I refused to stop because it was too dangerous and there were soldiers behind us and there was a lot of shooting. But she insisted and I ended up stopping. We ran from the car and went under a huge bridge.

There, we saw something amazing. A Korean lady had just given birth to a baby under the bridge. The lady had taken off all her clothes and wrapped her new baby in her underwear and other clothes. Then, she had curled herself around the baby to protect it from the icy cold winter.

The baby was alive and crying but the mother was frozen to death. That baby was you and your mother gave her life to save you.

When the young Korean-American man heard this story he was moved with great emotion and began trembling. He said to his father, "Please take me to the bridge where you found me. Please take me to the spot where you discovered me."

The parents agreed and arranged to take him to the spot where he was found. When they got to the spot under the bridge, the young Korean man did something amazing. He took off all his clothes and lay stark naked on the ground and began crying and wailing.

He cried, "O Mama, it was cold on that night when you took off all your clothes and gave them to me. O Mama, it was so cold when you gave your life for me.

O Mama, I love you and I thank you for dying for me. I will never forget what you did for me."

He lay there naked and crying and had to be consoled and dragged away from that spot under the bridge in Korea.

This story teaches us about the love that makes a person give his life for another. When the Good Samaritan approached this dying traveller, he risked his life so that the traveller would have a chance to live.

Do you think it was policemen or soldiers that made that woman take off her clothes and freeze to death for her child?

Do you think she did it for financial gain?

Do you think it was soldiers who frightened her to do what she did? Certainly not! She gave her life because of her great love for her baby.

Why God Sent His Son

For God so loved the world, that he gave his only begotten Son, that whosoever believeth in him should not perish, but have everlasting life.

John 3:16

1. **Why did God love the world so much? Because we are His creation.**

All things were made by him; and without him was not any thing made that was made.

John 1:3

2. **God's creation was going to perish in hell. God's creation was in difficulty, in darkness and in pain.**

I once met a man who had been to prison at the age of twenty-one. He was released fifteen years later when he was thirty-six years old. He was very jittery and was always looking behind him to see if there was anyone who would attack him from behind.

I found his behaviour very strange until he explained to me the horrors of prison life. He explained how people are attacked and raped all the time in prison. I thought to myself, "How terrible and how frightening it must be to be in prison."

How even more frightening it must be to go to hell! This is why God sent His Son, because He knew His creation was on the road to hell.

3. Why did God send His Son and not an angel? God wanted to send a powerful person who could save us.

One day, a beloved church member of mine was arrested by the police. He had been accused of doing something wrong. When I heard the news I was desperate and I wanted to save him from the clutches of the police and from being mistreated in the prison.

I wondered whom I could send to save the young man from being manhandled by the police. Then I thought of my wife and decided to send her to bail him because she was a lawyer. I sent my wife because I wanted to send a powerful person who could do the job.

Being a lawyer, I felt she was the best person to extract him from the problem. God also sent a powerful person, His only Son, to save us from our sins.

4. If you had been God, you would also have sent someone to save us.

I once sent a missionary to an island far away in the Indian Ocean.

There was a revolution in that country and after a series of unfortunate incidents my missionary was arrested and imprisoned by some revolutionary soldiers.

When I heard the news that my pastor had been arrested, I called one of my pastors in South Africa and told him to fly out to the island immediately to save my missionary and set him free. It is just natural to send a saviour to deliver someone you know and love.

When God sent His Son, He had to pay for the sins of the world with His Life and His Blood. He had to pay with His life: Life for life! Blood for blood! Jesus had to pay with His life.

And almost all things are by the law purged with blood; and without shedding of blood is no remission.

Hebrews 9:22

If you had to pay a price to set your son free from ignorance and backwardness would you not pay the price?

When I sent the pastor from South Africa to the island in the Indian Ocean, I asked him to pay for all tickets, lawyers, bills and any expense that would come up.

Supposing my missionary who was in prison on the island in the Indian Ocean refused the assistance of the pastor I had sent to save him?

Suppose he told the pastor that he did not want to leave the prison?

Suppose he told the pastor to mind his own business?

Supposing he told the pastor that he preferred to stay in prison?

This is what it is like when you refuse to accept Jesus Christ as your Saviour.

Can you see how crazy it looks when you do not accept Jesus Christ the Saviour? It is madness to reject Jesus Christ!

SALVATION MESSAGE 7:

A Saviour's Serenade

Now will I SING TO MY WELL BELOVED A SONG OF MY BELOVED touching his vineyard. My well beloved hath a vineyard in a very fruitful hill:

And he fenced it, and gathered out the stones thereof, and planted it with the choicest vine, and built a tower in the midst of it, and also made a winepress therein: and he looked that it should bring forth grapes, and it brought forth wild grapes.

And now, O inhabitants of Jerusalem, and men of Judah, judge, I pray you, betwixt me and my vineyard.

What could have been done more to my vineyard, that I have not done in it? Wherefore, when I looked that it should bring forth grapes, brought it forth wild grapes?

Isaiah 5:1-4

The Lord hath appeared of old unto me, saying, yea, I have loved thee with an everlasting love: therefore with loving kindness have I drawn thee.

Again I will build thee, and thou shalt be built, O virgin of Israel: thou shalt again be adorned with thy tabrets, and shalt go forth in the dances of them that make merry.

Thou shalt yet plant vines upon the mountains of Samaria: the planters shall plant, and shall eat them as common things.

For there shall be a day, that the watchmen upon the mount Ephraim shall cry, arise ye, and let us go up to Zion unto the Lord our God.

For thus saith the Lord; SING WITH GLADNESS FOR JACOB, and shout among the chief of the nations: publish ye, praise ye, and say, O Lord, save thy people, the remnant of Israel.

Jeremiah 31:3-7

A serenade is a love song. It is a song sang by a young man for the girl he loves. He may stand outside her window and plays his guitar whilst he sings to her. All this is to charm her, to woo her and to win her love. Throughout the Bible, you see the Lord singing songs to His people! Whilst serenading, the young man makes many points very clear to the girl. He tells her who he is and how his love is better than any other that she could ever have. As you go through the Bible, you will see that Jesus is singing a special love song to you.

1.   God is singing a song and saying that He loves you.

SCRIPTURE: For God so loved the world, that
                    he gave his only begotten Son,
                    that whosoever believeth in him
                    should not perish, but have everlasting
                    life.

John 3:16

SONG: "Jesus loves you this I know"

                    "For God so loved the world, that He
                    gave His only Son…"

52

2. **God is singing a song to you and telling you that His love is greater than any other love. His love is amazing. You will enjoy His love!**

> SCRIPTURE: Greater love hath no man than this, that a man lay down his life for his friends.
>
> John 15:13
>
> SONG: "Amazing love, how can it be…"
>
> SONG: "Greater love has no man..."

3. **God is singing a song to you that He is beautiful and glorious. He is worth taking as a beloved.**

> SCRIPTURE: Glorious things are spoken of thee, O city of God. Selah.
>
> Psalm 87:3
>
> SONG: "Glorious things of thee are spoken…"
>
> SONG: "O Lord, you are beautiful"

4. **God is singing a song to you and asking you to come to Him.**

> SCRIPTURE: Come unto me, all ye that labour and are heavy laden, and I will give you rest.
>
> Matthew 11:28
>
> SONG: "Come unto Jesus, give Him your life today…"
>
> SONG: "Come closer to me…"

5.   **God is proposing to you in a song. He is asking you to open the door to your heart and love Him. He is asking you to receive Him, follow Him and love Him.**

SCRIPTURE: Behold, I stand at the door, and knock: if any man hear my voice, and open the door, I will come in to him, and will sup with him, and he with me.

Revelation 3:20

SONG: "Softly and tenderly Jesus is calling…"

6.   **God is singing a song to you and saying, "You must respond to the love of God." You must give Him your heart and love Him back.**

SCRIPTURE: Let us therefore come boldly unto the throne of grace, that we may obtain mercy, and find grace to help in time of need.

Hebrews 4:16

SONG: "Come unto Jesus, give Him your life today."

SONG: "O, how I love Jesus…"

7.   **God is singing a song to you and saying, "Say 'Yes' to God. Say 'Yes' to the Saviour!" Answer Him now with an equally beautiful song!**

SCRIPTURE: I will sing unto the Lord, because he hath dealt bountifully with me.

Psalm 13:6

SONG: "I'll say 'Yes'; Lord, 'Yes' to Your will
                    and to Your way…"

**8.   God is singing a song to you and saying, "Give me
your heart." God is standing outside your window
waiting to hear your song that says you will give Him
your heart.**

SCRIPTURE: I will sing unto the Lord, because he
                    hath dealt bountifully with me.

                                            Psalm 13:6

SONG: "Lord I give you my heart …"

                    "I surrender all."

SALVATION MESSAGE 8:

John 3:16

For GOD so LOVED THE WORLD, that he gave his only begotten SON, that WHOSOEVER BELIEVETH in him should NOT PERISH, but have EVERLASTING LIFE.

John 3:16

The analysis of this great verse will reveal the greatest salvation ever known to man.

1. **God is the GREATEST PERSON EVER and He loves the world.**

God is greater than any person, so if He loves you then the greatest Person loves you!

2. **God shows the GREATEST LOVE EVER shown to anyone.**

The love of God is greater than the love of women, the love of a father, the love of a mother, the love of a boyfriend, the love of a girlfriend, the love of a nation. God showed the greatest love ever shown by anyone.

3. **God loves the GREATEST NUMBER OF PEOPLE EVER.**

Some people can only love a few people. Many women can only love their husband and their two children. Some people only love their tribesmen. Some people only love their country. Many people despise people of another colour. But God loved the whole wide world! God loved the greatest number of people ever.

4. **God gave the GREATEST GIFT EVER, which was His Son.**

All lovers give something. God's love made Him give something precious. Those who have children will understand how precious and valuable a child is. God gave the greatest gift ever, His Son.

5. **God gives the GREATEST INVITATION EVER, offering whosoever the gift of salvation.**

The gospel of Jesus Christ offers the widest invitation ever. God invites everyone to experience salvation whether living in Alaska, USA, U.K. Afghanistan, Ghana, South Africa or Germany.

6. **God gives us the GREATEST and simplest METHOD EVER of entering heaven – believing.**

This ensures that whether you are rich or poor, whether you are educated or uneducated, whether you are black or white, simple faith will work for you and give you access to heaven. This verse shows that everyone can be saved. Most privileges are reserved for the rich and powerful; but salvation is not only for the rich and the powerful.

The poor can believe and the rich can also believe the Word.

The uneducated can believe and the educated can believe the Word too.

Faith is the simplest and greatest method for entering heaven.

7.   God gives the GREATEST ESCAPE EVER.

God's love is directed to us to make sure we do not perish in hell. God's love was not given to make us rich people, with cars and houses. Not having a house is not the same as perishing. Not having a car, not having a visa is not the same as perishing. To perish is a very serious tragedy.

8.   God gives us the GREATEST OPPORTUNITY EVER to have everlasting life.

Receive Jesus Christ and seize the great opportunity of salvation.

SECTION 3:

SALVATION AND THE BLOOD OF JESUS

The Story of the Cross
(Jesus Christ Died for You)

For when we were yet without strength, in due time Christ died for the ungodly.

Romans 5:6

For I delivered unto you first of all that which I also received, how that Christ died for our sins according to the scriptures; And that he was buried, and that he rose again the third day according to the scriptures:

1 Corinthians 15:3-4

1. **God sent His son Jesus Christ who was born by a virgin.**

And we have seen and do testify that the Father sent the Son to be the Saviour of the world.

1 John 4:14

2. **Jesus Christ came to this world and preached many wonderful things that had never been heard before:**

Jesus saith unto him, I am the way, the truth, and the life: no man cometh unto the Father, but by me.

John 14:6

3. **Jesus healed the sick, performed many wonderful miracles and solved problems. For example, He healed the mad man of Gadara.**

And they come to Jesus, and see him that was possessed with the devil, and had the legion, sitting, and clothed, and in his right mind: and they were afraid.

Mark 5:15

4. **Jesus was betrayed by His disciple Judas, for thirty pieces of silver.**

Then one of the twelve, called Judas Iscariot, went unto the chief priests, And said unto them, What will ye give me, and I will deliver him unto you? And they covenanted with him for thirty pieces of silver. And from that time he sought opportunity to betray him.

Matthew 26:14-16

5. **Jesus warned Judas at the last Passover dinner not to betray Him.**

The Son of man goeth as it is written of him: but woe unto that man by whom the Son of man is betrayed! It had been good for that man if he had not been born.

Matthew 26:24

6. **Jesus went to the Garden of Gethsemane and prayed, sweating blood. He prayed that He would not have to die on the cross.**

And he went a little further, and fell on his face, and prayed, saying, O my Father, if it be possible, let this cup pass from me: nevertheless not as I will, but as thou wilt.

Matthew 26:39

7. **Whilst Jesus was in the garden, Judas Iscariot brought people with knives and swords and identified Jesus with a kiss.**

And while he yet spake, behold a multitude, and he that was called Judas, one of the twelve, went before them, and drew near unto Jesus to kiss him. But Jesus said unto him, Judas, betrayest thou the Son of man with a kiss?

Luke 22:47-48

8. Jesus was taken to the pastors and accused, beaten and slapped by the pastors of the day. He was accused of claiming to be the Son of God.

But Jesus held his peace. And the high priest answered and said unto him, I adjure thee by the living God, that thou tell us whether thou be the Christ, the Son of God.

Jesus saith unto him, Thou hast said: nevertheless I say unto you, Hereafter shall ye see the Son of man sitting on the right hand of power, and coming in the clouds of heaven.

Then the high priest rent his clothes, saying, He hath spoken blasphemy; what further need have we of witnesses? Behold, now ye have heard his blasphemy. What think ye? They answered and said, He is guilty of death.

Matthew 26:63-66

9. When Peter realized that it was becoming a serious threat to be associated with Jesus and that Jesus was in danger of death, Peter denied Christ.

Now Peter sat without in the palace: and a damsel came unto him, saying, Thou also wast with Jesus of Galilee. But he denied before them all, saying, I know not what thou sayest.

And when he was gone out into the porch, another maid saw him, and said unto them that were there, This fellow was also with Jesus of Nazareth. And again he denied with an oath, I do not know the man.

And after a while came unto him they that stood by, and said to Peter, Surely thou also art one of them; for thy speech bewrayeth thee.

Then began he to curse and to swear, saying, I know not the man. And immediately the cock crew.

Matthew 26:69-74

10. When Judas saw that they intended to kill Jesus, he sent the money back and went and hanged himself.

Then Judas, which had betrayed him, when he saw that he was condemned, repented himself, and brought again the thirty pieces of silver to the chief priests and elders,

Saying, I have sinned in that I have betrayed the innocent blood. And they said, what is that to us? see thou to that.

And he cast down the pieces of silver in the temple, and departed, and went and hanged himself.

Matthew 27:3-5

11. Jesus was taken to the Pilate, the governor, and tried. When Pilate saw that they were intent on murdering Jesus, he offered an alternative; to release Barabbas.

And they had then a notable prisoner, called Barabbas. Therefore when they were gathered together, Pilate said unto them, whom will ye that I release unto you? Barabbas, or Jesus which is called Christ?

Matthew 27:16-17

12. When Pilate saw that they were intent on murdering Jesus, he washed his hands off the case.

And the governor said, Why, what evil hath he done? But they cried out the more, saying, Let him be crucified. When Pilate saw that he could prevail nothing, but that rather a tumult was made, he took water, and washed his hands before the multitude, saying, I am innocent of the blood of this just person: see ye to it. Then answered all the people, and said, His blood be on us, and on our children.

Matthew 27:23-25

13. Jesus Christ was whipped on His back. "Then Pilate therefore took Jesus, and scourged him." (John 19:1)

They took his clothes away. "And they stripped him…" (Matthew 27:28)

The crown of thorns was put on His head. "And when they had platted a crown of thorns, they put it upon his head…" (Matthew 27:29)

He was spat on. "And they spit upon him…" (Matthew 27:30)

They mocked Him. "And after that they had mocked him…" (Matthew 27:31)

They nailed Him to a cross. "…and led him away to crucify him." (Matthew 27:31)

They pierced Him with a spear. "But one of the soldiers with a spear pierced his side…" (John 19:34)

14. Two thieves were crucified with Jesus. One of them mocked Him but the other one believed in Him.

Then were there two thieves crucified with him, one on the right hand, and another on the left.

Matthew 27:38

15. Jesus was buried in a tomb donated by Joseph of Arimathaea. Three days later, Jesus rose from the dead and appeared to His disciples.

When the even was come, there came a rich man of Arimathaea, named Joseph, who also himself was Jesus' disciple: He went to Pilate, and begged the body of Jesus. Then Pilate commanded the body to be delivered.

And when Joseph had taken the body, he wrapped it in a clean linen cloth, and laid it in his own new tomb, which he had hewn out in the rock: and he rolled a great stone to the door of the sepulchre, and departed.

Matthew 27:57-60

And they rose up the same hour, and returned to Jerusalem, and found the eleven gathered together, and them that were with them, Saying, The Lord is risen indeed, and hath appeared to Simon.

And they told what things were done in the way, and how he was known of them in breaking of bread. And as they thus spake, Jesus himself stood in the midst of them, and saith unto them, Peace be unto you.

Luke 24:33-36

16. Jesus died for you and suffered for you in order to take away your sins.

All we like sheep have gone astray; we have turned every one to his **own** way; and the Lord hath laid on him the iniquity of us all.

Isaiah 53:6

17. You must believe and receive Christ; otherwise you would have neglected a great way of salvation.

How shall we escape, if we neglect so great salvation; which at the first began to be spoken by the Lord, and was confirmed unto us by them that heard him;

Hebrews 2:3

18. Do you know any other man, prophet or religious leader who shed his blood for you? Do you know anyone in this world who has shed his blood to wash away your sins and cleanse you from unrighteousness? I don't!

65

Neither is there salvation in any other: for there is none other name under heaven given among men, whereby we must be saved.

Acts 4:12

SALVATION MESSAGE 10:

Without the Shedding of Blood there is No Forgiveness

For the life of the flesh is in the blood: and I have given it to you upon the altar to make an atonement for your souls: for it is the blood that maketh an atonement for the soul. Therefore I said unto the children of Israel, NO SOUL OF YOU SHALL EAT BLOOD,...

Leviticus 17:11-12

1. **God revealed the importance of blood through the prophet Moses and therefore commanded that blood should not be eaten.**

Perhaps we would have thought it was our heart, our brain or our kidneys that were most important. But through Moses, we learn that the life of a person is in his blood. None of us would have known the importance of our blood. All the parts of an animal could be eaten but the blood was not supposed to be eaten because it represented life.

2. **Long before medical science discovered it, Moses taught us that the blood of a person contained his life.**

For the life of the flesh is in the blood: ...

Leviticus 17:11

Today, we know that the blood carries life to all parts of the body. Moses could not have known that by medical science. He knew this because God revealed it to Him.

The Lady's Life

In medical school, I was privileged to be taught by a famous gynaecologist. After surgical operations, we would sit around him in the changing room whilst he taught us. Sometimes we wrote notes and sometimes we just listened to his amazing stories.

One day, he told us about an experience he had whilst working in the rural areas. He described a lady who had a ruptured ectopic pregnancy. She was bleeding internally and very near death.

"I was desperate," he said, "And there was no anaesthetist to make this woman sleep whilst I operated on her. There was also no blood to transfuse her with and I knew she was dying."

Desperate situations require desperate measures! Extremes must sometimes be fought with extremes! He described how he operated on her without anaesthesia and "plugged" the source of bleeding within her abdomen.

After he stopped the bleeding, he realised that most of the lady's blood had collected in her abdomen and she needed blood desperately. Since she was dying, he decided to give her her own blood. He told us how he scooped out the lady's blood, put it in a bottle and connected it to the lady. He transfused her with her own blood that had leaked out.

We, the students, were awe-struck as he described how the lady came back to life as her own blood re-entered her circulatory system.

You see, the life is in the blood! As the lady's blood re-entered her she came back to life.

3. **Because the blood contains the life of a person it represents his life.**

    For it is the life of all flesh; the blood of it is for the life thereof: ...

    Leviticus 17:14

    A bowl of human blood therefore represents a human life. A bowl of goat blood represents the goat's life. A bowl of elephant's blood represents the elephant's life. The bowlful of the blood of the Jesus that flowed down on the cross therefore represented the life of the Son of God. He gave His life and we saw it when His blood flowed out. This is what we mean when we say that Jesus Christ gave His life for us. It meant that He gave His blood! To give your life is to give your blood! To give your blood is to give your life!

4. **The blood has been chosen by God as the only thing that can be offered to appease Him and to atone for sin.**

    For the life of the flesh is in the blood: and I HAVE GIVEN IT TO YOU UPON THE ALTAR TO MAKE AN ATONEMENT FOR YOUR SOULS: ...

    Leviticus 17:11

5. **The New Testament confirms the truth that only blood can save.**

    And almost all things are by the law purged with blood; and without shedding of blood is no remission.

    Hebrews 9:22

    Thus this great truth revealed to Moses has passed on to Paul and the New Testament church. The apostle Paul makes it abundantly clear that without the shedding of blood (without the giving of a life) no one can be saved.

The Coconut Water

Many years ago, my mother showed me something that I have never forgotten. She picked out one of my father's shirts and pointed to a stain in it.

"Do you know what these stains are? These are stains from coconut water. Your father likes coconuts very much and he is always drinking coconut water."

She said, "So many of his shirts are stained with this coconut water and I cannot get rid of them."

She explained, "I can wash away everything with soap. I can wash out palm oil, dirt, chocolate, tea, coffee, stew, soup, toothpaste but I cannot wash out the stain of coconut water."

"Wow,' I said, "I never knew that coconut stains were so difficult to get rid of."

Indeed, soaps and detergents such as key soap, Omo, Ariel, Duck soap, Sunlight soap, Rexona, Lux, Imperial Leather are not able to wash away the coconut stains.

"So what can wash away the coconut stain?" I asked.

"Nothing," she said.

Every time I think of the coconut stain I think of the stain of sin.

I ask myself, "What can wash away our sins? What can wash away our lies, our stealing, our fornication and our murders?"

Nothing but the blood of Jesus can wash away our sins. Nothing but the blood of Jesus!! Only the blood of Jesus has the power to wash away these terrible stains.

6. Do you know anyone else who has shed his blood for you? Do you know anyone in this world who has shed his blood to wash away your sins and cleanse you from unrighteousness? I don't!

Neither is there salvation in any other: for there is none other name under heaven given among men, whereby we must be saved.

Acts 4:12

Eternal Life Through the Blood of Jesus

For the life of the flesh is in the blood...

Leviticus 17:11

1.   **Blood was created to carry life.**

Then Jesus said unto them, Verily, verily, I say unto you, Except ye eat the flesh of the Son of man, and DRINK HIS BLOOD, YE HAVE NO LIFE IN YOU."

John 6:53

Blood is a red, oxygen-containing liquid that gives life to everything it comes into contact with. Blood carries life by carrying life-giving oxygen and taking away poisonous carbon dioxide. Just as human blood carries life to every part of the body, the blood of Jesus carries eternal life.

The Life is in the Blood

One day I watched a man's leg being amputated in the theatre. Never had I felt such depression as I watched the operation unfold. I felt very sorry for the man as I watched his leg being carried away by hospital attendants. But a week later, I found this man whose leg was amputated sitting up in his bed, smiling and laughing with visitors. A few days later, I saw him going home happily.

He still had life in him and was going home to continue living happily ever after with his family.

I realized the truth in the scripture that says that the life of the flesh is in the blood. His life was not in his leg. If life were in his leg, he would have died when they cut it off. The life is indeed in the blood.

2.   The blood gives life because it can reach every part of the body.

After this I beheld, and, lo, a great multitude, which no man could number, of ALL NATIONS, AND KINDREDS, AND PEOPLE, and tongues, stood before the throne, and before the Lamb, clothed with white robes, and palms in their hands; ...And one of the elders answered, saying unto me, What are these which are arrayed in white robes? And whence came they? And I said unto him, Sir, thou knowest. And he said to me, these are they which came out of great tribulation, and have washed their robes, and MADE THEM WHITE IN THE BLOOD OF THE LAMB.

Revelation 7:9, 13-14

Just as human blood by its fluid nature reaches every part of the human body, the blood of Jesus Christ can reach every single member of the body of Christ.

Blood gives life because it unites the whole body. It unites the rest of the body with vital organs like the heart and the lungs. Just as our human blood unites the entire body, all members of the body of Christ are related to one another and to Christ the Head by the blood that flows everywhere. Through the blood of Jesus, everyone can be connected to God.

Just as the blood reaches every part of the body, the blood of Jesus is able to reach every part of the world. The blood of Jesus is effective universally. Every tribe and nation of the world can be reached by this blood. The blood of Jesus will connect the remotest village in the world to the throne of God and the Lamb that takes away the sins of the world.

The blood of Jesus is therefore the basis for strong relations and bonds that develop in the body of Christ between apparently unrelated people of varied backgrounds.

3.   **The blood carries life because it has the ability to carry nourishment.**

Whoso eateth my flesh, and DRINKETH MY BLOOD, HATH ETERNAL LIFE; and I will raise him up at the last day. For my flesh is meat indeed, and my blood is drink indeed.

John 6:54-55

Blood is a red liquid, containing dissolved food, that gives life to everything it comes into contact with. Within the blood are molecules of life-giving protein, carbohydrates, fats, vitamins and minerals. No wonder there is life in the blood! Just as red blood cells in human blood bring food to every part of the body, the blood of Jesus Christ brings life and well-being to everyone it comes in contact with.

Anyone who eats and drinks the blood of Jesus is going to enjoy eternal life.

4.   **The blood gives life because it has the ability to cleanse you regularly.**

But if we walk in the light, as he is in the light, we have fellowship one with another, and the BLOOD OF JESUS Christ his Son CLEANSETH us from all sin.

If we confess our sins, he is faithful and just to forgive us our sins, and to cleanse us from all unrighteousness.

1 John 1:7,9

Blood is a red, carbon dioxide removing liquid that gives life to everything it comes in contact with. Just as human blood carries away unwanted carbon dioxide, and disposes of it in the lungs, the blood of Jesus carries away our sin and filthiness.

5. **The blood gives life because it has the ability to purge and to sanctify.**

WHEREFORE JESUS ALSO, THAT HE MIGHT SANCTIFY THE PEOPLE WITH HIS OWN BLOOD, suffered without the gate. Let us go forth therefore unto him without the camp, bearing his reproach.

Hebrews 13:12-13

Blood is a red liquid that gives life to everything it comes in contact with by removing deadly poisons. Human blood also carries away unwanted poisonous chemicals like urea and disposes of them through the kidney. Indeed, the blood of Jesus fights the sin that destroys us.

The blood washes and removes poisonous and dangerous sins, attitudes and stains from our lives. Just as the blood in the human body fights to prevent you from dying from all sorts of illnesses, the blood of Jesus keeps you away from death. The blood of Jesus is what keeps you from eternal death in hell.

6. **The blood gives life because it contains elements that overcome spiritual and physical diseases.**

And I heard a loud voice saying in heaven, Now is come salvation, and strength, and the kingdom of our God, and the power of his Christ: for the accuser of our brethren is cast down, which accused them before our

God day and night. AND THEY OVERCAME HIM BY THE BLOOD OF THE LAMB, and by the word of their testimony; and they loved not their lives unto the death.

Revelation 12:10-11

You can overcome physical diseases and spiritual diseases through the blood of Jesus. Spiritual diseases like bitterness, jealousy, hatred and insecurity can be overcome through the blood of Jesus.

Blood is a red, liquid containing cells that fight diseases, infections and other evils that can kill the body. This is why blood gives life to everything it comes in contact with. Just as we overcome infection through the white blood cells in blood and fight battles against germs and other invaders, it is through the blood of Jesus that we overcome the devil and other invading evil spirits.

Blood is a red, liquid containing special cells called platelets that bring healing to injured parts of the body. Blood heals. Just as the platelets and other clotting factors within the blood help to form clots and plugs in wounds, the blood of Jesus helps our wounds to heal. Through the blood of Jesus we are forgiven for our terrible sins and receive the inspiration to forgive others and overcome bitterness.

7. **Do you know any other man, prophet or religious leader who shed his blood for you? Do you know anyone in this world who has shed his blood to wash away your sins and cleanse us from unrighteousness? I don't!**

    Neither is there salvation in any other: for there is none other name under heaven given among men, whereby we must be saved.

    Acts 4:12

Steps to Salvation Through the Blood of Jesus

Through the blood of Jesus salvation has come to the world. The scripture reveals five different steps that are taken on the road to salvation through the blood of Jesus.

1. First Step - Forgiveness through the Blood

In whom we have redemption THROUGH HIS BLOOD, THE FORGIVENESS OF SINS, according to the riches of his grace; wherein he hath abounded toward us in all wisdom and prudence;

Ephesians 1:7-8

Through the blood of Jesus you receive the first step towards your salvation – forgiveness. Forgiveness means that God has stopped feeling angry towards you. He has pardoned you and written off your debts. You are discharged from your obligation and God is no more resentful towards you.

The Blood versus the Orange Juice

I once worked with someone on an important project. He was a great assistant and worked very hard. One day, our church was preparing for its grand dedication. This gentleman was in charge of the preparation. It was a crucial and very significant moment in my ministry. Everything hinged on him doing his work.

One day, I came to the church building site and found that this gentleman was not around. I asked where he was, because I had repeatedly emphasized to him that he needed to finish the work in time for the programme. To my shock this gentleman had left the country and abandoned me mid-air. I was launched into a terrible crisis and had to organise several emergency measures to save myself from terrible disgrace and embarrassment. I was very upset with the gentleman because I had given myself to work with him and had trusted him greatly. After the programme I decided not to work with him anymore.

One day, I was at home when a delegation arrived in my house. This was a delegation that had come on the behalf of this gentleman to plead for me to forgive him and accept him to continue working for me. I listened to all that they had to say. At the end of their speech they presented me with a basket that contained some orange juice and apple juice.

As I looked at the basket I smiled to myself because I remembered the blood of Jesus. These people were trying to wipe out the sins of this man with the orange juice and apple juice. But orange juice cannot wash away sins. Only the blood of Jesus can wash away sins. I forgave him, and accepted him back smiling to myself every time I drank some of their orange juice. Perhaps that is how God feels when He sees the blood of Jesus and forgives and pardons our sins.

2.   Second Step- Cleansing through the Blood

But if we walk in the light, as he is in the light, we have fellowship one with another, and the BLOOD OF JESUS CHRIST HIS SON CLEANSETH us from all sin....

1 John 1:7

After being forgiven you need cleansing. This process takes you one-step further than forgiveness did. You may be forgiven but there is often a scent of the past evils that contaminate us.

The Armed Robber Who Needed Cleansing

One day, a young man was being chased by a crowd who suspected that he was an armed robber. Unfortunately, he fell into a huge watery septic tank. This young man could not swim, much less in this swirling stew of faeces. He screamed for help and someone stretched a rod out to him. He was pulled out and saved from an ignominious death. He stood by the pool, thankful just to be alive. After a while, someone said to him, "You better go and have a bath. Your life has been saved but you still smell bad!" And with that the young man was ushered away for a thorough, disinfecting bath. That is how salvation is. You are forgiven but there is a need for your cleansing.

3. Third Step - Sanctification through the Blood

For the bodies of those beasts, whose blood is brought into the sanctuary by the high priest for sin, are burned without the camp. Wherefore Jesus also, that he might SANCTIFY THE PEOPLE WITH HIS OWN BLOOD, suffered without the gate. Let us go forth therefore unto him without the camp, bearing his reproach.

Hebrews 13:11-13

Sanctification takes you even further than forgiveness and cleansing do. It means you have been set apart for a sacred religious purpose. It is only the sanctifying power of the blood of Jesus that can move you so far from your previous evil state. This is the power that can utterly transform a criminal into a priest of God! This power is the sanctifying power of the blood of Jesus.

Peter called himself "elect" according to the sanctification of the Spirit and sprinkling of the Blood. "Elect according to the foreknowledge of God the Father, through sanctification of the

Spirit, unto obedience and sprinkling of the blood of Jesus Christ: grace unto you, and peace, be multiplied" (1 Peter 1:2). He had been elevated from being a fisherman to becoming the head of the worldwide church. How did that happen? It happened through the sanctifying power of the blood of Jesus.

4.   Fourth Step - Redemption through the Blood

And they sung a new song, saying, Thou art worthy to take the book, and to open the seals thereof: for thou wast slain, and HAST REDEEMED US TO GOD BY THY BLOOD out of every kindred, and tongue, and people, and nation; And hast made us unto our God kings and priests: and we shall reign on the earth.

Revelation 5:9-10

In whom we have REDEMPTION THROUGH HIS BLOOD, the forgiveness of sins, according to the riches of his grace.

Ephesians 1:7

The next step in this process is redemption. To redeem is to get, to win, or to buy someone or something back. To redeem a slave means to buy back a slave. Christ has legally bought us back from the devil's slave camp. He paid for us with His blood. *When God went shopping, He paid the bill with Jesus' blood.*

You may use something but you may not buy it. You may use a car but you may not buy it. You may wear a dress but you may not buy it. God decided to forgive us and to buy us back from the devil. He wanted to have a permanent relationship with us.

God bought you from the devil's slave camp, you now belong to Him permanently. Your forgiveness, your cleansing and your sanctification are permanent. You belong to God. The devil has no legal access to you.

5. **Fifth Step - Reconciliation through the Blood**

For all have sinned, and come short of the glory of God; Being justified freely by his grace through the redemption that is in Christ Jesus: Whom God hath set forth to be A PROPITIATION THROUGH FAITH IN HIS BLOOD, to declare his righteousness for the remission of sins that are past, through the forbearance of God; To declare, I say, at this time his righteousness: that he might be just, and the justifier of him which believeth in Jesus.

Romans 3:23-26

Finally, reconciliation with God comes because you are forgiven, cleansed, sanctified and redeemed. You can now enjoy a reconciled relationship with God. This is what propitiation is all about. Propitiation involves a regaining of the favour and the goodwill that you lost with God. Through the blood of Jesus you will appease the heavenly Father and restore a beautiful relationship with Him.

6. **Do you know any other man, prophet or religious leader who shed his blood for you? Do you know anyone in this world who has shed his blood to wash away your sins and cleanse us from unrighteousness? I don't!**

Neither is there salvation in any other: for there is none other name under heaven given among men, whereby we must be saved.

Acts 4:12

The Blood of the Lamb

1. Jesus Christ is the Lamb of God Who Takes Away the Sins of the World.

The next day John seeth Jesus coming unto him, and saith, Behold the Lamb of God, which taketh away the sin of the world.

John 1:29

2. The Blood of the Lamb Has The Supernatural Power to Save You from the Consequences of Your Sin.

Forasmuch as ye know that ye were not REDEEMED with corruptible things, as silver and gold, from your vain conversation received by tradition from your fathers; But WITH THE PRECIOUS BLOOD OF CHRIST, as of a lamb without blemish and without spot:

1 Peter 1:18-19

The Search for Blood

I once knew somebody who was dying in the hospital and needed blood so that he could be saved. I got involved and went personally to the blood bank. When I entered the bank I saw blood in packets lying all over the place. There was some blood on the table and there was also blood in the fridge. I looked into the fridge myself and saw several shelves laden with blood. But there was a problem. They did not have the right blood for my friend. My friend's blood was a rare type.

"Sorry, we don't have the type of blood that you need," they said.

"What do you mean by that? Is this animal blood? Is it the blood of goats or the blood of bulls?"

"*We don't have goat blood here!*" They exclaimed. "Goat blood does not go with human blood. Your friend needs a special type of human blood which we do not have."

Then I asked about the blood on the table. They said, "*This blood has expired.* It cannot be used any more."

"What do you mean by 'expired'?" I asked.

"*It is too old,*" they said. "It has lost its power."

"Wow, " I thought to myself. "Then the Blood of Jesus is really powerful, to have lasted for more than two thousand years without losing its power."

That night I realized how true it was that there were different kinds of blood. There were many kinds of blood but none of them was appropriate. That night I realized that all the blood in the bank could not save my friend. It was simply not the right kind of blood. It was either expired blood, or the wrong type of blood. I began to make calls to other hospitals to see if I could find some appropriate blood for my friend.

You see, dear friend, the blood of bulls and goats could never have the power to save you from your sins. Only the blood of the sinless Lamb of God has the power to wash away sins.

This is why we sing about the blood of Jesus. This is why we sing:

"There is power, power, wonder working power in the blood of the Lamb."

This is why we also sing that the Blood will never lose its power. The blood of Jesus will last forever. It is eternal Blood and it will always have the power to wash away sins.

The Murderer Who Could Not Be Redeemed

One day I visited a high security prison in Africa. I was slated to preach on death row that morning. Everybody in the section I went to was condemned to death. I was met at the sectional gate of that prison by a bible-wielding gentleman who introduced himself as the leader of the fellowship. He looked and sounded like any ordinary pastor you would meet in a church. I asked him who he was.

He said, "I'm the leader of the fellowship of the condemned cells." I was amazed that such a spiritual, bible-wielding person would be in this place. I gathered courage and asked him, "What did you do that brought you to this prison?"

He smiled sheepishly at me and said, "Oh, murder. Everyone in this section has been convicted of murder."

I was silent for a while and wondered how such a nice person could kill anyone.

Then I asked him, "Who did you kill?"

He said, "I killed my son."

"Mercy!" I thought. "How awful."

I arrived at the meeting place and I looked at the congregation. The hall was filled with sincere looking men who were praying earnestly to God. Suddenly, I was gripped with a strong desire to set them free. I felt in my heart that these were good people who had repented of their mistakes. I wanted to rush to the main gate and command that the prisoners be set free.

It was then that I realized that I had no power to set these men free from prison. No matter what I thought and no matter how much money I had, it would take a very, very high power to get them out of jail.

I thought of how difficult it would be to get a presidential pardon for the entire fellowship of murderers that attended my service. They were in there for life and most of them would have to while away their time on earth in that prison.

That's when I realized how powerful the blood of Jesus was.

Blood Redeems and Changes Your Destiny

We were bound in the devil's chains! We were drowning in our sins! We were guilty of all the charges! We were headed for hell!

What could change our destiny? What could get us out of eternal prison? Only something extremely powerful could work out deliverance for you and me. After all, we are clearly guilty and there is no argument about that. The powerful thing that has the ability to free us from our well-deserved prison is the blood of Jesus Christ. The blood of Jesus is the only thing with that kind of power. That is why we sing the song "What can wash away my sins; Nothing but the blood of Jesus! What can make me whole again? Nothing but the blood of Jesus!"

What has the power to save us from our wretched existence as prisoners? The King James Bible calls our wretched existence "our vain conversation".

3.   **The Blood of the Lamb Has the Supernatural Power to Prevent Death.**

For the life of the flesh is in the blood: and I have given it to you upon the altar to MAKE AN ATONEMENT FOR YOUR SOULS:

Leviticus 17:11

The blood of Jesus has within it a supernatural ability to prevent death. The blood of Jesus has within it a supernatural ability to prevent you from going to hell. Because the life is in the blood, the absence of life-giving blood causes death.

Medical science has discovered that any part of the human body that is deprived of blood dies. For instance, sections of brain tissue die when the blood supply to that section is blocked. This is what we call a stroke. Sections of the world are condemned to death when the blood of Jesus is stopped from flowing there. Entire regions of the world are condemned to death and hell because no evangelist has been able to go there. Life will come to many people when they receive the blood of Jesus.

The Leg Which Died

Years ago, I was in a consulting room of the hospital and my professor called me in to see a man whose leg was "dead". The man's leg had turned black and cold because the blood supply to the leg had been cut off in an accident.

This was the first time I had seen anything like that. I did not know that a section of the body could actually die and still be attached to the body. This man was in danger of developing gangrene in the dead leg, which would spread and kill him quickly. He had to have his leg amputated because the blood had stopped flowing to it.   Just as blood had been prevented from flowing into a section of the man's body, the blood of Jesus is being prevented from flowing to some sections of the world. These sections of the world are dominated by evil religions, which put men in captivity and lead them to hell.

That is why I am a preacher: to make the blood of Jesus avail for the souls of this world! I preach so that the blood of Jesus and the sacrifice of the cross will not be wasted. O what praises we shall sing because of the great gift of salvation that we have through the blood of Jesus!

4. The Blood of the Lamb Has Supernatural Power to Bring You Back from the Dead.

Now the God of peace, that BROUGHT AGAIN FROM THE DEAD our Lord Jesus, that great shepherd of the sheep, THROUGH THE BLOOD of the everlasting covenant,

Hebrews 13:20

The scripture teaches us that the blood of Jesus is the power that raised Jesus from the dead. The blood of Jesus has the power to raise the dead. It is the only power that could raise Jesus Christ out of the grave. It is by this same power of the Blood that you will be raised from the dead. You will die, but you will not remain dead because of the power of the blood of Jesus.

The Man Who Vomited His Life Away

Blood has the power to bring back people from the dead. Even natural blood does that. That is why there are blood banks. These banks store blood so that blood can be accessed quickly in emergencies to bring people back to life.

One night, I was on duty at the emergency ward when a young man was brought to the hospital. This gentleman had an unusual problem where he was vomiting blood. He retched and vomited all night long. Each time he vomited, it was bright red blood which came out. He never vomited a single morsel of food. His stomach was empty and he was bringing out pure blood. By 2.00 am his condition began to deteriorate and I had to get blood for him.

I walked to and fro from the blood bank that night, fetching blood for this man. I was trying to bring him back from the dead. It was a race for life. By the morning the space around his bed was covered with bright red blood because he had vomited all around him all night long. Sad to say, in the end we were unable to prevent him from going to the grave because he had brought out more blood than we were able to replace.

The race that night was a race to get as much blood to the man as quickly as possible.

Only a supply of blood could prevent the man from dying and going to the grave.

Indeed, the race today is the race to get the blood of Jesus to as many places as possible and quickly enough. Only the blood of Jesus can prevent people from dying and going to hell.

5. **The Blood of the Lamb Has The Supernatural Ability to Open the Gates of Heaven For You.**

After this I beheld, and, lo, A GREAT MULTITUDE, which no man could number, of all nations, and kindreds, and people, and tongues, stood before the throne, and before the Lamb, clothed with white robes, and palms in their hands; nd cried with a loud voice, saying, Salvation to our God which sitteth upon the throne, and unto the Lamb.

And one of the elders answered, saying unto me, WHAT ARE THESE WHICH ARE ARRAYED IN WHITE ROBES? and whence came they? And I said unto him, Sir, thou knowest. And he said to me, THESE ARE THEY which came out of great tribulation, and HAVE WASHED THEIR ROBES, and made them white IN THE BLOOD OF THE LAMB.

Revelation 7:9-10, 13-14

Indeed, one of the wonders of heaven is about how people like us could get into a place like heaven.

How did we escape the prison we deserved to go to? How did we get out of the company of murderers and fellow fornicators?

How did we weave our way out of the sentence of death against us? How did we avoid the verdict of hell?

Who do we know who made a way for us to come to heaven? Which important person chipped in a word on our behalf? What are people like us doing in heaven?

Where are our dirty clothes and filthy rags? How come we are dressed in white? Is this not a company of thieves, murderers and evildoers?

How did people who hardly went to church manage to come to heaven? How come they are singing hymns? Are they here on a visit? Are they going to be here forever?

One of the elders has the answer to these questions. He explains that the multitudes have been able to come to heaven by washing their robes in the blood of the Lamb.

The Day I Entered the Anointed Car

One day, a great man of God visited our country. After the program, thousands of people thronged him and a large security force had to help the man of God enter the waiting limousine. Everyone wanted to get a glimpse of the man of God or to touch the hem of his garment.

Eventually this man was whisked away by the driver and the hosting Bishop. Sitting in front of the car was one extra person. Who was this extra person and how did he get to be in the car when thousands of people just wanted to get a glimpse of him?

Who was the fourth man in the car? It was no other person than "yours truly"- myself! People always wondered how I got into such a privileged position. How did I enter the anointed car? I had the ride of a lifetime as well as a most important time of fellowship and impartation of the Spirit. It was a momentous occasion for me and I received a great anointing from one of God's generals just two weeks before he died. People asked, "How did you get into such a privileged and holy spot?" That is my secret.

Perhaps another question to ask is, "How did someone like you get into a church? How did someone like you become a minister of the gospel? What on earth is someone like you doing in a Holy Place?"

The only explanation that can be given for you and I going to a place like heaven will be the blood of Jesus. This incredibly great privilege is given to us only by the blood of Jesus. One day I hope to stand in heaven. Like everybody else I will be asked why the gates of heaven should be opened unto me. I do not hope to enter heaven because I was a pastor or because I preached to large crowds. I hope to enter the gates of heaven for the same reason as everybody else – the blood of Jesus! It is the blood of Jesus that we depend on for entry into Heaven.

6. The Blood of the Lamb Has the Supernatural Power to Overcome the Devil.

And they OVERCAME HIM BY THE BLOOD OF THE LAMB, and by the word of their testimony; and they loved not their lives unto the death.

Revelation 12:11

The blood of Jesus has power. Through the blood of Jesus you will gain superiority over the devil and you will defeat him. Through the blood of Jesus you will win all the battles of life and ministry. Through the blood of Jesus you will deal with all the demonic problems of this world. It is time to overpower and overwhelm the devil through the powerful and precious everlasting blood of Jesus.

We live in a world dominated by an evil spirit of pride, rebellion and wickedness. This evil spirit is assisted by thousands of demons with the same evil character. All the struggles of our lives are related to the presence of evil spirits in the atmosphere. The atmosphere in different parts of the country and different parts of the world are determined by these evil spirits.

The scripture has good news for us. We can overcome the devil and his cohorts. We have been told exactly how we will overcome the devil – through the blood of Jesus.

Do you know any other man, prophet or religious leader who shed his blood for you? Do you know anyone in this world who has shed his blood to wash away your sins and cleanse us from unrighteousness? I don't!

Neither is there salvation in any other: for there is none other name under heaven given among men, whereby we must be saved.

Acts 4:12

SALVATION MESSAGE 14:

The Power in the Blood of Jesus

Through the blood of Jesus salvation has come to the world. The scripture reveals eight different steps that are taken on the road to salvation through the blood of Jesus.

1. **God Sent His Son, Jesus Christ to Save the World from their Sins.**

   For God so loved the world, that he gave his only begotten Son, that whosoever believeth in him should not perish, but have everlasting life.

   John 3:16

   And she shall bring forth a son, and thou shalt call his name JESUS: for he shall save his people from their sins.

   Matthew 1:21

2. **What Weapon or Equipment Did Jesus Have to Save the World from their Sins? He Had His Own Blood as the Tool to Save the World.**

   There was a man who was parachuted from a plane into war. As he was landing all his weapons fell out. This man happened to be with a lady, who asked: "Now that all your weapons have fallen out, what are you going to fight with when you meet your enemy?"

In response, the man pulled out a long knife hidden in his trousers, which made the lady feel assured that the fight would go well.

What power or weapon did Jesus use when He came to save us? The power of His blood!

3.   **Jesus Christ Did Not Hold Back Even When the Weapon He Had to Use Was His Own Blood.**

There are times when a part of your body can be used to save another person. This happens, for instance, in a blood donation or in a kidney donation.

The Story of the Kidney Donation

One day, there was a prayer meeting at which prayers were offered up for a brother who needed a kidney donation. Those present at the meeting declared their love for the sick brother and their desire for him to continue to live through a kidney donation.

However, as the prayer meeting went on, it was realised that no one was prepared to donate their kidney even though that was what they were praying about. Finally, the leader of the prayer meeting decided to allow God to choose whose kidney should be donated. So he took a feather and told the gathering that he was going to throw the feather in the air and whomever it landed on would have to donate his kidney. Everyone agreed to this process of divine selection.

He threw the feather up into the air. Up it went and came sailing down, amazingly in the direction of the leader himself. Suddenly, the leader began to shout and blow at the feather to re-direct it, so that it would not come to him.

It was evident that no one was prepared to donate his kidney; not even the leader! It is one thing to say you love someone but it is another thing to have the "greater love" which makes you sacrifice yourself for him.

4.   You Will Have Forgiveness through the Blood.

In whom we have redemption THROUGH HIS BLOOD, THE FORGIVENESS OF SINS, according to the riches of his grace; wherein he hath abounded toward us in all wisdom and prudence.

Ephesians 1:7-8

Through the blood of Jesus you receive forgiveness. Forgiveness means that God has stopped feeling angry towards you. He has pardoned you and written off your debts. You are discharged from your obligation and God is no more resentful towards you.

The Blood versus the Orange Juice

I once worked with someone on an important project. He was a great assistant and worked very hard. One day, our church was preparing for its grand dedication. This gentleman was in charge of the preparation. It was a crucial and very significant moment in my ministry. Everything hinged on him doing his work.

One day, I came to the church building site and found that this gentleman was not around. I asked where he was, because I had repeatedly emphasized to him that he needed to finish the work in time for the programme. To my shock this gentleman had left the country and abandoned me in mid-air. I was launched into a terrible crisis and had to organise several emergency measures to save myself from a terrible disgrace and embarrassment. I was very upset with the gentleman because I had given myself to work with him and had trusted him greatly. After the programme I decided not to work with him any more.

One day, I was at home when a delegation arrived in my house. This was a delegation that had come on the behalf of this gentleman to plead for me to forgive him and accept him to continue working for me. I listened all that they had to say. At the end of their speech they presented me with a basket that contained some orange juice and apple juice.

As I looked at the basket I smiled to myself because I remembered the blood of Jesus. These people were trying to wipe out the sins of this man with the orange juice and apple juice. But orange juice cannot wash away sins. Only the blood of Jesus can wash away sins. I forgave him, and accepted him back smiling to myself every time I drank some of their orange juice. Perhaps that is how God feels when He sees the blood of Jesus and forgives and pardons our sins.

5.   You Will Be Cleansed through the Blood.

But if we walk in the light, as he is in the light, we have fellowship one with another, and the BLOOD OF JESUS CHRIST HIS SON CLEANSETH us from all sin…

1 John 1:7

After being forgiven you need cleansing. This process takes you one-step further than forgiveness did. You may be forgiven but there is often a scent of the past evils that contaminate us.

The Armed Robber Who Needed Cleansing

One day, a young man was chased by a crowd who suspected that he was an armed robber. Unfortunately, he fell into a huge watery septic tank.

This young man could not swim, much less in this swirling stew of faeces. He screamed for help and someone stretched a rod out to him. He was pulled out and saved from an ignominious death.

The people who had been chasing him felt so sorry for him that they forgave him. The armed robber was now a free man. He stood by the pool, thankful just to be alive. Then he went home, happy to be alive.

His family was happy to see him, but after a while, one of them said to him, "You better go and have a bath. Your life has been saved but you still smell bad!" And with that the young man was ushered away for a thorough disinfecting bath. That is how salvation is. You are forgiven but there is a need for your cleansing.

6. You Will Be Sanctified through the Blood.

For the bodies of those beasts, whose blood is brought into the sanctuary by the high priest for sin, are burned without the camp. Wherefore Jesus also, that he might SANCTIFY THE PEOPLE WITH HIS OWN BLOOD, suffered without the gate. Let us go forth therefore unto him without the camp, bearing his reproach.

Hebrews 13:11-13

Sanctification takes you even further than forgiveness and cleansing do. It means you have been set apart for a sacred religious purpose. It is only the sanctifying power of the Blood of Jesus that can move you so far from your past evil state. This is the power that can utterly transform a criminal into a priest of God! This power is the sanctifying power of the Blood of Jesus.

Peter called himself "elect" according to the sanctification of the Spirit and sprinkling of the Blood. "Elect according to the foreknowledge of God the Father, through sanctification of the Spirit, unto obedience and sprinkling of the blood of Jesus Christ: grace unto you, and peace, be multiplied" (1 Peter 1:2). He had been elevated from being a fisherman to becoming the head of the worldwide church. How did that happen? It happened through the sanctifying power of the Blood of Jesus.

7.   You Will Be Redeemed through the Blood.

And they sung a new song, saying, Thou art worthy to take the book, and to open the seals thereof: for thou wast slain, and HAST REDEEMED US TO GOD BY THY BLOOD out of every kindred, and tongue, and people, and nation; And hast made us unto our God kings and priests: and we shall reign on the earth.

Revelation 5:9-10

In whom we have REDEMPTION THROUGH HIS BLOOD, the forgiveness of sins, according to the riches of his grace.

Ephesians 1:7

The next step in this process is redemption. To redeem is to get, to win, or to buy someone or something back. To redeem a slave means to buy back a slave. Christ has legally bought us back from the devil's slave camp. He paid for us with His blood. *When God went shopping, He paid the bill with His blood.*

You may use something but you may not buy it. You may use a car but you may not buy it. You may wear a dress but you may not buy it. God decided to forgive us and to buy us back from the devil. He wanted to have a permanent relationship with us.

When God bought you from the devil's slave camp, you now belong to Him permanently. Your forgiveness, your cleansing and your sanctification are permanent. You belong to God. The devil has no legal access to you.

8.   You Will Be Reconciled To God through the Blood.

For all have sinned, and come short of the glory of God; Being justified freely by his grace through the redemption that is in Christ Jesus: Whom God hath set forth to be A PROPITIATION THROUGH FAITH IN HIS BLOOD, to

declare his righteousness for the remission of sins that are
past, through the forbearance of God; To declare, I say, at
this time his righteousness: that he might be just, and the
justifier of him which believeth in Jesus.

Romans 3:23-26

Final reconciliation with God comes because you are
forgiven, cleansed, sanctified and redeemed. You can now enjoy
a reconciled relationship with God. This is what propitiation is
all about. Propitiation involves a regaining of the favour and the
goodwill that you lost with God. Through the blood of Jesus
you will appease the heavenly Father and restore a beautiful
relationship with Him.

Do you know anyone else who shed his blood for you? Do
you know anyone in this world who has shed his blood to wash
away your sins and cleanse you from unrighteousness? I don't!

Neither is there salvation in any other: for there is none
other name under heaven given among men, whereby we
must be saved.

Acts 4:12

SECTION 4:

SALVATION, JUDGMENT AND HELL

SALVATION MESSAGE 15:

Life, Death and Judgment

1. **Life is always followed by death and judgment: Your life is a vapour that appears for a short time. Because your life is a vapour it quickly disappears and is followed by two other things: your death and your judgment.**

Your chances of dying are 100%. It is a reality that death and judgment will come quickly to all men. Billy Graham says his greatest surprise is the brevity of life.

Whereas ye know not what shall be on the morrow. For what is your life? It is even a vapour, that appeareth for a little time, and then vanisheth away.

James 4:14

And as it is appointed unto men once to die, but after this the judgment:

Hebrews 9:27

The Famous Epitaph

One day, a man was strolling through a cemetery when he chanced upon an epitaph that stunned him. It read:

Martin Gooseberry

Born: December 25, 1844

Died: April 18, 1896

"I was once like you and you will soon be like me."

He was amazed and began to ponder on the inscription on the epitaph - "I was once like you".

The epitaph meant, "I once walked through cemeteries just like you. I once felt I could never die. I once felt I did not belong to the world of graves and cemeteries. I once never imagined myself sweating in a coffin six feet below the earth. Just like you, I once went home to my wife and children. I once had supper everyday with my family. I once drove out of my home every morning.

But today I lie silently in this grave. My condition is now so terrible that my family has brought me out here to rest in peace. I am now all alone in this coffin under the earth. To my left and to my right are other dead people whom I never knew or spoke to whilst on earth.

But you will soon be like me and we will be together in this cemetery, forgotten by men. As you go home do not forget, I was once like you and you will soon be like me."

2.   **Life is always followed by death and judgment: Your life is something that was given to you by God. You did not choose to live. You were created. Your life is therefore not something that you can end.**

You cannot end your life or escape from this life. The rich man and Lazarus did not end their lives when they died. They continued to live. You will continue to be alive when you die.

Thou art worthy, O Lord, to receive glory and honour and power: for thou hast created all things, and for thy pleasure they are and were created.

Revelation 4:11

And it came to pass, that the beggar died, and was carried by the angels into Abraham's bosom: the rich man also died, and was buried; And in hell he lift up his eyes, being in torments, and seeth Abraham afar off, and Lazarus in his bosom.

And he cried and said, Father Abraham, have mercy on me, and send Lazarus, that he may dip the tip of his finger in water, and cool my tongue; for I am tormented in this flame.

Luke 16:22-24

3. **Life is always followed by death and judgment: Your life is followed by death. Death is both an enemy to man and a blessing to man.** Death is an enemy because we were not created to die. We were created to live forever.

Death destroys everything that we try to do on earth. It makes nonsense of our achievements and our successes.

Death is also a blessing because it brings an end to the evil that men do. Death terminates the existence of evil men on the earth. Can you imagine if people like Hitler, Stalin, Idi Amin, Bokassa, Caligula, Nero, Genghis Khan and so on lived forever and continued to practice their wickedness on humankind?

So when this corruptible shall have put on incorruption, and this mortal shall have put on immortality, then shall be brought to pass the saying that is written, Death is swallowed up in victory. O death, where is thy sting? O grave, where is thy victory?

1 Corinthians 15:54-55

4. Life is always followed by death and judgment: Your life is followed by death, the date of which is already determined.

Seeing his DAYS ARE DETERMINED, the number of his months are with thee, thou hast appointed his bounds that he cannot pass;

Job 14:5

¹The Prisoner on Death Row

One day, a man was sentenced to death for a crime that he claimed he did not commit. He was sentenced to death but his lawyers fought for a stay of execution. After several years and several legal battles, it was finally decided that he should be executed. That night, his family was invited to have a special dinner with him after which he was sent to the death chamber. The long drawn out battle to save his life ended that night with his death.

After the execution there was a press conference and the pastor who stayed with the convict until his very last moment was interviewed.

"Did he confess to the murder before he died?" They wanted to know.

"No, he maintained his innocence until he was executed," the pastor said.

"What did you tell him? How did you comfort him? Did you say anything? Did he say anything?"

The minister's answer was simple, but profound. *"I told him that we were all under a death sentence only that we do not know when it will be implemented.* You know that your death sentence will be implemented tonight but we don't know when ours will be implemented."

I thought to myself, "How true that is. We are all indeed under a death sentence." [1]

As the scripture says, our days are determined. That famous prisoner had the advantage of knowing when it was determined that he should die. Indeed, we are all destined to die and to disappear into the grave. The thing is that we don't know when we will be asked to get into our graves.

That is why you must prepare to meet your God at any time!

5.　**Life is always followed by death and judgment: Your life is followed by death for which you must be prepared. You must not prepare for everything else without preparing for death also.**

Therefore thus will I do unto thee, O Israel: and because I will do this unto thee, PREPARE TO MEET THY GOD, O Israel.

Amos 4:12

Tears and Joy

One day, a young pastor took an international flight from his country to another. As he walked across the tarmac towards the aircraft he noticed an important man being seen off by a large tearful crowd. They seemed to weep and wail endlessly, not wanting him to leave.

After a very long flight they disembarked at their destination. When this pastor walked down the stairs he was amazed at the crowd of people that was waiting for this same man who had been seen off by the other tearful crowd. This time the crowd was not crying. It was a happy crowd of people throwing their caps and flowers into the air. They seemed ecstatic as they screamed, clapped and cheered the new arrival.

It was then that it occurred to the pastor that when a person dies there may be a tearful group on this side mourning his death, but in heaven there will be a joyful, cheering welcoming party.

What will happen when you die? Will you have a joyful reception on the other side? Will you be received with excitement and gladness in heaven? Or will you be banished into outer darkness?

6. **Life is always followed by death and judgment: Your life is followed by death, which is only a shadow for Christians.**

Even though I walk through the valley of THE SHADOW OF DEATH, I will fear no evil, for you are with me; Your rod and Your staff, they comfort me.

Psalm 23:4 (NASB)

Death for a Christian is a different experience because to be absent from the body is to be present with the Lord (2 Corinthians 5:8). Christians only experience a shadow of death because they belong to the Lord.

²The Shadow of the Truck

One day, a Presbyterian minister's wife died tragically leaving behind three little children. He decided to preach at his wife's funeral himself. On the day of the funeral, as he drove his three little children to the graveside of their mother, a massive 16-wheeler truck overtook them and cast a huge shadow over their car.

The father turned to his children and asked, "Would you rather be run over by the truck or by its shadow?"

His daughter answered, "We prefer to be run over by the shadow because a shadow can't hurt you."

Then he said to his children, "Your mother has been overrun not by death but by the shadow of death because Mummy is alive with the Lord today."[2]

When you are a Christian you only experience the shadow of death and not death because Jesus said, "And whosoever liveth and believeth on me shall never die …" (John 11:26).

We are confident, I say, and willing rather to be absent from the body, and to be present with the Lord.

2 Corinthians 5:8

7. **Life is always followed by death and judgment: Your life is followed by death, which is also followed by your judgment. If you fail your judgment you will be sent to hell.**

And as it is appointed unto men once to die, but AFTER THIS THE JUDGMENT:

Hebrews 9:27

And I saw the dead, small and great, stand before God; and the books were opened: and another book was opened, which is the book of life: and the dead were judged out of those things which were written in the books, according to their works.

And the sea gave up the dead which were in it; and death and hell delivered up the dead which were in them: and they were judged every man according to their works.

And death and hell were cast into the lake of fire. This is the second death. And whosoever was not found written in the book of life was cast into the lake of fire.

Revelation 20:12-15

Why Your Soul is Important

For what shall it profit a man, if he shall gain the whole world, and lose his own soul?

Mark 8:36

1. Your soul is important because it is the inner man, the real man who will live forever when the flesh is dead. Jesus described how the soul of a rich man suffered in hell whilst the soul of a poor man was in heaven.

There was a certain rich man, which was clothed in purple and fine linen, and fared sumptuously every day:

And there was a certain beggar named Lazarus, which was laid at his gate, full of sores, And desiring to be fed with the crumbs which fell from the rich man's table: moreover the dogs came and licked his sores.

And it came to pass, that the beggar died, and was carried by the angels into Abraham's bosom: the rich man also died, and was buried; And in hell he lift up his eyes, being in torments, and seeth Abraham afar off, and Lazarus in his bosom.

And he cried and said, Father Abraham, have mercy on me, and send Lazarus, that he may dip the tip of his finger in water, and cool my tongue; for I am tormented in this flame.

But Abraham said, Son, remember that thou in thy lifetime receivedst thy good things, and likewise Lazarus evil things: but now he is comforted, and thou art tormented.

And beside all this, between us and you there is a great gulf fixed: so that they which would pass from hence to you cannot; neither can they pass to us, that would come from thence.

Luke 16:19-26

2. To gain the whole world is to gain all the wealth, the money, the fame, the popularity, the acclaim and the honours this world can offer.

Whenever I think of the scripture in Mark 8:27, I remember those who have gained the wealth, the acclaim, the prosperity and the honours of this world. When I think of those who have gained this world and have died, I am frightened by the possibility that they may have lost their souls even though they gained the whole world.

Whenever I think about this scripture I remember **Princess Diana** who gained the palaces, the fame and the acclaim of this world. Could she be in hell today with the rich man Jesus spoke about? Could she be screaming with the millions of lost souls who are perishing in the lake of fire today?

Whenever I think about this scripture I remember **Michael Jackson** who gained the popularity, the fame, the wealth and the acclaim of this world. Could he be in hell today with the rich man Jesus spoke about? Could he be screaming with the millions of lost souls who are perishing in the lake of fire? What a frightening thought for someone whom so many people loved.

Whenever I think about this scripture I remember **Nelson Mandela** who gained the acclaim of this world by forgiving his tormentors and oppressors and allowing peace to come to South Africa. Could he be in hell today and suffer alongside the rich man Jesus spoke about who was calling for a drop of water? Could he one day be screaming with the millions of lost souls who are perishing in the lake of fire?

Whenever I think about this scripture I remember the powerful presidents who have ruled this world and affected the lives of millions. They gained the world's attention but could they be in hell today? Where will Chancellor Hitler be? What about Stalin? What about Churchill, Reagan, Nixon, Kennedy, Abraham Lincoln and Ghana's Kwame Nkrumah? Could any of these powerful people be in hell? Could they be screaming alongside millions of lost souls who are perishing in the lake of fire?

3. **Your soul is important because Jesus said there was nothing valuable enough that you could give in exchange for your soul.**

    For what is a man profited, if he shall gain the whole world, and lose his own soul? Or WHAT SHALL A MAN GIVE IN EXCHANGE FOR HIS SOUL?

    Matthew 16: 26

4. **Your soul is so important that God has appointed shepherds to guide your soul to heaven. Every preacher has been sent by God to shepherd and guide souls safely to green pastures.**

    For ye were as sheep going astray; but are now returned unto THE SHEPHERD and Bishop of your souls.

    1 Peter 2:25

5.   Your soul is important because your soul can be lost.

For what is a man profited, if he shall gain the whole world, and LOSE HIS OWN SOUL? Or what shall a man give in exchange for his soul?

Matthew 16:26

6.   Your soul is important because the soul can be destroyed.

And fear not them which kill the body, but are not able to kill the soul: but rather fear him which is ABLE TO DESTROY BOTH SOUL AND BODY IN HELL.

Matthew 10:28

7.   A soul is important because the soul can die.

Behold, all souls are mine; as the soul of the father, so also the soul of the son is mine: THE SOUL THAT SINNETH, IT SHALL DIE.

Ezekiel 18:4

8.   Your soul is important because it can go to hell.

For David speaketh concerning him, I foresaw the Lord always before my face, for he is on my right hand, that I should not be moved:

Therefore did my heart rejoice, and my tongue was glad; moreover also my flesh shall rest in hope:

BECAUSE THOU WILT NOT LEAVE MY SOUL IN HELL, neither wilt thou suffer thine Holy One to see corruption.

Acts 2:25-27

9.   Your soul is important because it can be required from you at any time. No matter who you are, your soul will be required of you. You will leave your skeleton behind, but your soul will be required of you.

And he spake a parable unto them, saying, The ground of a certain rich man brought forth plentifully: And he thought within himself, saying, What shall I do, because I have no room where to bestow my fruits?

And he said, this will I do: I will pull down my barns, and build greater; and there will I bestow all my fruits and my goods.

And I will say to my soul, Soul, thou hast much goods laid up for many years; take thine ease, eat, drink, and be merry.

But God said unto him, THOU FOOL, THIS NIGHT THY SOUL SHALL BE REQUIRED OF THEE: then whose shall those things be, which thou hast provided?

So is he that layeth up treasure for himself, and is not rich toward God.

Luke 12:16-21

The King's Last Command

Once upon a time, there lived a certain king who loved to acquire palaces, properties and accumulate great wealth. His palace could be compared to only the best in the world. This king was used to being in power, having ruled all his life.

One day, he summoned his courtiers and, among other things, gave specific instructions concerning his eventual death and burial. He instructed that a lovely room be prepared to serve as his tomb. He instructed them that they should not let him lie in a coffin. He wanted to sit on his royal throne and continue to reign over his wealth and palaces even in his death.

He also asked that an open book be placed on the table before him as he sat on his royal throne.

In the course of time the king died and the members of his court carried out all his instructions. His royal chair was placed before a table, his body was placed in his chair and a huge Bible was placed on the table before his body.

A hundred years later, another king was enthroned. He had heard of this old king's command and wondered if it had been followed and whether the king was reigning in his death. He sent his servants to open up the tomb and find out the state of this reigning king. When they opened up the tomb they were amazed at the sight they beheld:

A skeleton in tattered kingly robes! The skeleton was seated on the chair with a crown tipped sideways on a skull. A bone that used to be his forefinger was pointed to a portion of the Bible.

The servants drew near to see what the finger was pointing to. Believe it or not it was pointing to Mark 8:36: "For what shall it profit a man, if he shall gain the whole world, and lose his own soul?"

10. Your soul can be saved by having faith in God. Your soul can be saved by having faith in the blood of Jesus Christ.

Now the just shall live by faith: but if any man draw back, my soul shall have no pleasure in him.

But we are not of them who draw back unto perdition; but of them THAT BELIEVE TO THE SAVING OF THE SOUL.

Hebrews 10:38-39

Who Will Go To Hell?

There was a certain rich man, which was clothed in purple and fine linen, and fared sumptuously every day:

And there was a certain beggar named Lazarus, which was laid at his gate, full of sores,

And desiring to be fed with the crumbs which fell from the rich man's table: moreover the dogs came and licked his sores. And it came to pass, that the beggar died, and was carried by the angels into Abraham's bosom: the rich man also died, and was buried;

And in hell he lift up his eyes, being in torments, and seeth Abraham afar off, and Lazarus in his bosom.

Luke 16:19-23

1. **Many rich people will go to hell.**

Christ died to save you from perishing in hell. A place is made intolerable by the type of people that are there. The intolerable nature of hell is created by the presence of the most evil men who ever lived as well as the presence of evil spirits, the false prophet, the dragon and fallen angels. Jesus told us the story of the rich man who went to hell.

The Sick Politician

I remember a rich politician of a certain country who went to jail for various crimes. When he entered the prison he was so frightened by the kind of people that were there that he feigned sickness immediately and asked to be admitted to the hospital.

In that country, if you had enough money you could pay to be in a hospital that was outside the prison. This rich man continued to pay thousands of dollars so that he could stay out of the frightening prison. In the end, his money ran out and he had to go back to face the people in prison. Hopefully, this rich man would serve his sentence and come out of prison alive.

That is the fate of many rich men who descend into hell with no chance of parole. They are shocked to find that they have descended into a horrible pit; wherein dwell the most evil men that ever lived!

...THE RICH MAN ALSO DIED, AND WAS BURIED; AND IN HELL HE LIFT UP HIS EYES, being in torments, and seeth Abraham afar off, and Lazarus in his bosom.

Luke 16:22-23

2.   **Wicked people will go to hell.**

The wicked shall be turned into hell, and all the nations that forget God.

Psalms 9:17

The Frightened Prisoner

One day after preaching, a man walked up to me and introduced himself as an ex-convict. He described how he had been in prison for fifteen years. As he talked with me, I realised how nervous and edgy he was, casting furtive glances across his shoulder every few seconds.

At a point, I asked him what was wrong. He apologised for his unusually restless and jumpy attitude. He explained, "I am always scared because I think somebody is going to attack me from behind. I was twenty-one years old when I went to prison and I am now thirty-six years old."

He went on, "In jail there were so many murderers and rapists. You are always in danger of being attacked from behind. That is why I am so nervous."

That is what makes prison frightening. I began to understand what it meant to be in a prison. I understood even more what it meant to go to hell and be caged in with frightening characters like witches, wizards and murderers. Hell is a place to avoid at all costs. There will be many wicked people in hell.

3.   **People who have forgotten God and those who do not acknowledge God will go to hell.**

The wicked shall be turned into hell, AND ALL THE NATIONS THAT FORGET GOD.

Psalms 9:17

There are many people who have taken God out of their lives and their careers. They have forgotten that there is a God somewhere. Many people in Europe believe that there is no God. They do not believe in God, they do not pray to God and they do not go to church any more.

They may do good deeds and finance huge humanitarian programs but they will be turned into hell because they forget that there is a God. It is a fool who says in his heart that there is no God.

The fool hath said in his heart, There is no God. They are corrupt, they have done abominable works, there is none that doeth good.

Psalms 14:1

And just as they DID NOT SEE FIT TO ACKNOWLEDGE GOD ANY LONGER, God gave them over to a depraved mind, to do those things which are not proper, being filled with all unrighteousness, wickedness, greed, evil; full of envy, murder, strife, deceit, malice; they are gossips, slanderers, haters of God, insolent, arrogant, boastful, inventors of evil, disobedient to parents, without understanding, untrustworthy, unloving, unmerciful; and, although they know the ordinance of God, that THOSE WHO PRACTICE SUCH THINGS ARE WORTHY OF DEATH, they not only do the same, but also give hearty approval to those who practice them.

Romans 1:28-32, (NASB)

4. The pompous, the mighty and proud, the chief ones of the earth will go to hell.

The big shots of the earth will crowd themselves into the dark spaces of hell. The Bible speaks of the chief ones of the earth. The Bible describes how their ostentation and showiness will be brought down. Unfortunately, this will be the portion of the glamorous and flamboyant peoples of the earth.

Hell from beneath is moved for thee to meet thee at thy coming: it stirreth up the dead for thee, even all THE CHIEF ONES OF THE EARTH; it hath raised up from their thrones all the kings of the nations.

All they shall speak and say unto thee, Art thou also become weak as we? art thou become like unto us?

THY POMP IS BROUGHT DOWN to the grave, and the noise of thy viols: the worm is spread under thee, and the worms cover thee.

Isaiah 14:9-11

5.   The beast and the false prophet will go to hell.

The beast, who is the anti-Christ and the most evil prophet that ever lived, will also be among the community in hell. They will have their place there forever and all those who go to hell will have to contend with them.

And the BEAST was taken, and with him the FALSE PROPHET that wrought miracles before him, with which he deceived them that had received the mark of the beast, and them that worshipped his image. These both were CAST ALIVE INTO A LAKE OF FIRE burning with brimstone.

Revelation 19:20

6.   The devil will go to hell.

Another personality who will be among the community of hell is the devil himself. All those who have been afraid of demons and devils and ghosts will have to deal with the devil himself. The devil himself will be one of the most prominent and important members of the vast community of hell.

And THE DEVIL that deceived them WAS CAST INTO THE LAKE OF FIRE and brimstone, where the beast and the false prophet are, and shall be tormented day and night forever and ever.

Revelation 20:10

7. Anyone whose name is not in the book of life will go to hell.

And whosoever was not found written in the book of life was cast into the lake of fire.

Revelation 20:15

Finally, all those whose names are not in the Book of Life will go to hell. It is important that your name is in the Book of Life. Jesus came to die on the cross so that your name could be written in the Book of Life. Today is the day of salvation. You must accept Jesus Christ as your Saviour so that your name can be written in the Book of Life.

What Will Happen To You When You Die?

There was a certain rich man, which was clothed in purple and fine linen, and fared sumptuously every day:

And there was a certain beggar named Lazarus, which was laid at his gate, full of sores,

And desiring to be fed with the crumbs which fell from the rich man's table: moreover the dogs came and licked his sores.

And it came to pass, that the beggar died, and was carried by the angels into Abraham's bosom: the rich man also died, and was buried;

And in hell he lift up his eyes, being in torments, and seeth Abraham afar off, and Lazarus in his bosom.

And he cried and said, Father Abraham, have mercy on me, and send Lazarus, that he may dip the tip of his finger in water, and cool my tongue; for I am tormented in this flame.

But Abraham said, Son, remember that thou in thy lifetime receivedst thy good things, and likewise Lazarus evil things: but now he is comforted, and thou art tormented.

And beside all this, between us and you there is a great gulf fixed: so that they which would pass from hence to you cannot; neither can they pass to us, that would come from thence.

Then he said, I pray thee therefore, father, that thou wouldest send him to my father's house:

For I have five brethren; that he may testify unto them, lest they also come into this place of torment.

Abraham saith unto him, They have Moses and the prophets; let them hear them.

And he said, Nay, father Abraham: but if one went unto them from the dead, they will repent.

And he said unto him, If they hear not Moses and the prophets, neither will they be persuaded, though one rose from the dead.

Luke 16:19-31

One of the most important questions to ask yourself is: "What will happen to me when I die?" This is a question that cannot be easily answered by university lecturers or schoolteachers. There are no textbooks that boldly and adequately answer the question of what happens to a man when he dies. The Bible is the only book that confidently answers this controversial and difficult question.

Both the rich and the poor will die. The Bible declares that after death there will be judgment. Rich men are likely to live longer than the poor. However, both will eventually die. Death is the leveller that will level out things for both the rich and the poor.

Fifteen Things That Will Happen When You Die

1.   When you die you will either go to heaven or hell.

The rich man went to hell and Lazarus went to heaven. You will not just stop existing! You are not just converted into a piece of meat! You will head for a permanent destination away from this earth – heaven or hell.

> And it came to pass, that the beggar died, and was carried by the angels into Abraham's bosom: the rich man also died, and was buried; And in hell he lift up his eyes, being in torments, and seeth Abraham afar off, and Lazarus in his bosom.

> Luke 16:22-23

2.   For those going to heaven, you will be escorted by angels from this earth into the presence of God and into heaven.

This is what happened to Lazarus and I expect nothing less than a similar angelic escort for all of us who know the Lord.

> And it came to pass, that the beggar died, and was CARRIED BY THE ANGELS INTO ABRAHAM'S BOSOM: …

> Luke 16:22

3.   For those going to hell; you will not be escorted by angels. You will be met on arrival by evil spirits and other dead people.

This will be one of the most unpleasant experiences of your life. Your arrival into the permanent abode of darkness, demons and wicked fallen beings will not be noticed. Hell will be moved to meet you at your coming.

HELL FROM BENEATH IS MOVED FOR THEE TO
MEET THEE at thy coming: it stirreth up the dead for
thee, even all the chief ones of the earth; it hath raised up
from their thrones all the kings of the nations.

Isaiah 14:9

**4.   For those going to hell, you will descend and go
downwards. Hell is below. Hell is beneath us.**

The scripture says, "Hell from beneath is moved for thee".
That is why the rich man had to lift us his eyes to see Abraham
afar off. The rich man was down below and Lazarus was up
above him.

And it came to pass, that the beggar died, and was carried
by the angels into Abraham's bosom: the rich man also
died, and was buried; And in hell he LIFT UP HIS EYES,
being in torments, and seeth Abraham afar off, and Lazarus
in his bosom.

Luke 16:22-23

**5.   When you die you will discover that you have a
spiritual body, which is what the Bible refers to as the
inward man.**

When Jesus told the story of Lazarus, he referred to different
body parts such as the tongue, the finger and the eyes. It is
evident that there is another man within. This inward man will
live forever; either in heaven or in hell.

And he cried and said, Father Abraham, have mercy on me,
and send Lazarus, that he may dip the tip of his FINGER
in water, and cool my TONGUE; for I am tormented in
this flame.

Luke 16:24

**6.   If you go to hell when you die, you will find yourself in
a prison where there is endless unimaginable distress
and torment with intolerable agony.**

The endless nature of the agonies of hell is depicted by the worm that does not die and the fire that is not quenched.

And if thy hand offend thee, cut it off: it is better for thee to enter into life maimed, than having two hands to go into hell, into the fire that never shall be quenched: Where their WORM DIETH NOT, and the FIRE IS NOT QUENCHED.

Mark 9:43-44

7. If you go to hell when you die you will discover a place where people scream and cry for a drop of water.

Nobody asks for a bottle of water in hell. No one asks whether the water is cold or not. No one asks for ice. No one even asks for a small glass of water. Just a drop of water would make all the difference in hell. I honestly cannot imagine what kind of place hell is.

And he cried and said, Father Abraham, have mercy on me, and send Lazarus, that he may DIP THE TIP OF HIS FINGER IN WATER, AND COOL MY TONGUE; for I am tormented in this flame.

Luke 16:24

8. If you go to hell when you die you will discover a place of unbelievable and indescribable anguish and torment.

And he cried and said, Father Abraham, have mercy on me, and send Lazarus, that he may dip the tip of his finger in water, and cool my tongue; for I AM TORMENTED in this flame.

Luke 16:24

9. When you die you will discover that many people who received good things on earth will receive evil things in hell and many people who received evil things on earth will receive good things in heaven.

Many who suffered on earth will be happy and many who received evil things on earth will receive good things in heaven.

But Abraham said, Son, remember that thou in thy lifetime receivedst thy GOOD THINGS, and likewise Lazarus EVIL THINGS: but now he is comforted, and thou art tormented.

Luke 16:25

10. When you die you will discover that the first shall be last and the last shall be first.

In hell, the poor man was in a better place than the rich man. There was a complete reversal of status. The rich man was down, down, down! The rich man was powerless! The rich man was suffering! The rich man needed water! The rich man needed help! The rich man was crying out of his pain and his need!

Do you remember that all these things were happening to the poor man on earth? On earth, the poor man was down, down, down, needing help, and needing water. On earth, the poor man was powerless as he suffered and cried out in pain from his sores.

The words of Jesus will come to pass with such frightening accuracy, making nonsense of all the things we valued whilst on earth.

But Abraham said, Son, remember that thou in thy lifetime receivedst thy good things, and likewise Lazarus evil things: but NOW HE IS COMFORTED, AND THOU ART TORMENTED.

Luke 16:25

11. When you die, your circumstances will change radically.

If you were a rich man who used to send people on errands, you will no longer be able to do that. In the story that Jesus told, the rich man tried to send the poor man Lazarus on an errand, but he was blocked. Things had changed and the rich man was no longer allowed to have his own way. What a drastic change of circumstances.

> And he cried and said, Father Abraham, HAVE MERCY ON ME, AND SEND LAZARUS, that he may dip the tip of his finger in water, and cool my tongue; for I am tormented in this flame.
>
> Luke 16:24

12. When you die you will remember everything that happened on earth.

You will remember the opportunities you had. You will remember the messages you heard. You will remember your sins, and you will remember the altar calls you did not respond to. You will wish you had lived your life with the reality of heaven and hell always on your heart.

> But Abraham said, SON, REMEMBER that thou in thy lifetime receivedst thy good things, and likewise Lazarus evil things: but now he is comforted, and thou art tormented.
>
> Luke 16:25

13. When you die you will discover that there is a big gap between heaven and hell.

People cannot cross over from hell to heaven no matter who they are and no matter how much money they had on earth. If you want to cross into heaven, you must cross now because you cannot transfer when you die. This reality will be difficult for people who are used to taking advantage of their connections and friends in high places to get what they want. There will be no one in any high place to contact.

One of my children was privileged to gain admission into a prestigious school in Ghana. This school originally only had the capacity for two hundred and fifty children but it has been expanded to house one thousand, five hundred children. After the school had admitted the new entrants who really qualified, other students were mysteriously added to the school population everyday. My child told me how a new student arrived in the school every single day. Every one in the school knew that these were children who were connected to the rich and powerful in the Ghanaian society.

People who live in the African world are so used to getting things done through "whom you know". The reality of heaven and hell will be a great shock to this African culture. People cannot be transferred from hell to heaven every week because of whom they know. Salvation will be through the blood of Jesus and not through "whom you know".

> And beside all this, between us and you there is a GREAT GULF FIXED: so that they which would pass from hence to you cannot; neither can they pass to us, that would come from thence.
>
> Luke 16:26

14. When you die you will discover the importance of evangelists who go all over the world preaching the gospel.

You will appreciate the value of gospel crusades, evangelistic breakfast meetings, gospel concerts, Christian literature and tracts, and Christian television outreach programs. You will wish there had been more of these highly criticized preachers. You will wish you could swallow any words of criticism you have ever uttered against pastors and evangelists.

> Then he said, I pray thee therefore, father, that thou wouldest SEND HIM TO MY FATHER'S HOUSE: For I have five brethren; that he may testify unto them, lest they also come into this place of torment. Abraham saith unto him, they have Moses and the prophets; let them hear them. And he said, Nay, father Abraham: but if one went unto them from the dead, they will repent.
>
> Luke 16:27-30

126

15. When you die you will only be concerned about people not going to hell.

One day, you will not care about your money or your property. Today, most ministers of the gospel do not have the drive for soul winning that the rich man had when he was in hell. One day, you will be glad that Jesus Christ came to die on the cross to shed His Blood for you. You will be glad that God so loved the world that He gave His only begotten Son that whosoever believes in Him should not perish but have everlasting life.

Then he said, I pray thee therefore, father, that thou wouldest send him to my father's house: For I have five brethren; that he may testify unto them, lest they also come into THIS PLACE OF TORMENT.

Luke 16:27-28

127

SALVATION MESSAGE 19:

Why You Must Not Perish in the Lake of Fire

And the devil that deceived them was cast into the lake of fire and brimstone, where the beast and the false prophet are, and shall be tormented day and night for ever and ever.

And I saw a great white throne, and him that sat on it, from whose face the earth and the heaven fled away; and there was found no place for them. And I saw the dead, small and great, stand before God; and the books were opened: and another book was opened, which is the book of life: and the dead were judged out of those things which were written in the books, according to their works.

And the sea gave up the dead which were in it; and death and hell delivered up the dead which were in them: and they were judged every man according to their works. AND DEATH AND HELL WERE CAST INTO THE LAKE OF FIRE. This is the second death. And whosoever was not found written in the book of life was cast into the lake of fire.

Revelation 20:10-15

Christ died to save us from perishing in the lake of fire. All through the Bible we are told that there is a place called "hell". The lake of fire is the final destination for all who go to hell.

The Room Mate Who Went To Hell

I once heard a startling story of how the Lord Jesus appeared to an Assemblies of God pastor in a vision and told him, "I want you to become more evangelistic so I am going to take you to hell so you see how real it is."

This pastor had known the Lord from his youth but when he became a teenager he backslid and forsook God. This backsliding continued until he went to the university, where he re-dedicated his life to the Lord.

In fact, he became so zealous that he left college and decided to go into Bible School and into the ministry. One Sunday night, the Lord appeared to him, urging him to be more evangelistic.

During the vision the Lord took him to hell, where he saw all the sights and sounds of hell. He saw the weeping, the gnashing and the wailing of the lost. He said, "If the Lord had not been with me, I would have been really frightened of what I saw in hell."

Suddenly, they came across someone in hell whom he recognized. This person was his roommate whilst in second year in college.

He exclaimed, "What are you doing here? "

To his amazement his roommate said, "I was killed in an automobile accident on Friday."

Remember that this vision took place on Sunday night.

When he came out of the vision, he was so disturbed and wanted to call his mother to find out if she knew anything about his roommate but it was too late to call. So he called his mother on Monday. After exchanging niceties with her he asked, "Have you heard from so and so, my roommate?"

His mother answered, "I was going to tell you, he was killed in a terrible car accident on Friday."

The pastor could not believe his ears. He was in shock. It was real. He had actually seen his former roommate in hell. He had actually seen the inside of the prison with his own friend and roommate in it.

Dear friend, hell is real and the people in hell know and remember how they died! They know when they died! They have found out first hand that the Bible is true!

1. You must not perish in hell because hell is a vast lake of burning brimstone (sulphur).

There are many huge lakes of burning sulphur on the earth today. We call them volcanoes and indeed they are a sober reminder of the reality of the eternal lake of fire.

Burning sulphur has an acrid odour that is found in volcanoes. It is a marvel that modern sceptics cannot imagine lakes that are continually on fire. Volcanoes are burning lakes of fire found in different mountains all over the earth. Many of these volcanoes have been simmering for hundreds of years and no one has asked how the liquid fire in these vast lakes is kept ablaze.

And the devil that deceived them was cast into the LAKE OF FIRE AND BRIMSTONE [burning sulphur], where the beast and the false prophet are, and shall be tormented day and night for ever and ever.

Revelation 20:10

2. You must not perish in hell because it is a place of sorrows.

There are many well-known sorrows on this earth. However the Bible warns of the sorrows of hell. If the sorrows of this earth are difficult to bear how much more terrible will the sorrows of hell be? Hell is a place to avoid because of the sorrows there.

The SORROWS OF HELL compassed me about; the snares of death prevented me;

2 Samuel 22:6

3.   You must not perish in hell because it is a place where you never die and where the suffering never ends.

And IN THOSE DAYS SHALL MEN SEEK DEATH, and shall not find it; and shall desire to die, and death shall flee from them.

Revelation 9:6

The Husband Who Thought He Could End It All

The endless nature of hell is perhaps the most frightening aspect of all. I once heard the true story of a Swiss lady who was suffering in the hospital from terminal cancer. Her husband visited her everyday and watched his wife suffer and her health deteriorate. His wife was constantly writhing in agony and desperately wanted to die.

One day, he decided to end it all himself. Since he was a member of the reserve army of Switzerland, he went home, took his gun, went back to the hospital and shot his wife. Then he handed himself over to the police. He could not stand the suffering of his wife any longer and he decided to end it all. This gentleman was happy with the outcome because he knew he had ended his wife's suffering on this earth.

As I thought of this story, I remembered what Jesus had said about a place where the suffering never ends. You will not be able to take a gun and end anything. The worm never dies and the heat is never turned off.

And if thy hand offend thee, cut it off: it is better for thee to enter into life maimed, than having two hands to go into hell, into the fire that never shall be quenched: WHERE THEIR WORM DIETH NOT, AND THE FIRE IS NOT QUENCHED.

Mark 9:43-44

4. You must not perish in hell because it is a place worth giving up your eyes, arms and legs in order to avoid.

I know of no place on earth that is worth giving up your arms or your eyes for. Perhaps there is no stronger description to help us comprehend the kind of place that hell must be. A place so terrible that you should gladly offer your hand, your foot or your eye so as to escape from there!

And if thy hand offend thee, cut it off: it is better for thee to enter into life maimed, than HAVING TWO HANDS TO GO INTO HELL, into the fire that never shall be quenched: Where their worm dieth not, and the fire is not quenched.

And if thy foot offend thee, cut it off: it is better for thee to enter halt into life, than having two feet to be cast into hell, into the fire that never shall be quenched: Where their worm dieth not, and the fire is not quenched. And if thine eye offend thee, pluck it out: it is better for thee to enter into the kingdom of God with one eye, than having two eyes to be cast into hell fire:

Mark 9:43-47

5. You must not perish in hell because in the lake of fire, you will be bound in chains forever.

To be bound for a few hours is a hard enough experience. I cannot fathom what it must be like to be bound forever in chains of darkness.

For if God spared not the angels that sinned, but cast them down to hell, and delivered them into CHAINS OF DARKNESS, to be reserved unto judgment;

2 Peter 2:4

6.   You must not perish in hell because you will remain alive in the lake of fire.

You will not drown in the lake! Neither will you be burnt to ashes! You will be alive in this fire! This is not comparable to death by firing squad, drowning, hanging, poisoning or even electrocution. In those cases, death comes after a few minutes; and the horrors of the execution scene will pass away quickly whilst you are transported into another world. In this lake of fire, you will be alive whilst burning in a lake of fire.

And the beast was taken, and with him the false prophet that wrought miracles before him, with which he deceived them that had received the mark of the beast, and them that worshipped his image. These both were CAST ALIVE INTO A LAKE OF FIRE burning with brimstone.

Revelation 19:20

7.   The lake of fire will never be full because the Bible says hell is never full.

There is space for you in hell if you stubbornly refuse the gospel salvation through Christ.

Hell and destruction are never full; so the eyes of man are never satisfied.

Proverbs 27:20

8.   The lake of fire is constantly being expanded.

Because the majority of people are on the broad way, there are endless numbers of people heading towards hell. Multitudes await the good news of Jesus Christ in the corners of the earth whilst Christians rejoice over nothing in their big city churches.

The lake of fire is being expanded because more and more people are rejecting God, in their pride.

Therefore HELL HATH ENLARGED HERSELF, and opened her mouth without measure: and their glory, and their multitude, and their pomp, and he that rejoiceth, shall descend into it.

Isaiah 5:14

9.   You cannot afford to perish in the lake of fire.

Today must be the day of your salvation. You must not wait even one minute. You must not juggle with your very life.

The Italian Juggler

One day, an Italian man was returning home to Italy after living in America for a number of years. He was on a steamboat that was crossing the Atlantic Ocean from America to Europe. The journey across the ocean took several days and everyone on board was looking for some entertainment.

One day, this Italian man came across a young boy who was juggling a couple of oranges on the deck of the ship.

It happened that this Italian man was a professional juggler and that was the job he had been doing in America for so many years. He approached the young boy and offered to juggle his oranges for him. Because he was so good at juggling, a little crowd gathered around him. The juggler became excited and took on more and more oranges. Each time he took one more orange the crowd became more frenzied and cheered him on. The Italian juggler became even more excited and told the crowd, "I am going to show you something."

He excused himself from the crowd and went to his cabin to take something. When he came back on the deck he showed the crowd what he had in his hand. Everyone gasped! It was a huge valuable diamond belonging to this Italian juggler. He had bought it with all the money and savings he had earned from his years of work in America. He told the crowd, "I am going to juggle this diamond. It is my life's savings."

People told him not to do it but he told them that his hands were very sure and that juggling was his profession. He threw the diamond into the air with the other oranges and began juggling. The crowd was silent as they watched the Italian juggler play with his whole life's fortune.

Up went the diamond, glistening and sparkling in the sunshine. Just when the diamond came back to the juggler's hand the ship lurched and the diamond missed the juggler's hand and fell on the deck and bounced off the deck into the sea to the disbelief of the entire crowd.

This is what many people are doing in their lives. They are juggling with their souls. They are playing around with the reality of eternity. Like the Italian juggler, they do not realise how high the stakes are. It is their very lives that are at stake. Walking away from Jesus is walking away from your life. Walking away from Jesus Christ is to walk into the lake of fire.

The Day of Judgment

1. **No one will escape the Day of Judgment: Death and judgment are appointments that you cannot avoid. Some people appear to have escaped human judgment, but the Day of Judgment will certainly come to pass for everyone.**

And thinkest thou this, O man, that judgest them which do such things, and doest the same, that thou shalt escape the judgment of God?

Romans 2:3

And as it is appointed unto men once to die, but after this the judgment:

Hebrews 9:27

[3]The Appointment in Accra

There was a certain rich Nigerian man who lived in the city of Lagos, the capital of Nigeria. This man had many servants, but he was particularly fond of the chief servant who was a Ghanaian and had been with him for many years.

One day, the chief servant went to the market to buy some things for the master. And whom did he meet? He met a person called Death. Death had appeared in the market in bodily form. Death stared at the chief servant who in turn became frightened by the long stare of this stranger. He was so frightened that he abandoned his mission and forgot to buy the goods his master had sent him to buy.

When he got back home his master asked him, "Where are the things I sent you to buy?"

He told his master about how he had met Death in a bodily form. The chief servant was very shaken; and the master quickly realized that the chief servant was truly shaken because he had not behaved that way before.

The chief servant begged his master saying, "I am so terrified by the way Death stared at me that I want to leave Lagos immediately. I would like to go back to Accra before tonight. I really feel that Death wants to kill me."

The master really loved his servant and so released him to leave immediately for Accra. After the chief servant left, the master decided to go to town himself and see if he would find Death there. Indeed, if he did find him, the master would sort Death out because he was a very powerful person.

In the market, he was surprised to meet Death in bodily form, just as his servant had said. The master was fearless and approached Death, confronting and challenging him, "How dare you stare at my servant that way? Who do you think you are? What do you mean by that?"

Death stared silently at the master and then spoke. He said, "I was staring at him because I was surprised to find him in the market this morning seeing I have an appointment with him in Ghana tonight."[3]

The master was aghast. His servant was on his way to Ghana! He then knew that there was no way his servant would escape the appointment with Death.

2. **No one will escape the Day of Judgment: The Day of Judgment often comes suddenly. No one knows the hour or the day that God will call on us for judgment.**

For when they shall say, peace and safety; then SUDDEN DESTRUCTION cometh upon them, as travail upon a woman with child; and they shall not escape.

1 Thessalonians 5:3

But God said unto him, THOU FOOL, THIS NIGHT thy soul shall be required of thee: then whose shall those things be, which thou hast provided?

Luke 12:20

3. **No one will escape the Day of Judgment: The delay in the coming of the Day of Judgment is because of God's love and mercy to us.**

But, beloved, be not ignorant of this one thing, that one day is with the Lord as a thousand years, and a thousand years as one day. The Lord is not slack concerning his promise, as some men count slackness; but IS LONGSUFFERING TO US-WARD, NOT WILLING THAT ANY SHOULD PERISH, but that all should come to repentance.

2 Peter 3:8-9

4. **No one will escape the Day of Judgment: As the Day of Judgment is delayed, men become more hardened and more set in their evil ways.**

Because sentence against an evil work is not executed speedily, therefore the heart of the sons of men is fully set in them to do evil.

Ecclesiastes 8:11

5. **No one will escape the Day of Judgment: The mercies of God are intended to lead you to repentance before the Day of Judgment.**

Or despisest thou the riches of his goodness and forbearance and longsuffering; not knowing that THE GOODNESS OF GOD LEADETH THEE TO REPENTANCE?

Romans 2: 4

Do you think that God will judge and condemn others for sinning and not judge you when you do them, too?

Don't you realize how kind, tolerant, and patient God is with you? Or don't you care? Can't you see how kind he has been in giving you time to turn from your sin?

Romans 2:3-4 (NLT)

6. **No one will escape the Day of Judgment: As at today, you are not condemned. A final decision has not been taken about you in spite of your sins. A verdict has not been passed on you. God has not taken a decision on whether you should go to heaven or hell. You still have a chance to repent.**

For God sent not his Son into the world to condemn the world; but that the world through him might be saved.

He that believeth on him is not condemned: but he that believeth not is condemned already, because he hath not believed in the name of the only begotten Son of God.

And this is the condemnation, that light is come into the world, and men loved darkness rather than light, because their deeds were evil.

John 3:17-19

7. **No one will escape the Day of Judgment: Now is the time to repent because you are not condemned yet. God will receive you today. How can you escape if you neglect such an opportunity to be saved?**

Again, he limiteth a certain day, saying in David, To day, after so long a time; as it is said, TO DAY IF YE WILL HEAR HIS VOICE, HARDEN NOT YOUR HEARTS.

Hebrews 4:7

(For he saith, I have heard thee in a time accepted, and in the day of salvation have I succoured thee: behold, NOW IS THE ACCEPTED TIME; behold, now is the day of salvation.)

2 Corinthians 6:2

HOW SHALL WE ESCAPE, if we neglect so great salvation; which at the first began to be spoken by the Lord, and was confirmed unto us by them that heard him;

Hebrews 2:3

Did They Escape?

I know of several people who seem to have escaped judgment. The infamous Slobodan Milosevic who was the president of Serbia and Yugoslavia from 1989 until 2000, died of a heart attack before his five-year long trial for war crimes ended.

Adolf Hitler seemed to escape from the judgment of the allies who descended on Berlin in 1945, by committing suicide just before they arrived in his bunker.

As many as thirty-seven per cent of all murders in the United States go unsolved and the murderers seem to have escaped judgment.

But do these people really escape judgment? They may have escaped the judgment of human beings but they cannot escape the judgment of God. The Bible says that evil men will not go unpunished. (Jeremiah 30:11)

Christ the Judge

I charge thee therefore before God, and the Lord Jesus Christ, who shall judge the quick and the dead at his appearing and his kingdom;

2 Timothy 4:1

1. **Christ is the True and Righteous Judge: If man, in his sinful state, practices a system of judgment whilst on earth, why do you think God will not have a system of judgment Himself?**

All over the world, nations pass judgment on its citizens and imprison them for their wrongdoings. The presence of courts, tribunals and prisons is evidence of how men practice the concept of judgment.

And moreover I saw UNDER THE SUN THE PLACE OF JUDGMENT, that wickedness was there; and the place of righteousness, that iniquity was there.

Ecclesiastes 3:16

2. **Christ is the True and Righteous Judge: Man's judgment is often fraught with error. Man often judges by the outward appearance and this often leads to wrong decisions.**

Judge not according to the appearance, but judge righteous judgment.

John 7:24

But the Lord said to Samuel, "DON'T JUDGE BY HIS APPEARANCE or height, for I have rejected him. The Lord doesn't make decisions the way you do! People judge by outward appearance, but the Lord looks at a person's thoughts and intentions."

1 Samuel 16:7 (NLT)

Since 1989, over two hundred and sixty convicted prisoners in the United States of America have been set free after DNA tests established their innocence. So as you can see, the history of man contains recorded incidents of people who were wrongfully imprisoned by the justice system.

I remember the story of a government official who was murdered by a mob when they suspected that he was carrying a murdered victim in his car. This man was no murderer and it turned out he was actually taking the body of his mother-in-law to the mortuary when he was lynched.

The judgment of man is flawed because man looks on the outward appearance. There are people who naturally have funny faces. Everything they say sounds like a joke. There are others who have strange faces reminiscent of witches. Yet others have faces that look like those of criminals. These faces just happen to match the stereotypes that we have at the back of our minds. It does not mean that the people are what you think they are.

God does not look at these stereotyped faces. God does not judge according to vague perceptions. He judges according to truth.

3. **Christ is the True and Righteous Judge: God's judgment is according to the truth and not according to outward appearances.**

God's Judgment is a Righteous Judgment because God sees everything. God's judgment is a Righteous Judgment because He sees the hearts of men. There is nowhere to hide from God.

But we are sure that the JUDGMENT OF GOD IS ACCORDING TO TRUTH against them which commit such things.

Romans 2:2

Neither is there any creature that is not manifest in his sight: but ALL THINGS ARE NAKED and opened unto the eyes of him with whom we have to do.

Hebrews 4:13

Whither shall I go from thy spirit? Or WHITHER SHALL I FLEE FROM THY PRESENCE? If I ascend up into heaven, thou art there: if I make my bed in hell, behold, thou art there. If I take the wings of the morning, and dwell in the uttermost parts of the sea; even there shall thy hand lead me, and thy right hand shall hold me.

Psalms 139:7-10

4. **Christ is the True and Righteous Judge: Many men seem to escape judgment by justifying themselves and making excuses to men. The judgment of God will not allow you to justify yourself before Him.**

And he said unto them, YE ARE THEY WHICH JUSTIFY YOURSELVES BEFORE MEN; BUT GOD KNOWETH YOUR HEARTS: for that which is highly esteemed among men is abomination in the sight of God.

Luke 16:15

5. Christ is the True and Righteous Judge: Christ your Saviour today will be your Judge tomorrow.

The Saviour Who Became A Judge

A young man went swimming and nearly drowned. A passer-by jumped into the water and saved the drowning young man. Several years passed and this young man unfortunately became an armed robber. One day, this armed robber was arrested in a raid and was brought before the courts. He was very frightened because he knew he would receive the death sentence for his crimes.

When the case began, he soon realised that the judge sitting on the case was the same man who had saved his life by pulling him out of the lagoon years before. This realisation was a source of great relief to him, and the young armed robber relaxed, knowing that this man would treat him kindly. However to his amazement and disbelief, he did receive the death sentence for his crimes. He could neither believe his eyes nor his ears as the man who had saved his life earlier sentenced him to death for his crime. His saviour had become his judge.

Because HE HATH APPOINTED A DAY, IN THE WHICH HE WILL JUDGE the world in righteousness by that man whom he hath ordained; whereof he hath given assurance unto all men, in that he hath raised him from the dead.

Acts 17:31

6. **Christ is the True and Righteous Judge: Acknowledge your sins and confess that you are a sinner. Set things right before you meet the Judge.**

If we confess our sins, he is faithful and just to forgive us our sins, and to cleanse us from all unrighteousness.

1 John 1:9

Escape

How shall we escape, if we neglect so great salvation; which at the first began to be spoken by the Lord, and was confirmed unto us by them that heard him;

Hebrews 2:3

All through the Bible, God encourages people to escape from judgment and hell by accepting His free gift of salvation. Your need to escape from hell is very great because the conditions in hell will be intolerable. Escaping from the maximum-security prisons and the island prisons of the world is almost impossible. How much more to escape from the prison that God Himself has created for the devil and his cohorts and all the rebellious men of the world! There will be no escape once you are inside. Your chance to escape the judgment, the damnation and the torment of hell is now!

1. **You cannot escape the judgment of God: Just as a pregnant woman cannot escape labour, you cannot escape death.**

For when they shall say, peace and safety; then sudden destruction cometh upon them, as travail upon a woman with child; and THEY SHALL NOT ESCAPE.

1 Thessalonians 5:3

2.   You cannot escape the judgment of God: You cannot escape the judgment of God when you die.

And thinkest thou this, O man, that judgest them which do such things, and doest the same, THAT THOU SHALT ESCAPE THE JUDGMENT OF GOD?

Romans 2:3

3.   You cannot escape the judgment of God: You can escape hell by listening carefully and obeying the Word of God. If you do not listen and obey the Word of God you will not escape.

Watch ye therefore, and pray always, that YE MAY BE ACCOUNTED WORTHY TO ESCAPE all these things that shall come to pass, and to stand before the Son of man.

Luke 21:36

4.   You cannot escape the judgment of God: You can escape condemnation and hell if your sins are washed away by the blood of Jesus.

And from Jesus Christ, who is the faithful witness, and the first begotten of the dead, and the prince of the kings of the earth. Unto him that loved us, and washed us from our sins in his own blood,

Revelation 1:5

5.   You cannot escape the judgment of God: You will never escape without being washed by the blood of Jesus because we are all terrible sinners.

Ye serpents, ye generation of vipers, how can ye ESCAPE the damnation of hell?

Matthew 23:33

How SHALL WE ESCAPE, IF WE NEGLECT so great salvation; which at the first began to be spoken by the Lord, and was confirmed unto us by them that heard him;

Hebrews 2:3

How many of us have told a lie before? All of us!

How many of us have stolen something before? All of us!

How many of us have murdered someone before? All of us, because if you hate your brother you are a murderer.

How many of us have committed fornication before? All of us, because if you look at a woman lustfully you have already committed fornication with her.

There is no escape from our sinfulness. We must accept Jesus Christ and enjoy His wonderful salvation!

SALVATION MESSAGE 23:

Number Your Days

For all our days are passed away in thy wrath: we spend our years as a tale that is told. The days of our years are threescore years and ten; and if by reason of strength they be fourscore years, yet is their strength labour and sorrow; for it is soon cut off, and we fly away. Who knoweth the power of thine anger? even according to thy fear, so is thy wrath. So teach us to number our days, that we may apply our hearts unto wisdom.

Ps 90:9-12

1.   **Number your days: The Word of God commands you to number your days because God has given man a fixed number of days to be on earth.**

God originally gave us 120 years to live. But this has been reduced to 70 years because of sin.

And the LORD said, My spirit shall not always strive with man, for that he also is flesh: yet HIS DAYS SHALL BE AN HUNDRED AND TWENTY YEARS.

Genesis 6:3

149

The days of our years are THREESCORE YEARS AND
TEN; and if by reason of strength they be fourscore years,
yet is their strength labour and sorrow; for it is soon cut
off, and we fly away.

Psalms 90:10

The fear of the Lord prolongeth days: but the years of the
wicked shall be shortened.

Proverbs 10:27

2.   **Number your days: The Word of God commands you
to number your days because mankind often numbers
the wrong things.**

So teach us to number our days, that we may apply our
hearts unto wisdom.

Psalm 90:12

Indeed, men have passionately numbered everything except
their days. One rich man, sensing that he was going to die, asked
his children to take him out for a last ride through the city. He
made his children take him to all the different houses that he had
built in his lifetime. He was numbering his houses instead of
numbering his days.

Men are constantly numbering or counting the wrong things.
I remember the story of a man who was constantly counting the
amount of money that he had. When I first heard about him he
had about eight hundred million dollars. Every year, he would
assess his wealth as it gradually increased from eight hundred
million dollars to one billion dollars. He was obsessed with
crossing the one billion dollar mark.

Another rich man that I knew was constantly numbering the
coloured Mercedes Benz cars that were parked in his driveway.
He had the exact same car in different colours for different days
of the week and different occasions.

A lady I knew actually numbered her numerous dresses. I marvelled as I saw her dresses carefully numbered and lined in a long array. Her numerous shoes of different shades and colours filled large spaces in her closet.

I once saw a shoe shop in a certain country that reminded me of this lady who had numbered her shoes. The shop was called *"There is Nothing Like Too Many Shoes Limited".*

God advises His children to count their days rather than their shoes, their money, their cars or their houses. Sadly, men are doing the exact opposite.

3. **Number your days: The Word of God commands you to number your days because when you number your days you will discover that your life on earth is a contract.**

Your life on earth is like the limited time a hired person works for. He can only work as long as the contract allows.

Is THERE NOT AN APPOINTED TIME TO MAN UPON EARTH? are not his days also like the days of an hireling? As a servant earnestly desireth the shadow, and as an hireling looketh for the reward of his work:

Job 7:1-2

4. **Number your days: The Word of God commands you to number your days because when you number your days you will understand that the day of your death is already determined.**

There is a point beyond which you cannot go. God is the only One who knows that moment.

Seeing HIS DAYS ARE DETERMINED, the number of his months are with thee, thou hast appointed his bounds that he cannot pass;

Job 14:5

151

5. **Number your days: The Word of God commands you to number your days because Jesus numbered His days on earth. He knew His time was limited.**

Jesus saith unto them, My meat is to do the will of him that sent me, AND TO FINISH HIS WORK.

John 4:34

I must work the works of him that sent me, while it is day: THE NIGHT COMETH, WHEN NO MAN CAN WORK. As long as I am in the world, I am the light of the world.

John 9:4-5

6. **Number your days: The Word of God commands you to number your days because God does not want you to be deluded into thinking that you have more time than you actually do.**

SAY NOT YE, THERE ARE YET FOUR MONTHS, and then cometh harvest? behold, I say unto you, Lift up your eyes, and look on the fields; for they are white already to harvest. And he that reapeth receiveth wages, and gathereth fruit unto life eternal: that both he that soweth and he that reapeth may rejoice together.

John 4:35-36

7. **Number your days: The Word of God commands you to number your days because He wants you to be prepared for eternal judgment.** As you receive Jesus Christ as your Saviour, you will be washed in His blood today.

SALVATION MESSAGE 24:

What Shall It Profit a Man If He Shall Gain the Whole World and Lose His Soul?

For what shall it profit a man, if he shall gain the whole world, and lose his own soul? Or what shall a man give in exchange for his soul?

Mark 8:36-37

1. **What shall it profit a man to get all the money in the world and lose his soul? Earthly treasures and earthly money are not worth dying for. You cannot give up your soul for them.**

What shall it profit the miners in town to get all the gold in the world and lose their soul?

What shall it profit the stockbrokers to get all the money they can and go to hell?

What shall it profit the bankers to get all the money in the world and go to hell? What shall it profit the investors to gain the highest mark-ups on their investments and lose their souls?

You will have to leave all the money behind. Money will be a disappointing pursuit for you even on earth. The Bible predicts these realities. There is no need to use your life as an experiment to discover how true this famous scripture is!

WILT THOU SET THINE EYES UPON THAT WHICH
IS NOT? For riches certainly make themselves wings;
they fly away as an eagle toward heaven.

Proverbs 23:5

For riches are not for ever: and doth the crown endure to
every generation?

Proverbs 27:24

Thus I hated all the fruit of my labor for which I had
labored under the sun, for I must leave it to the man who
will come after me.

And who knows whether he will be a wise man or a fool?
Yet he will have control over all the fruit of my labor for
which I have labored by acting wisely under the sun. This
too is vanity.

Therefore I completely despaired of all the fruit of my
labor for which I had labored under the sun.

Ecclesiastes 2:18-20 (NASB)

For we brought nothing into this world, and it is certain we
can carry nothing out.

1 Timothy 6:7

2.   **What shall it profit a man to gain all the power the
world and lose his soul? Earthly power and position is
not worth dying for. You cannot give up your soul for
it.**

The Political Pilot

Years ago I knew of a pilot who had had a dramatic conversion
to Christ. His story was similar to the conversion of Paul because
he had seen a light and heard a voice calling him. He had become
a Bible study leader and an ardent Christian. I remember having
to rent instruments from his fellowship in order to have a crusade.

This well-known Christian, one day decided to join a political party and became an active politician. I watched, as he gradually became a popular politician. The more political he became, the less Christian he was until you could hardly recognize the Christian in him. It seems he forsook all his Christian principles in order to gain the world of political power.

He joined himself to wicked, die-hard politicians and hardened sinners who had no fear of God. Eventually, he left his wife and family and became just another unbeliever.

Years went by and he was struck with an incurable disease and was forced to turn to God again. One day, at about midnight, he felt deathly ill and he decided to make his way to a pastor's house. He banged on the gate and with a rasping faint voice, asked the security man to please let him in.

"Who are you?" he asked.

"I am the Minister of Rivers and Lakes. Let me in. I am dying."

The security man instantly recognized the important figure behind the gate. That night this Christian-turned-politician knelt and prayed in the pastor's living room.

He confessed how he had forsaken God and his family and strayed as far as the occult in his quest for political power.

"But it was not worth it," he told the pastor as he wept bitterly, repenting and gasping for every breath.

He died two weeks later, a stark example of someone who had tried to gain the whole world and almost lost his soul in the process.

Jesus said clearly, "What shall it profit a man to gain the world and lose his soul?" There is nothing more valuable than the soul of a man.

3.   **What will it profit a beautiful girl if she marries the prince and loses her soul? Earthly marriage is not worth dying for. You cannot give up your soul for it.**

The King's Wife

One day, a young beautiful African lady qualified from the university and began her career as an accountant. A bright future lay before her and she had planned to achieve many things for herself. One day, the traditional king of that country spotted her on one of his outings. He desired to marry her and offered her a chance to become his official queen.

This lady had a tough choice to make because taking up that position would mean that she would give up her career. It would also mean that she would become one of several women who would be wives to the king. She would also lose her privacy and her ability to see her friends and family as often as she was used to. She would not even have her bath on her own anymore because she would always have maids and guards waiting on her. To everyone's amazement she gave up her career, her ambitions, her friends, her privacy, and the assurance of being the only wife of her husband. Her only advantage was going to be that she would be the official queen.

Think of it, that God offers us the chance to become the royalty of Heaven. And yet many are not prepared to pay the price for it. Jesus taught that there is nothing more precious and more important than the soul of a man. And yet men and women are not prepared to pay anything for the salvation of their souls!

How much she hath glorified herself, and lived deliciously, so much torment and sorrow give her: for she saith in her heart, I sit a queen, and am no widow, and shall see no sorrow. Therefore shall her plagues come in one day, death, and mourning, and famine; and she shall be utterly burned with fire: for strong is the Lord God who judgeth her.

Revelation 18:7-8

4.   What shall it profit a woman to have a lot of children and lose her soul? Having a child is not worth dying for. You cannot give up your soul for it.

The Snake in the Woman

One day, I watched a documentary that showed a lady who was desperate to have a child. She had sought treatment in many places and had finally resorted to a herbalist who claimed to have a solution to her problem. In this real life documentary, she was being shown receiving treatment for infertility.

Can you guess what the treatment was? It involved the insertion of a snake (a serpent) into the birth canal of the woman. I watched in horror as the herbalist inserted a living writhing snake into the lady. This woman lay calmly in the lithotomy position whilst the herbalist inserted the entire snake into her body. This was the supposed treatment that would give this woman a child.

I realised the great extent to which people are prepared to go to have a child. But would they be prepared to do anything in order to go to Heaven and be saved? People are prepared to give up so much for other causes and yet when they are presented with Jesus they come up with a thousand excuses.

I also knew of a lady who was fifty-five years old and very determined to have a child. She underwent several risky procedures and took lots of dangerous medicines. She emphasized to the doctor that she would rather die than be without a child.

Miraculously, at the age of fifty-five she conceived and gave birth to twins. She died immediately after delivery. She had truly given up the whole world for her twins. But would this woman be prepared to do the same in order to be saved and go to Heaven? Would she be prepared to give up everything to save her soul? Most people are not prepared to do anything to have salvation.

5.   **What shall it profit a man if he becomes a European citizen and loses his soul? Becoming a European citizen is not worth dying for. You cannot give up your soul for it.**

The Stowaway

One day, a Ghanaian brother who lived in a port city of his country was watching television when it struck him about how beautiful the cities of Europe looked. He said within himself, "I must go to Europe. I don't mind whether it is Germany, England, Holland, Italy, …I am ready to go anywhere once it is in Europe." He had no means of flying to Europe and he did not qualify for a visa either. So he decided that he would become a stowaway and hide on one of the ships that sailed from his port to the glamorous cities of Europe. He was a determined young man and he eventually got himself onto a ship that was sailing for Europe. He hid deep in the hold, among the containers. Shortly after the ship took off he was discovered and brought back to the harbour.

He was not in the least perturbed and he decided to do it again. Unfortunately for this determined stowaway he was discovered again shortly after the ship left the harbour and was returned to his country.

He told his friends about his exploits and felt even more confident that he was going to make it on his third attempt. Indeed, he was more successful on his third attempt at being a stowaway and was only discovered when the ship was on the high seas.

Unfortunately for him the captain of this ship was a cruel, no-nonsense man and had him thrown overboard into the shark-infested ocean. I held my breath as this young man told me about how he spotted the shoreline from afar and decided to swim to land.

Miraculously he made it to the shore. He then asked some locals which country he was in, and they told him that he was in Liberia. He made his way back to Ghana and arrived safely in his port city. Yet again, for the fourth time he became a stowaway. This time he hid in the engine without eating for two weeks and was not discovered until the ship arrived in Amsterdam where he slipped out unnoticed.

I could not believe the determination, tenacity and self-sacrifice of this young man just to become a Dutch citizen.

As we sat talking in Holland he pulled out his European passport proudly and showed me pictures of his Dutch wife. Then I offered him an invitation to come to church. This was an invitation to Heaven. It was an invitation to become a proud citizen of the kingdom of God. Yet he refused, giving one lame excuse after another about how his work would not allow him to go to church.

I marvelled about how this man was prepared to give up the whole world to become a European citizen but was not prepared to give up anything to become a citizen of Heaven.

6.   **What shall it profit a man if he becomes an American citizen and loses his soul? Becoming an American citizen is not worth dying for. You cannot give up your soul for it.**

7.   **It is only your soul that is worth giving up everything for. Your soul is eternal and precious. Your soul will live forever. It is worth giving up everything for your soul to be saved.**

… it is better for thee to enter into life with one eye, rather than having two eyes to be cast into hell fire.

Matthew 18:9

Yea doubtless, and I count all things but loss for the excellency of the knowledge of Christ Jesus my Lord: for whom I have suffered the loss of all things, and do count them but dung, THAT I MAY WIN CHRIST, and be found in him, not having mine own righteousness, which is of the law, but that which is through the faith of Christ, the righteousness which is of God by faith:

Philippians 3:8-9

SALVATION MESSAGE 25:

Will You Be In Outer Darkness?

Then he which had received the one talent came and said, Lord, I knew thee that thou art an hard man, reaping where thou hast not sown, and gathering where thou hast not strawed:

And I was afraid, and went and hid thy talent in the earth: lo, there thou hast that is thine.

His lord answered and said unto him, Thou wicked and slothful servant, thou knewest that I reap where I sowed not, and gather where I have not strawed: Thou oughtest therefore to have put my money to the exchangers, and then at my coming I should have received mine own with usury.

Take therefore the talent from him, and give it unto him which hath ten talents.

For unto every one that hath shall be given, and he shall have abundance: but from him that hath not shall be taken away even that which he hath. And cast ye the unprofitable servant into OUTER DARKNESS: there shall be weeping and gnashing of teeth.

Matthew 25:24-30

1. People are sent into OUTER DARKNESS because they DESPISE THE OPPORTUNITY they have to be saved.

The man who received one talent received a great treasure. Hearing the gospel is receiving a great treasure.

Unfortunately, some people despise the treasure of the gospel that is placed in their hands. God wants people to hear the gospel preached.

Some people hear the gospel once, some hear it five times and some hear it ten times. You must make the most of the opportunity that you have. Different people have different numbers of opportunities to be saved. Some people have only one chance to be saved. This may be your one and only chance to be saved!

Or despisest thou the riches of his goodness and forbearance and longsuffering; not knowing that the goodness of God leadeth thee to repentance? But after thy hardness and impenitent heart treasurest up unto thyself wrath against the day of wrath and revelation of the righteous judgment of God;

Romans 2:4-5

2. People are sent into OUTER DARKNESS because they ARE LAZY.

"Thou slothful servant," said the master to the servant whom he was about to send into outer darkness. People are simply too lazy to pray, too lazy to go to church, too lazy to serve God and too lazy to study the Word.

The desire of the slothful killeth him; for his hands refuse to labour.

Proverbs 21:25

3. People are sent into OUTER DARKNESS because they are WICKED.

"Thou wicked servant..." said the master to the servant whom he was about to send into outer darkness.

Be not over much wicked, neither be thou foolish: why shouldest thou die before thy time?

Ecclesiastes 7:17

The wicked shall be turned into hell, and all the nations that forget God.

Psalms 9:17

4. People are sent into OUTER DARKNESS because THEY ACCUSE the people who come to preach to them.

"You reap where you don't sow," said the servant who was sent into outer darkness. The servant could not do anything with the talent because he was spending his time finding fault with the master.

Instead of receiving the Word, some rather accuse the men of God that are sent to them. The Bible declares boldly that salvation comes to places where the accusations have been silenced.

Constant criticism of evangelists makes it difficult for them to preach the simple gospel of Jesus Christ. They always have to defend themselves instead of preaching the gospel that needs to be heard.

And I heard a loud voice saying in heaven, Now is come salvation, and strength, and the kingdom of our God, and the power of his Christ: for the accuser of our brethren is cast down, which accused them before our God day and night.

Revelation 12:10

5. People are sent into OUTER DARKNESS because they are full of FEAR.

"I was afraid and I hid myself," said the servant who was sent into outer darkness. Many people are afraid of change. They are afraid of the unknown. They are afraid of leaving their boyfriends, they are afraid of joining the church; and because they are afraid, they hide. They don't come into the open to admit they are sinners.

You have to openly admit you are a sinner in order to be saved. You have to overcome your fears if you want to escape from outer darkness. Hell is full of fearful people. Fearful people are ranked alongside with the abominable, the idolaters and adulterers. Read it for yourself:

But the fearful, and unbelieving, and the abominable, and murderers, and whoremongers, and sorcerers, and idolaters, and all liars, shall have their part in the lake which burneth with fire and brimstone: which is the second death.

Revelation 21:8

6. People are sent into OUTER DARKNESS because they always feel that somebody is trying to CHEAT THEM.

"You want to reap what you have not sown," said the servant who was sent into outer darkness. The servant accused his master of reaping where he had not sown (which is cheating). Some people feel they are so smart that they always know when someone is trying to cheat them. Such people are "too clever" for God Himself and usually end up in hell. There is a kind of cleverness that is demonic, earthly and sensual. It emanates from hell and keeps people away from God.

Be not righteous over much; neither make thyself over wise: why shouldest thou destroy thyself?

Ecclesiastes 7:16

This wisdom descendeth not from above, but is earthly, sensual, devilish.

James 3:15

⁵The Village of the Cannibals

There were five sons who lived with their father in a beautiful mansion located on the top of a mountain. The eldest was an obedient son, but his four younger brothers were rebellious.

The father had warned the sons about a dangerous river nearby; but because the sons were rebellious they did not listen to his advice and kept going to this river. Each day, the rebellious children played in the river, swimming deeper and further each time.

One day, the four rebellious brothers decided to explore the banks of the river in a boat they had made. They did not know that this was the most dangerous thing they could ever do on that river. The river had carried away hundreds of people into unchartered and unknown territories.

That day, they launched out on the boat, and were swept away by the terrible currents that the river was known for. They fought to retain their balance and to gain control but they were no match for the raging currents of this powerful river. They held on to each other for hours as the river carried them downstream until it finally dumped them on the banks of a strange, unknown and frightening land inhabited by cannibals and brutal man-eating savages. For a long time the four children lay on the bank not knowing what to do.

The days passed and they attempted to go back upstream but the current was too strong. They also attempted to walk back by the side of the river but the terrain was icy, slippery, mountainous and impossible to climb. It seemed they were surrounded by the tallest mountains in the world on every side. Soon, reality set in, and they said to each other as the truth dawned on them, "We are trapped. There is no way back."

"We shouldn't have disobeyed our father," they admitted.

With the passage of time however, the sons learned to survive in the strange land. They found fruits for food and learnt how to make fire without matches. With time, they could kill animals, eat the meat and use the skin for clothes. They determined not to forget their homeland nor abandon hopes of returning to their father. Each day they set about the task of finding food and building shelter. Every evening they built a fire and told stories of their father and older brother. All four sons longed to see them again.

Then, one night, one brother failed to come to the fire. The others found him the next morning in the valley with the cannibals. He was building a hut of grass and mud.

"I've grown tired of our talks by the fireside," he told them. "What good does it do to remember? Besides, this land isn't so bad. I will build a great house and settle here."

"But this isn't a house, it is a hut" they objected. "It is a disgrace to live in such a place."

"What do you think our father will think of this?"

"But he isn't here. He isn't even near. Am I to spend forever waiting for him? I'm making new friends; I'm learning new ways. If he comes, he comes, but I'm not waiting forever."

A few days later, two of the other sons abandoned the riverside and followed their brother's example to settle and to build huts in the village of the cannibals. But the youngest son decided to live by the riverside in the hope that he would one day be rescued.

One day, the youngest brother heard a familiar voice behind him, "Father has sent me to bring you home."

The youngest lifted his eyes to see the face of his older brother. "You have come for us!" he shouted. For a long time the two embraced.

"And your brothers?" the eldest finally asked.

"They have made homes here and married cannibals in the villages around."

"Take me to them," said the oldest brother.

The youngest brother took him to the three other brothers. But the three brothers were not happy to see them.

"Who are you? What do you want?" the brothers asked their older brother.

"I have come to take you home," said the oldest brother.

"No, you have not come to take me home! You have come to take my mansion from me."

"But this is not a mansion. This is a hut," the firstborn countered in amazement.

"It is a mansion! This is the best area in Cannibal Village. I built it with my own hands. Now, go away. You cannot have my mansion."

"Don't you remember your father's house?"

"I have no father and I don't remember anything," he answered.

Nearby cannibals who had come to witness the scene did not hold their peace but joined in, "Don't listen to this stranger. He wants to take your mansion away from you. Send him away," they screamed.

The oldest son could not believe his ears: "But you were born in a mansion in a distant land where the streets are made of gold and where the modern lights never go out. You disobeyed our father and ended up in this strange land. I have come to take you home."

But the second brother's response was similar. "I don't need anything from you. I don't need my father and I don't need anything he has. I am happy as I am and everything is alright here." But really, he was afraid of the river and he was afraid of drowning.

He began hurling rocks at his older brother whilst the cannibals screamed threateningly at him, "Send him away! He wants to drown you in the river."

The third brother's response was equally discouraging. He said, "It's too far to walk. I have tried it before. It is impossible to go back up that river." But it was because he was the laziest person in the family that he did not want to go up the river. Once again the cannibals joined in to drive the oldest brother away saying, "He is trying to seduce you. All he wants is your money. Don't listen to this evil man. Your father will kill you when you get back. He has not forgiven you."

In the end, only the youngest son followed the elder brother back up the river to the father's mansion. There he was received with great joy but the other members of the household could not understand why the other children had not come back to their father.[5]

This is the story of the rejection of salvation by deceived men filled with diverse excuses and accusations. Through diverse excuses and accusations men have rejected the true salvation that comes from their Father's love. They never see the lengths to which their Father has gone to get them saved.

One of the brothers thought somebody wanted to take something from him. Another of the brothers was full of the fear of drowning.

The other was too lazy to walk up the river.

What excuses do you have that prevent you from receiving Christ today? Which of these excuses is going to lead you to outer darkness one day?

7. **People are sent into OUTER DARKNESS because they are too PROUD to put aside their fears and accusations.**

Humble yourself in the sight of the Lord and receive the blood of Jesus Christ for your salvation.

Salvation Before Suicide

One day, I appointed a brother as a pastor. As I introduced him to the congregation I noticed the tears streaming down his face. I had appointed many pastors to the ministry but it was unusual for anyone to cry during his appointment. After the ceremony, I asked him why he was crying. He explained that he had had many other brothers who were now dead.

"My brothers committed suicide before they could hear the gospel. They were drunkards and one of them hanged himself in the kitchen."

He continued, "Before I met Christ I tried to commit suicide three times."

He explained, "Somehow, my attempts at suicide always failed. That's how come I am still alive. I was determined to try a fourth time but before I had the chance to I found Christ."

He went on, "I shouldn't even have been saved. I am amazed that someone like me should even become a pastor."

This gentleman was grateful for the opportunity to serve the Lord. His tears of gratefulness demonstrated that he did not despise the great talent that the Lord had given to him.

In My Father's House There Are Many Mansions

1.   It is not enough to believe in God. You must believe in His Son.

God has a Son. Jesus Christ is the Son of God. Jesus Christ is not just a great prophet, He is the Son of God.

Let not your heart be troubled: ye believe in God, believe also in me.

John 14:1

2.   God is preparing a place in Heaven for those who believe in Jesus.

Jesus wants you to be with Him and not with the devil. If you do not go to the place that is being prepared for you, you will go to hell.

And if I go and prepare a place for you, I will come again, and receive you unto myself; that where I am, there ye may be also.

John 14:3

Do you want to go to this place? Many people will be surprised when they die. They will be surprised to find out there is a real world waiting on the other side. If you do not go to this mansion you will go to hell.

3. **There are many different kinds of mansions that have been prepared for Christians.**

The first will be last and the last will be first.

In my Father's house are many mansions: if it were not so, I would have told you. I go to prepare a place for you.

John 14:2

Many Mansions

One day a rich Christian woman died and went to Heaven. She was met by Apostle Peter and some other dignitaries who took it upon themselves to show her to her new quarters. As they drove through the streets of gold, they passed through amazingly beautiful estates that were littered with fantastic mansions. Finally they arrived at her new residence. When they took her in, she realized that it was some kind of dormitory or barracks.

She looked around feeling a little dazed and said to Peter, "There must be some mistake. Do you know who I am? Why am I being brought here?"

Peter said, "This must be where you belong otherwise you wouldn't have been assigned to these barracks." Knowing she did not have a choice, she resigned herself to her fate and went to see Peter off.

As she did that she couldn't help noticing the fantastic mansion just across the hill. "Who lives there?" she asked. "Oh, that is your maidservants' mansion."

"My maid servant?" "Yes", Peter answered. "Your maidservant from Earth". The woman continued to question, "But how come she lives in this mansion and I live in these barracks?"

"Oh that's simple", said Peter. "When you were on Earth you did not have time for God or for Heaven. You were so busy working for yourself and building up treasures on Earth. Even when it was time to give to help the church, you gave very little compared to what you actually had. Your maidservant was very faithful in serving the Lord and even though she had very little money, she gave it all to the Lord's work.

You will have to stay in these barracks for eternity but she will be in that beautiful mansion forever. The first will be last and the last will be first.

4.   How can we find the way to Heaven and to these mansions? By following someone who knows the way.

And whither I go ye know, and the way ye know. Thomas saith unto him, Lord, we know not whither thou goest; and how can we know the way?

John 14:4-5

Someone Who Knows The Way

One day I held a crusade in Freetown, Sierra Leone. After this crusade, we drove to another city further inland called Kenema. We drove on untarred roads, across dangerously narrow bridges and through some forests on our way out of the city. As we got deeper I felt more and more uncertain about where we were going.

"Are they sure they are leading us in the right direction?" I asked.

Suddenly, I heard some good news. I was told that the man in the lead car was involved in mining and had often used that very route.

From then on, I became relaxed and knew that we were headed in the right direction. We were not lost after all because we were following someone who knew the way because he had been there before.

There are some people who have not been to Heaven, and also boldly declare that they do not know where they are going. Do not follow such people. How can you follow someone who does not know where he is going? Jesus Christ knows the way to Heaven because He has been there before. Follow someone who knows the way to heaven.

5.   Jesus Christ is the Way. There is no other way.

We must accept Him and believe in Him so that we can go to Heaven. Open your heart and receive Jesus Christ as the Way, the Truth and the Life for yourself.

Jesus saith unto him, I am the way, the truth, and the life: no man cometh unto the Father, but by me.

John 14:6

The Lake of Fire

And the devil that deceived them was cast into the lake of fire and brimstone, where the beast and the false prophet are, and shall be tormented day and night for ever and ever.

And I saw a great white throne, and him that sat on it, from whose face the earth and the heaven fled away; and there was found no place for them.

And I saw the dead, small and great, stand before God; and the books were opened: and another book was opened, which is the book of life: and the dead were judged out of those things which were written in the books, according to their works. And the sea gave up the dead which were in it; and death and hell delivered up the dead which were in them: and they were judged every man according to their works.

And death and hell were cast into the lake of fire. This is the second death. And whosoever was not found written in the book of life was cast into the lake of fire.

Revelation 20:10-15

1. **There is a real Lake of Fire: Fire and brimstone speaks of fire and burning yellow sulphur.**

The idea that there can be a lake with fire is very real because of the existence of volcanoes that are literally lakes of fire.

And the devil that deceived them was cast into the lake of fire and brimstone, where the beast and the false prophet are, and shall be tormented day and night for ever and ever.

Revelation 20:10

2. **There is a real Lake of Fire: It is appointed to all men to die and to appear for judgment. The judgment will be held in front of the great white throne.**

And I saw a great white throne, and him that sat on it, from whose face the earth and the heaven fled away; and there was found no place for them.

Revelation 20:11

3. **There is a real Lake of Fire: At the white throne, two different books will be opened. One of them is the Book of Life which is a register of the names of all those who will be admitted into Heaven.**

This is the reason why you must ask God to write your name in the Book of Life. It is also important to inform the angels when you have made a change in your name.

And whosoever was not found written in the book of life was cast into the lake of fire.

Revelation 20:15

4. **There is a real Lake of Fire: At the White Throne another book will be opened which contains a register of your works.**

Long lists of your activities, sins, mistakes, errors, deceptions and failings will be read out. Only those things covered by the blood of Jesus will escape detection. This is the reason why you have to confess your sins regularly.

> And I saw the dead, small and great, stand before God; and the books were opened: and another book was opened, which is the book of life: and the dead were judged out of those things which were written in the books, according to their works.
>
> Revelation 20:12

5. **There is a real Lake of Fire: Is your name in the Book of Life? Will you escape the lake of fire?**

Will you perish in the mighty billowing waves of the lake of fire? Will you rise on the crest of the waves and fall into the depths of the lake of fire for the rest of eternity? Will you live in that lake of fire, surrounded by frightening creatures of darkness and men of wickedness? This is really the death you must fear!

> And death and hell were cast into the lake of fire. This is the second death.
>
> Revelation 20:14

6. **There is a real Lake of Fire: Be washed by the blood of Jesus and have your name registered in the Book of Life. Escape the lake of fire and secure yourself a place in Heaven.**

> And I saw a new heaven and a new earth: for the first heaven and the first earth were passed away; and there was no more sea.
>
> Revelation 21:1

Not Everyone That Sayeth Lord, Lord Shall Enter the Kingdom

Not every one that saith unto me, Lord, Lord, shall enter into the kingdom of heaven; but he that doeth the will of my Father which is in heaven.

Many will say to me in that day, Lord, Lord, have we not prophesied in thy name? And in thy name have cast out devils? And in thy name done many wonderful works? And then will I profess unto them, I never knew you: depart from me, ye that work iniquity.

Matthew 7:21-23

1. **Not everyone that says Lord, Lord, truly knows God: Many people are religious but do not know God. Jesus was speaking about religious people who do not know God.**

Many will say to me in that day, Lord, Lord, have we not PROPHESIED in thy name? And in thy name have CAST OUT DEVILS? And in thy name DONE MANY WONDERFUL WORKS? And then will I profess unto them, I never knew you: depart from me, ye that work iniquity.

Matthew 7:22-23

2.   Not everyone that says Lord, Lord, truly knows
     God: The reality is that many religious works are not
     acceptable to God because they are full of hypocrisy
     and pretence.

Many people give money for great works, just as a show.
People do not really serve the Lord Jesus.   Beware of just
practicing your works before men to be noticed by people.

> Take heed that ye do not your alms before men, to be seen
> of them: otherwise ye have no reward of your Father which
> is in heaven.   Therefore WHEN THOU DOEST THINE
> ALMS, DO NOT SOUND A TRUMPET BEFORE THEE,
> AS THE HYPOCRITES DO in the synagogues and in the
> streets, that they may have glory of men. Verily I say unto
> you, they have their reward.
>
> Matthew 6:1-2

> But ALL THEIR WORKS THEY DO FOR TO BE SEEN
> OF MEN: they make broad their phylacteries, and enlarge
> the borders of their garments,
>
> Matthew 23:5

3.   Not everyone that says Lord, Lord, truly knows God:
     God does not look on the outward appearance.

Outward things are not what God looks at.   God looks at the
heart.   God looks not on the outward parts.   God looks on the
heart. Don't waste time trying to deceive God with your outward
works.

> But the Lord said unto Samuel, Look not on his
> countenance, or on the height of his stature; because I
> have refused him: for the Lord seeth not as man seeth; for
> man looketh on the outward appearance, but THE LORD
> LOOKETH ON THE HEART.
>
> 1 Samuel 16:7

4. Not everyone that says Lord, Lord, truly knows God: No one can be saved by religious works and good deeds.

You are saved by the grace of God. You are not saved by going to church, paying tithes or contributing to the church building fund. You are not saved by building orphanages or bore holes for communities.

For by grace are ye saved through faith; and that not of yourselves: it is the gift of God: not of works, lest any man should boast.

Ephesians 2:8-9

Therefore we conclude that A MAN IS JUSTIFIED BY FAITH without the deeds of the law.

Romans 3:28

Be not thou therefore ashamed of the testimony of our Lord, nor of me his prisoner: but be thou partaker of the afflictions of the gospel according to the power of God; Who hath saved us, and called us with an holy calling, not according to our works, but according to his own purpose and grace, which was given us in Christ Jesus before the world began,

2 Timothy 1:8-9

5. Not everyone that says Lord, Lord, truly knows God: The important thing is whether you know Jesus and Jesus knows you.

I never knew you. You can be part of an organization but never be known by the leader. I once had some pastors who were part of our church. They were representing me in different cities but I did not know them. Yes, they were in the church; but I did not know them! Even though they were working in the church and for the church I did not know them!

Many will say to me in that day, Lord, Lord, have we not prophesied in thy name? And in thy name have CAST OUT DEVILS? And in thy name DONE MANY WONDERFUL WORKS? And then will I profess unto them, I NEVER KNEW you: depart from me, ye that work iniquity.

Matthew 7:22-23

6.   Not everyone that says Lord, Lord, truly knows God: Do you know Jesus as your Saviour? Do you know Jesus as your Lord? Do you have a personal relationship with Him or is He outside your life?

Jesus Christ wants to come into your life and have a personal relationship with you.

Behold, I stand at the door, and knock: if any man hear my voice, and open the door, I will come in to him, and will sup with him, and he with me.

Revelation 3:20

7.   Not everyone that says Lord, Lord, truly knows God: Through the blood of Jesus you will be cleansed from your sins and you can get to know God.

The blood of Jesus and the supreme sacrifice is what has paid the price for our sins so that we can know God.

If we say that we have fellowship with Him and yet walk in the darkness, we lie and do not practice the truth; but if we walk in the Light as He Himself is in the Light, we have fellowship with one another, and the blood of Jesus His Son cleanses us from all sin.

1 John 1:6-7 (NASB)

SALVATION MESSAGE 29:

The Hidden Man

But let it be THE HIDDEN MAN of the heart, in that which is not corruptible, even the ornament of a meek and quiet spirit, which is in the sight of God of great price.

1 Peter 3:4

That he would grant you, according to the riches of his glory, to be strengthened with might by his Spirit in THE INNER MAN;

Ephesians 3:16

For I delight in the law of God after THE INWARD MAN:

Romans 7:22

1. There is a hidden man within you: Everybody has a man who is hiding within him and who looks just like him. The rich man in hell recognized Abraham because the hidden man looks exactly like the outward man.

And it came to pass, that the beggar died, and was carried by the angels into Abraham's bosom: the rich man also died, and was buried; And in hell he lift up his eyes, being in torments, and seeth Abraham afar off, and Lazarus in his bosom.

Luke 16:22-23

2. **There is a hidden man within you: On the day that you die, the man who has been hiding within you for many years will be revealed. Lazarus had a hidden man who was revealed at death. The rich man also had a hidden man within him who was revealed by death.**

And it came to pass, that the beggar died, and was carried by the angels into Abraham's bosom: the rich man also died, and was buried;
And in hell he lift up his eyes, being in torments, and seeth Abraham afar off, and Lazarus in his bosom.
And he cried and said, Father Abraham, have mercy on me, and send Lazarus, that he may dip the tip of his finger in water, and cool my tongue; for I am tormented in this flame.

Luke 16:22-24

3. **There is a hidden man within you: After death, the hidden man can no longer hide in the body so it is forced to migrate to either heaven or hell.** At death, the body decomposes and is covered with worms. The hidden man cannot stay in the midst of these worms. This is when the hidden man comes out of hiding.

One dieth in his full strength, being wholly at ease and quiet. His breasts are full of milk, and his bones are moistened with marrow. And another dieth in the bitterness

of his soul, and never eateth with pleasure. THEY SHALL
LIE DOWN ALIKE IN THE DUST, AND THE WORMS
SHALL COVER THEM.

Job 21:23-26

4.   There is a hidden man within you: At death, the
      hidden man is forced to move on to the next world
      which is either Heaven or hell. The address of the
      hidden man will either be in Heaven or in hell.

5.   There is a hidden man within you: When your hidden
      man finally comes out of hiding, will your hidden man
      live in Heaven or in hell? The hidden man of Lazarus
      is in Heaven and the hidden man of the rich man
      resides in hell.

6.   There is a hidden man within you: Receive Jesus as
      your Saviour and ensure that your hidden man will
      live in Heaven for eternity.

All Dead People Are Still Alive

And as it is appointed unto men once to die, but after this the judgment:

Hebrews 9:27

All the dead people you know are alive somewhere:

Lazarus is still alive. The rich man in Luke 16 is still alive.

Deceased pompous men are still alive. Hitler is still alive.

Those who didn't want to die but did, are still alive.

Famous people who died are still alive; Michael Jackson is still alive! Princess Diana is still alive!

Dead and former presidents are still alive: Kwame Nkrumah is still alive! Nelson Mandela is still alive!

Rich people are still alive.

Those who didn't believe are still alive.

Those who believed are still alive.

1. **All dead people are still alive: Your life exists after it vanishes from this earth. You will be living on after you vanish from this earth.**

Whereas ye know not what shall be on the morrow. For what is your life? It is even a vapour, that appeareth for a little time, and then vanisheth away.

James 4:14

The fact that something has vanished does not mean that it does not exist. When something vanishes, it means it has gone away from your vision. Your life is like a vapour that is seen briefly and then is not seen again.

2. **All dead people are still alive: After you die, there is judgment awaiting you. You need to be alive for the judgment.**

And as it is appointed unto men once to die, but after this the judgment:

Hebrews 9:27

3. **All dead people are still alive: After you die, you need to be alive to go to "court" and receive your judgment.**

It is appointed to men once to die and after that the judgment. After your death, you have to be alive to go to "court" to hear the court proceedings and receive your judgment. Evidence will be brought forth in various forms. Videos of certain things you did in life will be brought out. There will be photographs of some of the things you engaged in. It is appointed for man to die once, after that is court and judgment.

4.   All dead people are still alive: Even though your life is a vapour you cannot put an end to it yourself.

Thou art worthy, O Lord, to receive glory and honour and power; for thou hast created all things, and for thy pleasure they are and were created.

Revelation 4:11

God is the one who makes us alive and you cannot end the life God has given you. God has created life and our lives exist for His pleasure. You cannot choose to end your life by yourself. You cannot end your life by committing suicide.

Judas thought he was ending everything by killing himself. But it did not end there. There were 42 failed attempts to kill Adolf Hitler. Hitler thought that after causing the death of fifty million people, he could choose to end it all by committing suicide. But it is not true! All dead people are still alive.

Death is both a blessing and an enemy! Death looks bad but it is also good! Imagine life without death. Wicked people like Hitler would have continued their wicked ways. We have been created to live forever but we will exit from this earth first.

5.   All dead people are still alive: All dead people are still alive!

Luke 16 talks of a rich man clothed in purple and a poor man called Lazarus. One day Lazarus died, and angels came to carry him into Abraham's bosom. The rich man also died but no angels came for him. Demons escorted him to hell. It will be a frightening experience to die without knowing God.

6.   All dead people are still alive: There are many examples of people who are dead but alive.

In hell, the rich men lifted up his eyes – this action showed that he was alive.

In hell, the rich man was in torments – this means he could still feel pain.

The rich man was alive and he could still speak. Abraham engaged in a conversation with the rich man who had died.

Remember, after death, you are so alive that you can go to court! Jesus came to save us from our sins so that we do not go to hell.

7. **All dead people are still alive: Give your heart to Jesus so that you will be ALIVE IN HEAVEN and not ALIVE IN HELL.**

Make sure that you are alive in Heaven and not alive in hell!

SECTION 5:

SALVATION AND VARIOUS INDIVIDUALS

Jesus and the Woman of Samaria
(Do You Know and Recognize Jesus?)

Jesus answered and said unto her, If thou knewest the gift of God, and who it is that saith to thee, Give me to drink; thou wouldest have asked of him, and he would have given thee living water.

John 4:10

1. **Many people meet with Jesus but they do not recognize who He is. As a result of this they miss Him. Jesus asked the woman of Samaria whether she recognized who He was.**

Jesus answered and said unto her, IF THOU KNEWEST the gift of God, and who it is that saith to thee, Give me to drink; thou wouldest have asked of him, and he would have given thee living water.

John 4:10

2. **The woman of Samaria was with Jesus but did not recognize who He was.**

The woman saith unto him, I KNOW THAT MESSIAS COMETH, which is called Christ: when he is come, he will tell us all things. Jesus saith unto her, I that speak unto thee am he.

John 4:25-26

3.   Pontius Pilate was with Jesus but it was his wife who recognized whom He was in a dream.

When he was set down on the judgment seat, HIS WIFE sent unto him, saying, Have thou nothing to do with that just man: for I have suffered many things this day in a dream because of him.

Matthew 27:19

4.   There were two thieves on the cross but only one recognized Him.

And one of the malefactors which were hanged railed on him, saying, if thou be Christ, save thyself and us.

But the other answering rebuked him, saying, Dost not thou fear God, seeing thou art in the same condemnation?

And we indeed justly; for we receive the due reward of our deeds: but this man hath done nothing amiss.

Luke 23:39-41

5.   The two men on the road from Emmaus did not recognize Jesus.

And, behold, two of them went that same day to a village called Emmaus, which was from Jerusalem about threescore furlongs.

And they talked together of all these things which had happened. But their eyes were holden that THEY SHOULD NOT KNOW HIM.

Luke 24:13-14, 16

6. **Peter recognized Jesus and said He was the Son of God.**

When Jesus came into the coasts of Caesarea Philippi, he asked his disciples, saying, whom do men say that I the Son of man am?

And they said, Some say that thou art John the Baptist: some, Elias; and others, Jeremias, or one of the prophets. He saith unto them, But whom say ye that I am?

And Simon Peter answered and said, THOU ART THE CHRIST, the Son of the living God.

Matthew 16:13-16

7. **Do you recognize and know that Jesus is knocking on the door of your heart?** If you knew, you would answer and open your heart to Him so that you can be saved.

Behold, I STAND AT THE DOOR, and knock: if any man hear my voice, and open the door, I will come in to him, and will sup with him, and he with me.

Revelation 3:20

SALVATION MESSAGE 32:

Jesus and Nicodemus

There was a man of the Pharisees, named Nicodemus, a ruler of the Jews:

The same came to Jesus by night, and said unto him, Rabbi, we know that thou art a teacher come from God: for no man can do these miracles that thou doest, except God be with him.

Jesus answered and said unto him, Verily, verily, I say unto thee, Except a man be born again, he cannot see the kingdom of God.

Nicodemus saith unto him, How can a man be born when he is old? can he enter the second time into his mother's womb, and be born?

Jesus answered, Verily, verily, I say unto thee, Except a man be born of water and of the Spirit, he cannot enter into the kingdom of God.

That which is born of the flesh is flesh; and that which is born of the Spirit is spirit. Marvel not that I said unto thee, ye must be born again.

John 3:1-7

192

1. Nicodemus, like many important people, was religious but he was not born again. **Being religious does not make you a Christian. Being religious will not get you to Heaven.** Nicodemus, an important man, came to Jesus and important people need to come to Jesus too. Religious people need to come to Jesus Christ.

Not every one that saith unto me, Lord, Lord, shall enter into the kingdom of heaven; but he that doeth the will of my Father which is in heaven.

Matthew 7:21

2. Nicodemus, like many important people, did not want to be publicly associated with Christ. **It is necessary to associate publicly with Christ.** Nicodemus came to Jesus at night. Why did he not come during the day?

Whosoever therefore shall be ashamed of me and of my words in this adulterous and sinful generation; of him also shall the Son of man be ashamed, when he cometh in the glory of his Father with the holy angels.

Mark 8:38

3. Nicodemus, like many important people, saw the miracles and knew that God was speaking to him. **The miracles in your life are a sign of God's mercy to you.** Nicodemus noticed the miracles in the ministry of Jesus and recognized that they were signs from God.

Ye men of Israel, hear these words; Jesus of Nazareth, A MAN APPROVED OF GOD AMONG YOU BY MIRACLES and wonders and signs, which God did by him in the midst of you, as ye yourselves also know:

Acts 2:22

4. **Nicodemus, like many important people, would not be able to enter the kingdom of God unless he was born again. Unless a man is born again he cannot enter the kingdom of God.**

And said, Verily I say unto you, except ye be converted, and become as little children, ye shall not enter into the kingdom of heaven.

Matthew 18:3

Repent ye therefore, and be converted, that your sins may be blotted out, when the times of refreshing shall come from the presence of the Lord;

Acts 3:19

5. **Nicodemus, like many important people, would go to hell if he were not born again. Unless a man is born again he will not go to heaven; he will go to hell. Chiefs, leaders, presidents, school prefects, millionaires and students will go to hell if they are not born again.**

I tell you, Nay: but, except ye repent, ye shall all likewise perish.

Luke 13:5

6. **Nicodemus, like many important people, did not understand that being born again was a spiritual experience. Being born again is not a physical experience like eating, drinking, bathing, cooking, singing or dancing. Being born again is a totally spiritual experience that you can only have through your faith in God.**

For by grace are ye saved through faith; and that not of yourselves: it is the gift of God: Not of works, lest any man should boast.

Ephesians 2:8-9

7. **Nicodemus, like all important people, had to be saved and baptized.**

He that believeth and is baptized shall be saved; but he that believeth not shall be damned.

Mark 16:16

8. **Nicodemus, like many important people, was surprised at the simplicity and humility required for salvation. Do not be surprised at God's method of saving the world through Jesus Christ. Do not be surprised at the simplicity of Christ. You must equally not be surprised if you go to hell because you reject Christ. God is showing you the way of salvation today.**

How shall we escape, if we neglect so great salvation; which at the first began to be spoken by the Lord, and was confirmed unto us by them that heard him.

Hebrews 2:3

Jesus and Zacchaeus

And Jesus entered and passed through Jericho. And, behold, there was a man named Zacchaeus, which was the chief among the publicans, and he was rich.

And he sought to see Jesus who he was; and could not for the press, because he was little of stature. And he ran before, and climbed up into a sycomore tree to see him: for he was to pass that way. And when Jesus came to the place, he looked up, and saw him, and said unto him, Zacchaeus, make haste, and come down; for to day I must abide at thy house. And he made haste, and came down, and received him joyfully.

And when they saw it, they all murmured, saying, that he was gone to be guest with a man that is a sinner. And Zacchaeus stood, and said unto the Lord; Behold, Lord, the half of my goods I give to the poor; and if I have taken any thing from any man by false accusation, I restore him fourfold.

And Jesus said unto him, this day is salvation come to this house, forsomuch as he also is a son of Abraham. For the Son of man is come to seek and to save that which was lost.

Luke 19:1-10

1.   Zacchaeus, like many rich men, encountered Jesus Christ when He was passing through his city.

And Jesus entered and PASSED THROUGH JERICHO.

Luke 19:1

"Jesus entered and passed through Jericho." Jesus Christ is passing through your city, giving you an opportunity for salvation. Jesus Christ is seeking to save you today.

For the Son of man is come to save that which was lost. How think ye? if a man have an hundred sheep, and one of them be gone astray, doth he not leave the ninety and nine, and goeth into the mountains, and seeketh that which is gone astray?

Matthew 18:11-12

2.   Zacchaeus, like many rich men, was a sinner and trusted in his riches.

And, behold, there was a man named Zacchaeus, which was the chief among the publicans, and HE WAS RICH.

Luke 19:2

Many rich people are sinners who trust in their riches. Zacchaeus was a rich sinner. Jesus taught that it was difficult for rich people to be saved. Indeed, the only person Jesus told us was in hell was a rich man. Rich people can be saved and this is proved by the salvation of Zacchaeus.

The rich man's wealth is his strong city, and as an high wall in his own conceit. Before destruction the heart of man is haughty, and before honour is humility.

Proverbs 18:11-12

Lo, this is the man that made not God his strength; but trusted in the abundance of his riches, and strengthened himself in his wickedness.

Psalms 52:7

… But Jesus answereth again, and saith unto them, Children, how hard is it for them that trust in riches to enter into the kingdom of God!

Mark 10:24

For because thou hast trusted in thy works and in thy treasures, thou shalt also be taken: and Chemosh shall go forth into captivity with his priests and his princes together.

Jeremiah 48:7

3. Zacchaeus, like many rich men, was seeking Jesus but had external obstacles to overcome.

And he sought to see Jesus who he was; AND COULD NOT FOR THE PRESS, because he was little of stature.

Luke 19:3

Zacchaeus sought to see Jesus but had obstacles that prevented him from seeing Jesus. The crowds of people thronging Jesus became external obstacles that prevented Zacchaeus from seeing Jesus. Because there were thousands of people around, Zacchaeus could not get anywhere near the Lord.

There are many external obstacles that people have to overcome in order to receive Christ. The external obstacle may be a boyfriend, a girlfriend, a relative or even a parent. Sometimes your job actually prevents you from knowing Christ.

Whatever the obstacle is, you must overcome it and make contact with the Saviour. Zacchaeus climbed a tree to overcome the obstacles that stood between him and Christ. You must do whatever it takes to overcome whatever is blocking your view of the Lord.

And shall say, Cast ye up, cast ye up, prepare the way, TAKE UP THE STUMBLINGBLOCK OUT OF THE WAY OF MY PEOPLE.

Isaiah 57:14

Every valley shall be exalted, and every mountain and hill shall be made low: and the crooked shall be made straight, and THE ROUGH PLACES PLAIN: And the glory of the LORD shall be revealed, and all flesh shall see it together: for the mouth of the LORD hath spoken it.

Isaiah 40:4-5

If any man come to me, and hate not his father, and mother, and wife, and children, and brethren, and sisters, yea, and his own life also, he cannot be my disciple.

Luke 14:26

4. Zacchaeus, like many rich men, also had personal obstacles to overcome in order to see Jesus.

And he sought to see Jesus who he was; and could not for the press, because HE WAS LITTLE OF STATURE.

Luke 19:3

Zacchaeus was a short man (a man of little stature) and this was a personal problem that he had to overcome in order to see Jesus.

Zacchaeus was simply too short to see over the crowds of people. Many people seeking Jesus have personal and internal problems that they need to overcome in order to receive Jesus.

Internal obstacles like pride, a life of sin, addictions and family background can form barriers that prevent people from knowing the Lord.

And IF THY HAND OFFEND THEE, CUT IT OFF: it is better for thee to enter into life maimed, than having two hands to go into hell, into the fire that never shall be quenched:

Mark 9:43

Let the wicked forsake his way, and the unrighteous man his thoughts: and let him return unto the Lord, and he will have mercy upon him; and to our God, for he will abundantly pardon.

Isaiah 55:7

5. Zacchaeus was known to Jesus by name.

And when JESUS came to the place, he looked up, and saw him, and SAID UNTO HIM, ZACCHAEUS, make haste, and come down; for to day I must abide at thy house.

Luke 19:5

Jesus knows your name and calls you by your name today. Jesus said, "Zacchaeus, make haste, and come down; for to day I must abide at thy house."

All through the Bible, God has called people out by their names. Just as Zacchaeus was called out by name, God is calling you by name.

a. And the Lord God called unto ADAM, and said unto him, where art thou?

Genesis 3:9

b. And the Lord said unto Cain, Where is ABEL thy brother? And he said, I know not: Am I my brother's keeper?

Genesis 4:9

c. Now the Lord had said unto ABRAM, Get thee out of thy country, and from thy kindred, and from thy father's house, unto a land that I will shew thee.

Genesis 12:1

d. ...And when Jesus beheld him, he said, Thou art SIMON the son of Jona: thou shalt be called Cephas, which is by interpretation, a stone.

John 1:42

e. He saw in a vision evidently about the ninth hour of the day an angel of God coming in to him, and saying unto him, CORNELIUS. And when he looked on him, he was afraid, and said, what is it, Lord? And he said unto him, Thy prayers and thine alms are come up for a memorial before God.

Acts 10:3-4

f. And there came a voice to him, Rise, PETER; kill, and eat.

Acts 10:13

6. Zacchaeus, like many rich men, had to respond quickly to Jesus. It is important to respond quickly and immediately to God.

And when Jesus came to the place, he looked up, and saw him, and said unto him, ZACCHAEUS, MAKE HASTE, AND COME DOWN; for to day I must abide at thy house.

Luke 19:5

Jesus told Zacchaeus: "MAKE HASTE and come down to me". If you are coming to God, it is important to hurry up. Hurry, because you do not know how much time you have.

While it is said, to day if ye will hear his voice, harden not your hearts, as in the provocation.

Hebrews 3:15

For this shall every one that is godly pray unto thee in a time when thou mayest be found: surely in the floods of great waters they shall not come nigh unto him.

Psalms 32:6

Thus saith the Lord, in an acceptable time have I heard thee, and in a day of salvation have I helped thee: and I will preserve thee, and give thee for a covenant of the people, to establish the earth, to cause to inherit the desolate heritages;

Isaiah 49:8

7.   Zacchaeus, like many rich men needed Jesus Christ in his house. Jesus wanted to come into the heart and life of Zacchaeus.

And Jesus said unto him, THIS DAY IS SALVATION COME TO THIS HOUSE, forsomuch as he also is a son of Abraham.

Luke 19:9

BEHOLD, I STAND AT THE DOOR, and knock: if any man hear my voice, and open the door, I will come in to him, and will sup with him, and he with me.

Rev 3:20

8.   Zacchaeus, like many rich men, had to repent and turn away from his sins. To be saved, you must repent and change your ways.

There will be a major change in your life when you truly receive Jesus Christ. Zacchaeus did that practically, he received Jesus and he changed. You cannot remain the same and claim to be a Christian.

Zacchaeus said,

...Behold, Lord, the half of my goods I give to the poor; and IF I HAVE TAKEN ANY THING FROM ANY MAN BY FALSE ACCUSATION, I RESTORE HIM FOURFOLD.

Luke 19:8

Therefore also now, saith the Lord, turn ye even to me with all your heart, and with fasting, and with weeping, and with mourning:

Joel 2:12

Repent ye therefore, and be converted, that your sins may be blotted out, when the times of refreshing shall come from the presence of the Lord;

Acts 3:19

What Shall I Do To Inherit Eternal Life?
(Jesus and the Man with Great Possessions)

And, behold, one came and said unto him, Good Master, what good thing shall I do, that I may have eternal life?

And he said unto him, Why callest thou me good? there is none good but one, that is, God: but if thou wilt enter into life, keep the commandments.

He saith unto him, Which? Jesus said, Thou shalt do no murder, Thou shalt not commit adultery, Thou shalt not steal, Thou shalt not bear false witness, Honour thy father and thy mother: and, Thou shalt love thy neighbour as thyself. The young man saith unto him, All these things have I kept from my youth up: what lack I yet?

Jesus said unto him, If thou wilt be perfect, go and sell that thou hast, and give to the poor, and thou shalt have treasure in heaven: and come and follow me.

But when the young man heard that saying, he went away sorrowful: for he had great possessions.

Matthew 19:16-22

1. **The rich young ruler asked an important question that led to salvation. Everyone should ask important questions that lead to salvation.**

He asked, "What shall I do that I may inherit eternal life?" It is this question that led to him coming close to salvation. When you ask the right questions, it shows that your mind is focusing on the realities of eternity. When you ask questions about where to find food and how much food costs, your mind is obviously on earthly issues.

When you ask questions like the rich young ruler asked, your mind is working on eternity. Begin to ask yourself important questions that will lead to your salvation. These are some good questions to ask yourself:

"What will happen to me when I die?"

"Is Heaven real? Is hell real?"

"Will I go to Heaven or hell when I die?"

"What will happen to me on the Judgment Day?"

"Why did Jesus have to die on a cross?"

"Why did Jesus shed His blood for me?"

2. **Jesus told the rich young ruler three things that he had to do to obtain eternal life.**

a) First of all; keep the Ten Commandments. The rich young ruler claimed that he was already doing the first thing, which is keeping the commandments. Jesus acknowledged that it was a good thing. But He gave the rich young ruler two other things to do.

b) Second thing Jesus told the rich young ruler: Go and sell all that you have. Being a Christian involves sacrifice. No one can come to Jesus Christ without paying the price. God will not lower the price for you or anyone.

c) Third thing Jesus told the rich young ruler: Come and follow me. If you want eternal life you have to follow Jesus Christ.

Being a Christian and finding eternal life is to follow Jesus Christ. Without following Jesus you will not be washed by His blood and you will not be saved.

3.   The rich young ruler came to Jesus Christ when he was a young man. Everybody must come to Jesus Christ when they are young.

It is important to remember God when you are young because you may never grow to become very old and therefore may never have a chance to repent in your old age. Many people forget about God when they are young. You must remember your Creator in the days of your youth.

Remember now thy Creator in the days of thy youth, while the evil days come not, nor the years draw nigh, when thou shalt say, I have no pleasure in them;

Ecclesiastes 12:1

4.   The rich young ruler came to Jesus Christ when he had the opportunity. Everybody must come to Jesus Christ when there is an opportunity.

Today, as you read this book you have an opportunity to receive Jesus. At a crusade, you have the opportunity to receive Jesus. When an altar call is made in the church an opportunity presents itself for you to receive Jesus. When someone talks to you about Jesus Christ, do not miss the opportunity to receive Him. Do not allow the summer to end or the harvest to pass without getting saved. This is your chance for salvation. You do not know what tomorrow holds for you. Make the most of the opportunity that God has given to you.

The harvest is past, the summer is ended, and we are not saved.

Jeremiah 8:20

Go to now, ye that say, to day or to morrow we will go into such a city, and continue there a year, and buy and sell, and get gain:

Whereas ye know not what shall be on the morrow. For what is your life? It is even a vapour, that appeareth for a little time, and then vanisheth away.

James 4:13-14

5. The rich young ruler heard the Words of Life from Jesus Christ but he turned away from them. When you hear the Words of Life do not turn away from them. Open your heart and receive Jesus Christ today.

Do not turn away from Jesus because of your money. The Bible described the young ruler as a man who had great possessions. People turn away from Jesus because of their sins and because of their pride. Do not put your trust in riches.

They trust in their wealth and boast of great riches. Yet they cannot redeem themselves from death by paying a ransom to God.

Redemption does not come so easily, for no one can ever pay enough to live forever and never see the grave.

Those who are wise must finally die, just like the foolish and senseless, leaving all their wealth behind.

The grave is their eternal home, where they will stay forever. They may name their estates after themselves, but they leave their wealth to others.

Psalms 49:6-11 (NLT)

Lo, this is the man that made not God his strength; but trusted in the abundance of his riches, and strengthened himself in his wickedness. But I am like a green olive tree in the house of God: I trust in the mercy of God for ever and ever.

Psalms 52:7-8

... if riches increase, set not your heart upon them. God hath spoken once; twice have I heard this; that power belongeth unto God.

Psalms 62:10-11

And if THY HAND offend thee, cut it off: it is better for thee to enter into life maimed, than having two hands to go into hell, into the fire that never shall be quenched: where their worm dieth not, and the fire is not quenched.

And if THY FOOT offend thee, cut it off: it is better for thee to enter halt into life, than having two feet to be cast into hell, into the fire that never shall be quenched:

Where their worm dieth not, and the fire is not quenched.

And if THINE EYE offend thee, pluck it out: it is better for thee to enter into the kingdom of God with one eye, than having two eyes to be cast into hell fire:

Mark 9:43-47

Yea doubtless, and I count all things but loss for the excellency of the knowledge of Christ Jesus my Lord: for whom I have suffered the loss of all things, and do count them but dung, that I may win Christ,

Philippians 3:8

SALVATION MESSAGE 35:

Jesus and the Rich Fool

And he spake a parable unto them, saying, The ground of a certain rich man brought forth plentifully:

And he thought within himself, saying, What shall I do, because I have no room where to bestow my fruits?

And he said, This will I do: I will pull down my barns, and build greater; and there will I bestow all my fruits and my goods.

And I will say to my soul, Soul, thou hast much goods laid up for many years; take thine ease, eat, drink, and be merry.

But God said unto him, Thou fool, this night thy soul shall be required of thee: then whose shall those things be, which thou hast provided? So is he that layeth up treasure for himself, and is not rich toward God.

Luke 12:16-21

1. **The rich fool was a fool because he did not remember that prosperity and blessings come from God.**

   Every good gift and every perfect gift is from above, and cometh down from the Father of lights, with whom is no variableness, neither shadow of turning.

   James 1:17

   For promotion cometh neither from the east, nor from the west, nor from the south. But God is the judge:he putteth down one, and setteth up another.

   Psalms 75:6-7

2. **The rich fool was a fool because in his earthly prosperity he was not rich towards God.** This is the pattern of so many people who become rich on earth but are not rich towards God.

   So is he that layeth up treasure for himself, and is NOT RICH TOWARD GOD.

   Luke 12:21

The Millionaire and the Pastor

One day, a pastor visited a multi-millionaire in his home.

After a supper that could be served to kings and queens, the millionaire took the pastor to his rooftop to have some fresh air and enjoy the magnificent view.

As they stood together in the open air, the millionaire took the pastor by the hand and walked with him to the northern side of the rooftop. He said to the pastor, "As far as your eye can see in this direction are my forest reserves."

"Wow," said the pastor.

Then the millionaire pointed to the south and said, "Everything in this direction are my oil fields. I am sure you can see the drilling rigs from here."

"Wow, that's amazing," said the pastor.

Then the millionaire pointed to the east and said, "In this direction are my soy bean, corn and wheat plantations."

"Wow, that is a vast investment."

Then the millionaire pointed to the west and said smugly, "All the houses in this direction are my real estate investments with over one thousand houses."

"Wow,' said the pastor. "You are a real magnate."

Then it was the pastor's turn to ask the millionaire an important question. "You have so much towards the north. You have so much towards the south. You have so much wealth towards the east and so much prosperity in the west.

"But do you have anything in this direction?" he asked, pointing up towards the starry sky.

The millionaire was taken aback.

That night the millionaire realised that he was not rich towards God. He had no investments upwards. He was yet another rich fool who had amassed treasures on earth but was not ready to meet his God.

3. **The rich fool was a fool because he thought he would live forever. You don't know the day you will die.** You don't know the day Jesus will come.

.... truly as the LORD liveth, and as thy soul liveth, there is but a step between me and death.

1 Samuel 20:3

Be ye therefore ready also: for the Son of man cometh at an hour when ye think not.

Luke 12:40

4. **The rich fool was a fool because he made plans that did not include God.** The rich fool made many projections and plans without considering God.

Go to now, ye that say, Today or tomorrow we will go into such a city, and continue there a year, and buy and sell, and get gain: whereas ye know not what shall be on the morrow. For what is your life? It is even a vapour, that appeareth for a little time, and then vanisheth away.

James 4:13-14

5. **The rich fool was a fool because he was not prepared to meet his God.** Prepare to meet God is the warning that resounds from Heaven to all mankind.

Therefore thus will I do unto thee, O Israel: and because I will do this unto thee, PREPARE TO MEET THY GOD, O Israel.

Amos 4:12

6. **The rich fool was a fool because he did not prepare his soul for eternity.** You must prepare to meet your God by giving your life to Christ and being washed in the blood of Jesus.

SALVATION MESSAGE 36:

Don't Waste Your Chance!
(Jesus And Judas Iscariot)

1. **Many people have a great opportunity to go to Heaven. Judas had an opportunity to go to heaven because he was called out by name. Just like Judas, Jesus Christ is calling you out by name and giving you an opportunity to be saved.**

And it came to pass in those days, that he went out into a mountain to pray, and continued all night in prayer to God.

And when it was day, HE CALLED UNTO HIM HIS DISCIPLES: AND OF THEM HE CHOSE TWELVE, whom also he named apostles;

Simon, (whom he also named Peter,) and Andrew his brother, James and John, Philip and Bartholomew,

Matthew and Thomas, James the son of Alphaeus, and Simon called Zelotes,

And Judas the brother of James, and Judas Iscariot, which also was the traitor.

Luke 6:12-16

Judas Iscariot had the opportunity to go to Heaven BUT went into damnation though he was called out by name. Do not lose the opportunity to go to Heaven, and do not go to hell because you have the greatest opportunity of your life to be saved today.

2.   Do not lose your opportunity by allowing the devil to come into your heart. Judas Iscariot lost the opportunity to go to Heaven because the devil entered into his heart.

Now before the feast of the Passover, when Jesus knew that his hour was come that he should depart out of this world unto the Father, having loved his own which were in the world, he loved them unto the end.

And supper being ended, THE DEVIL HAVING NOW PUT INTO THE HEART OF JUDAS ISCARIOT, Simon's son, to betray him; And after the sop Satan entered into him. Then said Jesus unto him, that thou doest, do quickly.

John 13:1-2, 27

Judas Iscariot lost his opportunity to go to Heaven because the devil entered into his heart and he turned against the Lord in spite of the warnings he had received.

Jesus made Judas Iscariot aware that He knew about what Judas was doing. Jesus wanted to save Judas Iscariot. Jesus loved Judas Iscariot but Judas would not listen nor did he change his mind in spite of being warned. The Bible warns that if you are often reproved and you do not change your mind you will be destroyed. "He, that being often reproved hardeneth his neck, shall suddenly be destroyed, and that without remedy." (Proverbs 29:1)

When Jesus had thus said, he was troubled in spirit, and testified, and said, Verily, verily, I say unto you, that one of you shall betray me. Then the disciples looked one on another, doubting of whom he spake.

Now there was leaning on Jesus' bosom one of his disciples, whom Jesus loved.

Simon Peter therefore beckoned to him, that he should ask who it should be of whom he spake.

He then lying on Jesus' breast saith unto him, Lord, who is it?

Jesus answered, He it is, to whom I shall give a sop, when I have dipped it. And when he had dipped the sop, he gave it to Judas Iscariot, the son of Simon.

And after the sop Satan entered into him. Then said Jesus unto him, That thou doest, do quickly.

Now no man at the table knew for what intent he spake this unto him.

For some of them thought, because Judas had the bag, that Jesus had said unto him, Buy those things that we have need of against the feast; or, that he should give something to the poor.

He then having received the sop went immediately out: and it was night.

John 13:21-30

3.   Judas Iscariot wasted his opportunity to go to Heaven because of money. He exchanged his salvation for money.

Then one of the twelve, called Judas Iscariot, went unto the chief priests, and said unto them, WHAT WILL YE GIVE ME, AND I WILL DELIVER HIM UNTO YOU?

And they covenanted with him for thirty pieces of silver.

And from that time he sought opportunity to betray him.

Matthew 26:14-16

Thirty pieces of silver is the amount Judas earned to lose his soul. But there is no amount of money that will be enough to exchange for your soul.

Today, you must not turn against the Lord Jesus Christ. The Pharisees offered Judas money – he was offered thirty pieces of silver.

The devil makes offers. What can be offered to you to keep you away from Christ? Is it a job, money, a woman, a car, or a house? What is your price for your salvation?

Judas was made an offer to betray Christ. Judas began to look for opportunity to betray Christ when he received the offer. What can be offered to you to betray Christ? What are you prepared to pay to betray Christ?

FOR THE LOVE OF MONEY IS THE ROOT OF ALL EVIL: which while some coveted after, they have erred from the faith, and pierced themselves through with many sorrows.

1 Timothy 6:10

For what is a man profited, if he shall gain the whole world, and lose his own soul? Or what shall a man give in exchange for his soul?

Matthew 16:26

One wonders at how people highly value money and are prepared to sacrifice so much for a little bit of money. This is exactly what Judas did to himself. He lost his salvation because of a little bit of money.

4.   Jesus Christ suffered on the cross and shed His blood for us.

For CHRIST also hath once SUFFERED FOR SINS, the just for the unjust, that he might bring us to God, being put to death in the flesh, but quickened by the Spirit:

1 Peter 3:18

5.   How shall you escape if you neglect such a way of salvation? How could Judas escape after throwing away his relationship with Jesus Christ?

HOW SHALL WE ESCAPE, IF WE NEGLECT SO GREAT SALVATION; which at the first began to be spoken by the Lord, and was confirmed unto us by them that heard him;

Hebrews 2:3

SECTION 6:

SALVATION AND THE GREAT INVITATION

The Great Invitation

And sent his servant at supper time to say to them that were bidden, Come; for all things are now ready.

And they all with one consent began to make excuse. The first said unto him, I have bought a piece of ground, and I must needs go and see it: I pray thee have me excused.

And another said, I have bought five yoke of oxen, and I go to prove them: I pray thee have me excused.

And another said, I have married a wife, and therefore I cannot come.

So that servant came, and shewed his lord these things. Then the master of the house being angry said to his servant, Go out quickly into the streets and lanes of the city, and bring in hither the poor, and the maimed, and the halt, and the blind.

And the servant said, Lord, it is done as thou hast commanded, and yet there is room. And the lord said unto the servant, Go out into the highways and hedges, and compel them to come in, that my house may be filled.

For I say unto you, That none of those men which were bidden shall taste of my supper.

Luke 14:17-24

1.   God is inviting you to come to a feast with Him. All through the Bible God invites people to come to Him.

Come unto me, all ye that labour and are heavy laden, and I will give you rest.

Matthew 11:28

And the Spirit and the bride say, Come. And let him that heareth say, Come. And let him that is athirst come. And whosoever will, let him take the water of life freely.

Revelation 22:17

Come, and let us return unto the LORD: for he hath torn, and he will heal us; he hath smitten, and he will bind us up.

Hosea 6:1

I have sent also unto you all my servants the prophets, rising up early and sending them, saying, Return ye now every man from his evil way, and amend your doings, and go not after other gods to serve them, and ye shall dwell in the land which I have given to you and to your fathers: but ye have not inclined your ear, nor hearkened unto me.

Jeremiah 35:15

2.   You have been invited to a feast: Little things and little excuses keep people away from God.

Take us the foxes, the little foxes, that spoil the vines: for our vines have tender grapes.

Song of Solomon 2:15

3.   You have been invited to a feast: Your land, your property and your business must not keep you away from God.

And take heed to yourselves, lest at any time your hearts be overcharged with surfeiting, and drunkenness, and cares of this life, and so that day come upon you unawares.

Luke 21:34

4. You have been invited to a feast: Your family cannot and must not keep you away from God.

If any man come to me, and hate not his father, and mother, and wife, and children, and brethren, and sisters, yea, and his own life also, he cannot be my disciple.

Luke 14:26

And he said unto another, Follow me. But he said, Lord, suffer me first to go and bury my father. Jesus said unto him, Let the dead bury their dead: but go thou and preach the kingdom of God.

Luke 9:59-60

5. You have been invited to a feast: Unfortunately, many reject the great invitation, therefore many unexpected people will fill the places in Heaven.

Nevertheless, if thou warn the wicked of his way to turn from it; if he do not turn from his way, he shall die in his iniquity; but thou hast delivered thy soul.

Ezekiel 33:9

6. You have been invited to a feast: It is a dangerous mistake to reject the invitation and the love of God.

How shall we escape, if we neglect so great salvation; which at the first began to be spoken by the Lord, and was confirmed unto us by them that heard him;

Hebrews 2:3

See that ye refuse not him that speaketh. For if they escaped not who refused him that spake on earth, much more shall not we escape, if we turn away from him that speaketh from Heaven:

Hebrews 12:25

Odododioodioo

There was a man called Odododioodioo who was invited to church by his friends. He had received invitations to church from his friends since he was nineteen years old. He always shrugged off their invitations and asked them to invite others. On some occasions he would laugh at them for being so religious. Yet on other occasions he would engage in discussions with his friends, questioning all the things they believed about God.

But his favourite response to his friends was, "Don't worry, I will come. I will come some day".

Eventually, one day, he did go to church. Mind you, this was after fifteen years of repeated invitations; and by this time, Odododioodioo was thirty-four years old. There was something unusual about the day he had chosen to come. On that day, the church was packed with worshippers. The choir sang a beautiful song entitled, "Come unto Jesus, give Him your life today"; but Odododioodioo did not seem interested in the song. He never nodded his head once, he never tapped his feet and he never sang along. The pastor also preached powerfully but Odododioodioo did not seem to hear the message. He never opened his Bible, he never clapped his hands and he never even said "Amen" once.

Indeed there could not have been a more powerful salvation message than the message that was preached that day. It was a message filled with emotion, truth and anointing! There were tears on almost every cheek and few people could control their feelings. Odododioodioo did not laugh at any of the stories the preacher told and neither did he shed a tear during the emotional parts of the sermon. It was truly strange that there was not the slightest response nor reaction from Odododioodioo. In fact he did not seem to understand or care about anything that was going on. The saddest of all, was the fact that Odododioodioo did not lift up his hand to give his life to Christ during the altar call. He did not go forward to the altar when the invitation was made.

Do you want to know why Odododioodioo did not respond to the message of the day? Do you want to know why he did not tap his feet or sing along? Do you want to know why he did not even bother to say "Amen" when the pastor preached that powerful message? Do you want to know why he did not give his life to Christ when so many people did so on that day?

The answer is simple: Because it was Odododioodioo's funeral! He had finally come to church as he had promised, but he only came in as a dead body in a coffin! He had promised that he would come but in the end he came too late. That is why he did not hear anything! That is why he did not feel anything! He never responded to the invitation to come to church when he was alive. If he had come when he was alive he would have heard the choir singing and the pastor preaching, and he could have responded to the altar call. It was only when he was dead that his body was carried into the church for his funeral.

Is that what you are going to do with this great invitation? Will you spurn the numerous calls and invitations to come to Christ? Will you wait until it is too late?

7. You have been invited to a feast: Accept the invitation of Jesus Christ and be born again.

Behold I Stand at the Door

Behold, I stand at the door, and knock: if any man hear my voice, and open the door, I will come in to him, and will sup with him, and he with me.

Revelation 3:20

1. God is outside your life because you have not received Jesus Christ as your Saviour and Lord.

That at that time ye were without Christ, BEING ALIENS from the commonwealth of Israel, and strangers from the covenants of promise, having no hope, and without God in the world:

Ephesians 2:12

2. God is outside your life because of your ignorance about Him. If you knew how great and loving God was you would be on your knees begging that He should come into your life.

Having the understanding darkened, being alienated from the life of God through THE IGNORANCE that is in them, because of the blindness of their heart:

Ephesians 4:18

3. **God is outside the lives of many people because they have gone far away from Him through their sinful ways.**

For, lo, THEY THAT ARE FAR FROM THEE SHALL PERISH: thou hast destroyed all them that go a whoring from thee.

Psalms 73:27

THE LORD IS FAR FROM THE WICKED: but he heareth the prayer of the righteous.

Proverbs 15:29

4. **Jesus is knocking at the door. Open the door and receive Christ because He wants to bring healing into your life.** Jesus went to Jairus' house and brought healing to his daughter.

5. **Jesus is knocking at the door of your house. Open the door and receive Christ because he wants to deliver you from your sins with which you are heavy laden.**

Come unto me, all ye that labour and are heavy laden, and I will give you rest.

Matthew 11:28

6. **Many people do not receive Jesus Christ because the wrong person (the devil) is inside their hearts and lives.** This is the day you must break away from your bondage to the devil. Break away from disobedience to God.

And you hath he quickened, who were dead in trespasses and sins; wherein in time past ye walked according to the course of this world, according to the prince of the power of the air, THE SPIRIT THAT NOW WORKETH IN THE CHILDREN OF DISOBEDIENCE:

Ephesians 2:1-2

Margaret

I once heard this story about a lady called Margaret. During the Second World War, many young Germans were forced to join the army to fight for their country. There was a young lady called Margaret who had just gotten married to a handsome young soldier. Unfortunately, shortly after their marriage he had to leave for the battlefield. In great sadness he wept over his new bride Margaret, and kissed her a hundred times. He said "Bye-bye" to her and left for the war.

He dearly wanted to come back to his beautiful bride Margaret. Unfortunately, he was sent to the front lines and was captured almost immediately by the Russian army. He thus became a Russian prisoner of war and was sent to work in the camps. In the prison, he prayed constantly that he would be released so that he could go back to his beautiful bride, Margaret. Being a prisoner of war was a terrible experience. He suffered very much and was subjected to the hard labour of a prisoner of war. Every day, when he got up, he would think of Margaret! In every step he made during the day, carrying rocks and boulders from place to place; in the cold and in the heat, he thought of only one thing – Margaret!

The years went by and Germany lost the war. The prisoners were excited because they hoped to be released alive. One day the commander of the prison camp came up with a list of prisoners who were to be released. This young soldier was excited because he thought he would be released. Unfortunately, when the names were read out, his name was not on the list. His hopes were dashed! He was greatly disappointed and his heart sank. He had lost the chance to see Margaret.

But the very next week, another list of prisoners to be released was read out by the commander of the prison and this young soldier's name was on the list. What a day of rejoicing that was! He could think of only one thing – Margaret! "I am going to see Margaret!" He packed his few belongings and took a train to Germany to see his beloved Margaret! Through every step of that long journey he thought of only one thing – Margaret!

When he finally arrived in his town he was shocked to find that almost every building had been bombed and the town that he once knew was now basically a pile of rubble. He walked down the streets and came to the road where he had lived with Margaret.

To his amazement, their house was one of the few still standing. His heart began to pound as he walked up to the door. The moment of truth had come. He knocked on the door and waited in silence, wondering if anybody lived in that house. Suddenly, he heard footsteps, which he recognized. "These are the footsteps of Margaret," he thought.

Suddenly the door opened and there she was; more beautiful than the noonday sun, even more splendid than she had looked on her wedding day! The young soldier lifted up his hands and screamed, "Margaret, I am back!"

Then something terrible happened. Margaret slammed the door and locked it. The young soldier was shocked. He began knocking and banging on the door, "Margaret, Margaret, I am your husband. Open the door! Margaret, Margaret, I am your husband. Open the door!"

But she did not open the door. He could not believe what was happening. Why was Margaret not opening the door? This young man who had looked forward to seeing his beautiful bride was now in a state of shock. He stood outside the door knocking and calling for Margaret but she simply did not open the door.

Do You Want to Know Why?

Do you want to know why Margaret did not open the door? I will tell you why. It is the same reason why the church is not opening the door of its heart to Jesus. There was somebody else in the house! That is why Margaret did not open the door! *Another* man had come to live in the house whilst Margaret's husband was away at war. *Something* and *someone* else was in there and the rightful owner was now on the outside begging to come in.

Jesus is equally standing at the door of the heart of the church today, asking to be let in to take His rightful place. Unfortunately, other things are in there and that is why Jesus is on the outside. The spirit of disobedience is in the heart of disobedient children.

The love for the world has filled the heart of the church and Jesus is outside knocking and asking to be let in.

Money, wealth, and the deceitfulness of them all, have possessed the pulpit and the pew alike. No wonder Jesus is asking to be let back into His wealthy, "last-days" church! Satan has crept in and occupied the chair that he has no right to.

If Jesus occupies our hearts, we will be filled with the knowledge of His will and be in love with Him and not with the world. It is sad that our hearts have gone after earthly and worldly things. It is indeed pathetic that mammon has been welcomed into the church and has replaced Christ. We are richer than we have ever been but if Christ is outside then our riches will become a snare to us. "But lusted exceedingly in the wilderness, and tempted God in the desert. And he gave them their request; but sent leanness into their soul." (Psalm 106:14-15).

Come with Your Burdens

Come unto me, all ye that labour and are heavy laden, and I will give you rest. Take my yoke upon you, and learn of me; for I am meek and lowly in heart: and ye shall find rest unto your souls. For my yoke is easy, and my burden is light.

Matthew 11:28-30

1. **Come with your burdens: There are different kinds of burdens.**

The human race is burdened with many evil things. Sin is a burden that people carry throughout their lives. Financial burdens, burdens of sickness, academic burdens and other troubles are also borne by human beings.

You may think this scripture does not apply to you because you are not carrying a big bag or burden. However, the burdens that Jesus is talking about are the burdens of your sins; the burden of your sicknesses; the burden of your worries and the burdens of your fears.

2. **Come with your burdens: Your sins are a burden because they are attracting God's anger, which is causing sickness and disease in your life.**

There is NO SOUNDNESS IN MY FLESH BECAUSE OF THINE ANGER; neither is there any rest in my bones because of my sin. For mine iniquities are gone over mine head: as an HEAVY BURDEN they are too heavy for me. My wounds stink and are corrupt because of my foolishness.

Psalm 38:3-5

3. **Come with your burdens: Your sin is a burden because it opens the door to demons. It gives a place to the devil to come to your life.**

Neither give place to the devil.

Ephesians 4:27

4. **Come with your burdens: Your sin is a burden because the anger and the fury of God are directed towards you.**

O Lord, according to all thy righteousness, I beseech thee, let THINE ANGER AND THY FURY be turned away from thy city Jerusalem, thy holy mountain: BECAUSE FOR OUR SINS, and for the iniquities of our fathers, Jerusalem and thy people are become a reproach to all that are about us.

Daniel 9:16

5. **Come with your burdens: Your sins are a burden because they are filling your life with grief. Even your strength is failing because of your sins.**

For my life is spent with grief, and my years with sighing: my strength faileth BECAUSE OF MINE INIQUITY, and my bones are consumed.

Psalms 31:10

6. **Come with your burdens: Your sins are a burden to you because you do not have any rest and you do not have any peace. Because of your sins, your life is like a troubled sea.**

But the wicked are like the troubled sea, when it cannot rest, whose waters cast up mire and dirt. There is no peace, saith my God, to the wicked.

Isaiah 57:20-21

But unto them that are contentious, and do not obey the truth, but obey unrighteousness, indignation and wrath,

Tribulation and anguish, upon every soul of man that doeth evil, of the Jew first, and also of the Gentile;

Romans 2:8-9

7. **Come with your burdens: Your sins are a burden because you know that one day you will reap what you have sown.**

Be not deceived; God is not mocked: for whatsoever a man soweth, that shall he also reap. For he that soweth to his flesh shall of the flesh reap corruption; but he that soweth to the Spirit shall of the Spirit reap life everlasting.

Galatians 6:7-8

8. **Come with your burdens: Your sins are a burden because you know that the Day of Judgment is coming. The day of reckoning and the day of accountability will soon be upon all of us.**

But after thy hardness and impenitent heart treasurest up unto thyself wrath against the day of wrath and revelation of the righteous judgment of God; Who will render to every man according to his deeds:

Romans 2:5-6

9. Come with your burdens: Leave your burdens at the cross of Christ. Through the blood of Jesus you will be set free from the burden of your sins.

This is My blood of the covenant, which is poured out for many for forgiveness of sins.

Matthew 26:28 (NASB)

Blessed is he whose transgression is forgiven, whose sin is covered. Blessed is the man unto whom the Lord imputeth not iniquity, and in whose spirit there is no guile.

Psalm 32:1-2

SALVATION MESSAGE 40:

Come

And the Spirit and the bride say, COME. And let him that heareth say, COME. And let him that is athirst COME. And whosoever will, let him take the water of life freely.

Revelation 22:17

All through the Bible, God invites people to come to Him. This is the season of God's kindness and love towards mankind. It is the season when He is inviting. It is the season when He is saying, "Come". Anyone who does not heed this invitation will pay dearly for refusing this great invitation.

1. **COME: God is inviting you to come and enjoy the waters of life freely. There is no charge because all charges have been paid already by the blood of Jesus Christ.**

    Ho, every one that thirsteth, come ye to the waters, and he that hath no money; come ye, buy, and eat; yea, come, buy wine and milk without money and without price.

    Isaiah 55:1

2. COME: God is inviting you to come to Jesus even though you are laden with sin and many other evils.

Most people do not want to associate with people who have problems. They do not want you to come around them any more. But God is not like that! He is calling you to come with your problems.

COME UNTO ME, all ye that labour and are heavy laden, and I will give you rest.

Matthew 11:28

3. COME: Jesus is inviting you to come because He wants to heal you.

There was a certain blind man in Jericho called Bartimaeus. He was a beggar who sat along a street that was an entry point into the city. One day as he sat there he heard a sound like the shuffling of many feet so he asked what was happening. Someone told him that Jesus was passing by. When Bartimaeus heard that it was Jesus he began to shout, "Jesus, thou Son of David, have mercy on me."

The disciples told him to be quiet, but he shouted all the more, "Thou son of David, have mercy on me." Bartimaeus continued shouting till Jesus told him to come.

And they came to Jericho: and as he went out of Jericho with his disciples and a great number of people, blind Bartimaeus, the son of Timaeus, sat by the highway side begging.

And when he heard that it was Jesus of Nazareth, he began to cry out, and say, Jesus, thou Son of David, have mercy on me. And many charged him that he should hold his peace: but he cried the more a great deal, Thou Son of David, have mercy on me. And Jesus stood still, and commanded him to be called. And they call the blind man, saying unto him, Be of good comfort, rise; HE CALLETH THEE.

And he, casting away his garment, rose, and came to Jesus.

Mark 10:46-50

4.   COME: Jesus is inviting you to come because He loves you. It is when you are loved that you are invited to come.

For God so loved the world, that he gave his only begotten Son, that whosoever believeth in him should not perish, but have everlasting life.

John 3:16

The King's Wife

There was a certain king who had many wives. One day, I met one of the wives of the king. She told me she was the king's favourite so I asked her how she knew she was the favourite.

She answered, "Because he asks me to come to him all the time. He calls for me all the time, but does not call the other wives as often."

I asked, "At what times does she call for you?"

"At any time," she replied. "He can call me to come in the morning, in the afternoon, in the evening or even at midnight."

So what do you do if he calls for you at midnight?"

She replied, "I have a bath, dress up, do up my hair and go happily."

5.   COME: God is inviting you to come to Him so that you will have life. If you come to Him you will have eternal life.

And ye will not COME TO ME, that ye might have life.

John 5:40

6. **COME: Jesus is inviting you to come because He has prepared a great supper for you. God is inviting you to a great supper.**

And sent his servant at supper time to say to them that were bidden, COME; FOR ALL THINGS ARE NOW READY.

Luke 14:17

Repent

All through the Bible, God challenges people to repent. Preachers have been sent to give the message of repentance and remission of sins.

And that repentance and remission of sins should be preached in his name among all nations, beginning at Jerusalem.

Luke 24:47

To repent means to turn away from your sins and from your old lifestyle. A person who repents makes a complete turnaround in his life, often going in the opposite direction.

1. **God commands men everywhere to repent: It is not an option that we have.**

It is the command of God that all men repent and turn away from their sins everywhere.

And the times of this ignorance God winked at; but now COMMANDETH ALL MEN EVERY WHERE TO REPENT:

Acts 17:30

The best example of repentance is the prodigal son who turned away from his past life and went back to his father.

2. God commands men everywhere to repent: Judas did not repent completely and ended up in hell.

The best example of someone who did not turn away completely from his evil ways was Judas Iscariot. Judas Iscariot felt sorry but did not come back to the Lord, humble himself and confess his wrongdoing.

> Then Judas, which had betrayed him, when he saw that he was condemned, REPENTED HIMSELF, and brought again the thirty pieces of silver to the chief priests and elders, And he cast down the pieces of silver in the temple, and departed, and went and HANGED HIMSELF.

> Matthew 27:3,5

3. God commands men everywhere to repent: God is asking you to repent and turn away from the wickedness of the thoughts of your heart.

When you turn away from your wicked ways, He will forgive you for your sins.

> REPENT THEREFORE OF THIS THY WICKEDNESS, and pray God, if perhaps the thought of thine heart may be forgiven thee.

> Acts 8:22

Many people who claim to be Christians have not really repented because they do not turn away completely from their wicked ways and wicked thoughts. God expects you to turn away from wickedness. God expects you to turn away from bad thoughts and bad ideas. It is not enough to turn away from the actions. You must turn away from it in your mind and in your thoughts.

4. God commands men everywhere to repent: God is calling you to repent of murder. Whoever hates his brother is a murderer.

Whosoever hateth his brother is a murderer: ...

1 John 3:15

NEITHER REPENTED THEY OF THEIR MURDERS, nor of their sorceries, nor of their fornication, nor of their thefts.

Revelation 9:21

5. God commands men everywhere to repent: God is calling you to repent of your sorceries and witchcraft.

Whoever dabbles in the occult brings upon himself a curse.

NEITHER REPENTED THEY of their murders, nor OF THEIR SORCERIES, nor of their fornication, nor of their thefts.

Revelation 9:21

The Idol in the Wardrobe

A Christian couple was living happily, enjoying their marriage and their lives together. One day, the mother of the husband visited their home. She had a private meeting with her son before she went back to her village. Everything seemed to be normal until one day the wife stumbled on an idol her husband had hidden in the wardrobe.

She confronted her husband, "What on earth is this?"

"Is this an idol? Are you into witchcraft? Are you into occultism?" she questioned.

After a while, her husband finally admitted and said, "This is our family idol and it is on a rotation. It stays with each member of the family for a year then it moves to the next family member. My mother brought it to me the last time she visited because she says it is my turn to keep the family idol."

He continued to explain, "It is this graven image that protects our family."

The Christian wife wanted her husband to take the idol out of the home and burn it. But he refused, saying that they all benefitted from the protective powers that it gave them.

This idol became a bone of contention in the home until the marriage broke up.

As you can see from this story, there are people who claim to be Christians but do not turn away from occultism and sorcery. If you have repented you must turn away from all these practices. Repentance means to turn around and to turn away from your past ways.

6. God commands men everywhere to repent: God is calling you to repent of your fornication.

All those who engage in sexual immorality will incur the wrath of God.

NEITHER REPENTED THEY of their murders, nor of their sorceries, nor OF THEIR FORNICATION, nor of their thefts.

Revelation 9:21

Many people who claim to have come to Christ have not turned away from the sin of fornication. Sadly, they have not turned away from their lifestyle of indiscriminate sexual encounters with multiple partners. This is why the rate of HIV in the world is the same as the rate of HIV in the Church.

The Blood Donation

One day, a laboratory technician who worked at the blood bank gave me a sad and disappointing testimony. He said they had organised blood donation campaigns in many communities, including churches. He said it was unfortunate that they were unable to use much of the blood donated from the church. I asked why they were unable to use the blood from the church. He said in a hushed voice, "So much of the blood from the church could not be used because it was infected with HIV."

He told us about the large percentage of blood that had to be thrown away because of the infection.

I thought to myself, "Where did the church members get the HIV infection from?"

Obviously, they had it from sexual intercourse with random partners. Today, many people in church are HIV positive.

To repent means to turn away from this lifestyle. When people do not turn away from indiscriminate sex and immorality it means they have not repented. Repentance is to turn away from your old and evil ways.

7. God commands men everywhere to repent: God is calling you to repent of your thefts.

There is a curse in the house of every thief. God is calling us to turn away from stealing of every kind.

NEITHER REPENTED THEY of their murders, nor of their sorceries, nor of their fornication, nor OF THEIR THEFTS.

Revelation 9:21

There are many people who claim to be Christians but who are in prison today because they never truly repented and stopped stealing. I know this for a fact because whilst preaching in a prison service we would hear some of the prisoners respond with common and popular Christian slogans.

Obviously, attending church is not the same as repenting and turning away from sins. Many people who claim to be Christians have not turned away from stealing. That is why there are so many Christians in prison for stealing. One Christian brother told us how he had been sent to jail for five years for stealing.

8. **God commands men everywhere to repent: God is challenging you to repent of religious dead works and dead religion.**

.... the foundation of REPENTANCE FROM DEAD WORKS, and of faith toward God,

Hebrews 6:1

To what purpose is the multitude of your sacrifices unto me? saith the LORD:

And when ye spread forth your hands, I will hide mine eyes from you: yea, WHEN YE MAKE MANY PRAYERS, I WILL NOT HEAR: your hands are full of blood.

Wash you, make you clean; put away the evil of your doings from before mine eyes; cease to do evil; Learn to do well; seek judgment, relieve the oppressed, judge the fatherless, plead for the widow. Come now, and let us reason together, saith the LORD: though your sins be as scarlet, they shall be as white as snow; though they be red like crimson, they shall be as wool.

Isaiah 1:11, 15-18

I used to go to Church every Sunday

I used to go to church every Sunday. Oh Sunday morning! I used to wear my best clothes and best shoes. I used to go to see my friends. Friends, oh friends, but I never knew that I had to be born again.

Many people are deluded because of their religious lifestyle just as I was. Being religious will not take you to Heaven. Jesus warned against people who served Him with religious rituals. All through the Bible God warns against religious sacrifice and behaviour that does not come from the heart.

Even though I religiously went to church, I hated the hymns, I hated the hymn books, I hated the preaching and I found the priests boring. I had never read the Bible. If I had died then, I would have gone straight to hell because I had not repented and turned away from dead worship and dead religion. When I found Jesus, I began to enjoy reading the Bible because I had come to know the author of this great book.

9. **God commands men everywhere to repent: God is inviting you to repent; otherwise you will perish and go to hell.**

I tell you, nay: but, EXCEPT YE REPENT, YE SHALL ALL LIKEWISE PERISH.

Or those eighteen, upon whom the tower in Siloam fell, and slew them, think ye that they were sinners above all men that dwelt in Jerusalem? I tell you, nay: but, except ye repent, ye shall all likewise perish.

Luke 13:3-5

10. **God commands men everywhere to repent: Repent and be converted. You must become a new person through conversion to Christianity.**

You must change your life and change your ways. This is your chance to change. This is your chance to have a new life.

REPENT YE THEREFORE, AND BE CONVERTED, that your sins may be blotted out, when the times of refreshing shall come from the presence of the Lord;

Acts 3:19

11. God commands men everywhere to repent: There will be much joy and celebration in Heaven over your repentance.

I say unto you, that likewise JOY SHALL BE IN HEAVEN OVER ONE SINNER THAT REPENTETH, more than over ninety and nine just persons, which need no repentance.

Luke 15:7

Receive Christ

In the beginning was the Word, and the Word was with God, and the Word was God. The same was in the beginning with God. All things were made by him; and without him was not any thing made that was made.

In him was life; and the life was the light of men. And the light shineth in darkness; and the darkness comprehended it not.

There was a man sent from God, whose name was John. The same came for a witness, to bear witness of the Light, that all men through him might believe. He was not that Light, but was sent to bear witness of that Light. That was the true Light, which lighteth every man that cometh into the world.

He was in the world, and the world was made by him, and the world knew him not.

He came unto his own, and his own received him not.

But AS MANY AS RECEIVED HIM, to them gave he power to become the sons of God, even to them that believe on his name:

John 1:1-12

1. **Receive Christ: Because He is the One who was there in the beginning. Only the Bible tells you what happened in the beginning.**

In the beginning was the Word, and the Word was with God, and the Word was God.

John 1:1

2. **Receive Christ: Because Jesus Christ became flesh and walked amongst us.**

And the Word was made flesh, and dwelt among us, (and we beheld his glory, the glory as of the only begotten of the Father,) full of grace and truth.

John 1:14

3. **Receive Christ: Because Jesus Christ was the shining Light that drove away the darkness. All forces of evil will bow in the presence of the Light. When Jesus Christ comes all demons run away.**

And the light shineth in darkness; and the darkness comprehended it not.

John 1:5

Whilst in medical school, I would go for lectures and come back to my hostel. One day, I opened the door to my room and switched on the lights. To my amazement three rats raced across the room and up the wall and disappeared into the ceiling. These rats had been having a good time in my absence; sleeping on my bed and occupying the room. However, when the lights came on they all ran for cover. They could not stand the light. This is what happens when the light of the gospel comes into your life. All the evil spirits and demons will leave you because of the shining light of the gospel.

4. Receive Christ: Because the world was made by Jesus Christ.

When the One Who created the world visited the world, they did not recognize Him. He allowed them to crucify Him because He wanted to shed His blood for us.

> He was in the world, and the world was made by him, and the world knew him not.
>
> John 1:10

The University Church

When I was a student on the university campus I started a fellowship that grew into a church. Many years after, I met a student from that same university. He told me that he was the pastor of that campus church.

As we talked I asked if he knew who had founded the church. He had no idea at all about the founder and was surprised to find out that the church which he was leading was actually founded by me. I realised then that you can be a part of something without knowing the founder and originator of it. That young man was in a church but did not recognize the founder and originator of his church when he showed up. He did not recognize who I was even though I stood in front of him. The world did not recognize Jesus Christ even though He walked in front of us.

5. Receive Christ: Because anyone who receives Christ receives the power to become a Son of God.

> He came unto his own, and his own received him not. But as many as received him, to them gave he power to become the sons of God, even to them that believe on his name:
>
> John 1:11-12

6. Receive Christ: Because if you receive Christ as the Son of God you have life.

And this is the record, that God hath given to us eternal life, and this life is in his Son. He that hath the Son hath life; and he that hath not the Son of God hath not life.

1 John 5:11-12

SALVATION MESSAGE 43:

Is Anyone Thirsty?

In the last day, that great day of the feast, Jesus stood and cried, saying, IF ANY MAN THIRST, LET HIM COME UNTO ME, AND DRINK. He that believeth on me, as the scripture hath said, out of his belly shall flow rivers of living water.

(But this spake he of the Spirit, which they that believe on him should receive: for the Holy Ghost was not yet given; because that Jesus was not yet glorified.)

Many of the people therefore, when they heard this saying, said, of a truth this is the Prophet.

John 7:37-40

1. **Is anyone thirsty? Yes, we are all thirsty.** Men are always seeking to quench their thirst in the wrong way. Men try to quench their thirst with money.

Wilt thou set thine eyes upon that which is not? for riches certainly make themselves wings; they fly away as an eagle toward heaven.

Proverbs 23:5

2. Is anyone thirsty? Yes, we are all thirsty. Men try to quench their thirst by seeking knowledge.

Ever learning, and never able to come to the knowledge of the truth.

2 Timothy 3:7

For in much wisdom is much grief: and he that increaseth knowledge increaseth sorrow.

Ecclesiastes 1:18

3. Is anyone thirsty? Yes, we are all thirsty. Men try to quench their thirst by seeking pleasure.

For the time past of our life may suffice us to have wrought the will of the Gentiles, when we walked in lasciviousness, lusts, excess of wine, revellings, banquetings, and abominable idolatries: Wherein they think it strange that ye run not with them to the same excess of riot, speaking evil of you:

1 Peter 4:3-4

4. Is anyone thirsty? Yes, we are all thirsty. Men try to quench their thirst through alcohol.

Woe unto them that rise up early in the morning, that they may follow strong drink; that continue until night, till wine inflame them!

Isaiah 5:11

Quenching Thirst With Alcohol

One day I was on night duty at the emergency ward. A twenty-five year old man was brought in on a stretcher. This young man was weak and dying because he had been vomiting blood all day. On further questioning I found out that this young man drank a locally manufactured alcoholic drink called akpeteshie from early morning to late evening. He had been doing this for many years even though he was only twenty-five years old.

We admitted him and rushed to get some blood for him. This young man continued retching and vomiting all night. By morning, the walls and the floor, around the bed in his ward were covered with bright red blood. Finally this young man died in the morning in spite of all the care and blood transfusions we gave him. This young man had oesophageal varices, which he developed from cirrhosis of the liver due to chronic alcoholism.

This young man had virtually drunk himself to death.

He had searched for happiness in alcohol. His friends, who brought him to the emergency room, told us that he would start drinking several tots of the locally-brewed alcohol from very early in the morning. The young man who had obviously become a chronic alcoholic, continued drinking throughout the day until he developed cirrhosis of the liver and oesophageal varices from which he died.

5. Is anyone thirsty? Yes, we are all thirsty. Men try to quench their thirst with sex.

I once spoke to a man who was tired of having sex. He said to me "I have had hundreds of girlfriends and I am sick and tired of them." He had drunk of these sexual waters for so long but was still not satisfied.

Let not thine heart decline to her ways, go not astray in her paths. For she hath cast down many wounded: yea, many strong men have been slain by her. Her house is the way to hell, going down to the chambers of death.

Proverbs 7:25-27

6. **Is anyone thirsty? Yes, we are all thirsty. Men try to quench their thirst by endless hard work.**

They go to the office from morning to evening, working tirelessly. They are driven from one project to the other, never finding what they are searching for.

There is one alone, and there is not a second; yea, he hath neither child nor brother: yet is there no end of all his labour; neither is his eye satisfied with riches; neither saith he, For whom do I labour, and bereave my soul of good? This is also vanity, yea, it is a sore travail.

Ecclesiastes 4:8

7. **Is anyone thirsty? Yes, we are all thirsty. Only Christ can quench the thirst of man. Only Christ can quench the search of man.**

But whosoever drinketh of the water that I shall give him shall never thirst; but the water that I shall give him shall be in him a well of water springing up into everlasting life.

John 4:14

The Salvation of the Ten Virgins

Then shall the kingdom of heaven be likened unto ten virgins, which took their lamps, and went forth to meet the bridegroom. And five of them were wise, and five were foolish.

They that were foolish took their lamps, and took no oil with them: But the wise took oil in their vessels with their lamps.

While the bridegroom tarried, they all slumbered and slept. And at midnight there was a cry made, Behold, the bridegroom cometh; go ye out to meet him.

Then all those virgins arose, and trimmed their lamps. And the foolish said unto the wise, Give us of your oil; for our lamps are gone out.

But the wise answered, saying, Not so; lest there be not enough for us and you: but go ye rather to them that sell, and buy for yourselves.

And while they went to buy, the bridegroom came; and they that were ready went in with him to the marriage: and the door was shut. Afterward came also the other virgins, saying, Lord, Lord, open to us. But he answered and said, Verily I say unto you, I know you not. Watch therefore, for ye know neither the day nor the hour wherein the Son of man cometh.

Matthew 25:1-13

1. **Virgins were invited for the marriage feast. Virginity stands for purity, holiness and sinlessness. Virgins are pure and untouched, even in the secret parts of their lives.**

2. **Virgins were invited for the marriage feast: Sin is referred to as dirt or filth. Sin takes away the virgin state.**

Through sin we are no longer "virgins" and are no longer qualified for the marriage feast.

The Lord looked down from heaven upon the children of men, to see if there were any that did understand, and seek God.

They are all gone aside, THEY ARE ALL TOGETHER BECOME FILTHY: there is none that doeth good, no, not one.

Psalm 14:2-3

Every one of them is gone back: THEY ARE ALTOGETHER BECOME FILTHY; there is none that doeth good, no, not one.

Psalms 53:3

But we are all as an unclean thing, and all our righteousnesses are as filthy rags; and we all do fade as a leaf; and our iniquities, like the wind, have taken us away.

Isaiah 64:6

But THE WICKED ARE LIKE the troubled sea, when it cannot rest, whose waters cast up mire and DIRT.

Isaiah 57:20

How much more abominable and FILTHY IS MAN, WHICH DRINKETH INIQUITY LIKE WATER?

Job 15:16

He that is unjust, let him be unjust still: and HE WHICH IS FILTHY, LET HIM BE FILTHY STILL: and he that is righteous, let him be righteous still: and he that is holy, let him be holy still.

Revelation 22:11

3. **Virgins were invited for the marriage feast. We have fallen and lost our state of virginity. But God wants to take away your filthy garments.**

Now Joshua was clothed with filthy garments, and stood before the angel.

And he answered and spake unto those that stood before him, saying, TAKE AWAY THE FILTHY GARMENTS FROM HIM. And unto him he said, Behold, I have caused thine iniquity to pass from thee, and I WILL CLOTHE THEE WITH CHANGE OF RAIMENT.

Zechariah 3:3-4

4. **Only the Blood of Jesus can cleanse us from the filth of our sins.**

But if we walk in the light, as he is in the light, we have fellowship one with another, and THE BLOOD OF JESUS CHRIST HIS SON CLEANSETH US FROM ALL SIN.

1 John 1:7

5. **Only the Blood of Jesus can wash us from the filth of our sins.**

And from Jesus Christ, who is the faithful witness, and the first begotten of the dead, and the prince of the kings of the earth. Unto him that loved us, and WASHED US FROM OUR SINS IN HIS OWN BLOOD,

Revelation 1:5

6. Through the Blood of Jesus your sins and filth will be washed away and you will be qualified to go to Heaven.

We will become virgins again and we will be welcomed to the wedding through the Blood of Jesus.

After this I beheld, and, lo, a great multitude, which no man could number, of all nations, and kindreds, and people, and tongues, stood before the throne, and before the Lamb, clothed with white robes, and palms in their hands; and cried with a loud voice, saying, Salvation to our God which sitteth upon the throne, and unto the Lamb.

And all the angels stood round about the throne, and about the elders and the four beasts, and fell before the throne on their faces, and worshipped God, saying, Amen: blessing, and glory, and wisdom, and thanksgiving, and honour, and power, and might, be unto our God for ever and ever. Amen.

And one of the elders answered, saying unto me, What are these which are arrayed in white robes? and whence came they? And I said unto him, Sir, thou knowest. And he said to me, These are they which came out of great tribulation, and have WASHED THEIR ROBES, and made them white IN THE BLOOD OF THE LAMB.

Revelations 7:9-14

SALVATION MESSAGE 45:

Ask, Seek and Knock

Ask, and it shall be given you; seek, and ye shall find; knock, and it shall be opened unto you: For every one that asketh receiveth; and he that seeketh findeth; and to him that knocketh it shall be opened.

Matthew 7:7-8

1.   ASK: Asking good questions will lead you to God.

There are many questions you should be asking. It was the asking of questions that led me to Christ.

"Where are all the dead people?"

"Where did they go?"

"Where do people go when they die?"

"Why did Jesus die on the cross?"   That is the most important question that I ever asked.

Thus saith the Lord, Stand ye in the ways, and see, and ASK FOR THE OLD PATHS, where is the good way, and walk therein, and ye shall find rest for your souls. But they said, We will not walk therein.

Jeremiah 6:16

2. SEEK GOD. Do not make the mistake of seeking the power of evil spirits and witchcraft, because Jesus is the One you need.

Do not seek after wizards, witches or evil powers.

Regard not them that have familiar spirits, NEITHER SEEK AFTER WIZARDS, to be defiled by them: I am the Lord your God.

Leviticus 19:31

3. SEEK GOD. Do not be so proud as to not seek God to help you.

The wicked, THROUGH THE PRIDE OF HIS COUNTENANCE, WILL NOT SEEK AFTER GOD: God is not in all his thoughts.

Psalm 10:4

4. SEEK GOD. God is looking to see if you are wise and understanding enough to seek Him.

The Lord looked down from heaven upon the children of men, to see IF THERE WERE ANY THAT DID UNDERSTAND, AND SEEK GOD.

Psalm 14:2

5. SEEK GOD. Seek God quickly and with all your heart.

Search to find God. Seek God early.

O God, thou art my God; EARLY WILL I SEEK THEE: my soul thirsteth for thee, my flesh longeth for thee in a dry and thirsty land, where no water is;

Psalm 63:1

6.   SEEK GOD. Seek God while He may be found.

God may not always be found. Seek Him while He may be found.

SEEK YE THE LORD WHILE HE MAY BE FOUND, call ye upon him while he is near: Let the wicked forsake his way, and the unrighteous man his thoughts: and let him return unto the Lord, and he will have mercy upon him; and to our God, for he will abundantly pardon.

Isaiah 55:6-7

7.   KNOCK: You must knock at the door of heaven.

The kingdom of heaven has a door. It must be opened for you. Woe to you if that door is not opened to you!

Strive to enter in at the strait gate: for many, I say unto you, will seek to enter in, and shall not be able. WHEN ONCE THE MASTER OF THE HOUSE IS RISEN UP, AND HATH SHUT TO THE DOOR, AND YE BEGIN TO STAND WITHOUT, AND TO KNOCK AT THE DOOR, SAYING, LORD, LORD, OPEN UNTO US; and he shall answer and say unto you, I know you not whence ye are: Then shall ye begin to say, We have eaten and drunk in thy presence, and thou hast taught in our streets.

But he shall say, I tell you, I know you not whence ye are; depart from me, all ye workers of iniquity.

Luke 13:24-27

8.   By asking, seeking and knocking, you will discover the Love of God and the Blood of Jesus that has been shed for you.

Come unto Me all ye that Labour, and are Heavy Laden and I Will Give You Rest

Come unto me, all ye that labour and are heavy laden, and I will give you rest.

Take my yoke upon you, and learn of me; for I am meek lowly in heart: and ye shall find rest unto your souls.

For my yoke is easy, and my burden is light.

Matthew 11:28-30

1. **Come with your burden: Jesus wants you to come to Him.**

Do not go anywhere else. Do not follow any other false religion or false hope.

"Come to me!" "Come to me!" "Come to me!" – this is the call of Jesus!

2. **Come with your burden: This is the call of the Lord to all who believe.**

Many years ago, Ghanaians did not need visas to go to England, America and France. All we needed to do was to buy a ticket and board the next flight to England. There would be no questions asked on the Ghanaian coast or on the English, American or French shores. In those days Ghana had one aeroplane, a VC 10 aircraft, and it cost six thousand cedis for a ticket to England.

Indeed, Ghanaians, Nigerians, Nigeriens, Togolese, Ivoirians and all other Africans freely travelled to the western world whenever they felt like it. However, as time went by, the African nations that had gained independence in the late fifties and early sixties became poorer due to the ineptitude of the African leaders who were completely out of their depth when it came to running a country.

All currencies lost their values, inflation soared and the basic essential commodities of life became rare. As their financial burdens increased and their poverty deepened, Africans decided to flee the shores of Africa and get as far away as possible from the incompetent administrators of the African continent.

When the European countries noticed that the burdens of the Africans had increased and were so poor and needy, they clamped up their borders and essentially said, "Don't come here any more."

They made new laws especially for the Africans, requiring them to get visas before coming to their countries. These laws had not existed before. They were created to keep people with financial burdens away.

Amazingly, these laws were not applied to other wealthy countries. They were applied to keep only the poor, the needy and the burdened away. Indeed, most human beings reject people who come to them heavily laden with financial or health burdens.

But with Jesus, it is not so. He specifically says, "Come to me with your burdens and I will give you rest."

Jesus Christ is not afraid of your financial burdens!

Jesus Christ is not afraid of your health burdens!

Jesus Christ is not afraid of your sins!

Today, Jesus is saying, "Come with your burdens".

3. Come with your burden: Jesus is saying to you today, "Come with your burden of sickness"

Jesus called for blind Bartimaeus to be brought to Him. He was not afraid of the burden of blindness.

And Jesus stood still, and commanded him to be called. And they call the blind man, saying unto him, be of good comfort, rise; HE CALLETH THEE.

Mark 10:49

4. Come with your burden: Jesus is saying to you today, "Come with the burden of your sins"

Jesus called for Zacchaeus even though he was heavy laden with sins.

And when JESUS came to the place, he looked up. And saw him, and SAID UNTO HIM, ZACCHAEUS, make haste, and COME DOWN; for to day I must abide at thy house. And he made haste, and came down, and received him joyfully. And when they saw it, they all murmured, saying, That he was gone to be guest WITH A MAN THAT IS A SINNER.

Luke 19:5-7

SECTION 7:

SALVATION AND CHOICES

SALVATION MESSAGE 47:

Choose

1. **Coming to Jesus Christ is making the greatest choice of your life. Choosing Jesus Christ is to choose a blessing instead of a curse.**

I call heaven and earth to record this day against you, that I have set before you life and death, blessing and cursing: therefore choose life, that both thou and thy seed may live:

Deuteronomy 30:19

2. **Coming to Jesus Christ is making the greatest choice of your life. Choosing Jesus Christ is choosing to walk through a narrow gate instead of a wide gate.**

Enter through the narrow gate; for the gate is wide and the way is broad that leads to destruction, and there are many who enter through it. For the gate is small and the way is narrow that leads to life, and there are few who find it.

Matthew 7:13-14 (NASB)

3. **Coming to Jesus Christ is making the greatest choice of your life. Choosing Jesus Christ is choosing to walk on a narrow way instead of a broad way.**

Enter through the narrow gate; for the gate is wide and the way is broad that leads to destruction, and there are many who enter through it. For the gate is small and the way is narrow that leads to life, and there are few who find it.

Matthew 7:13-14 (NASB)

4. **Coming to Jesus Christ is making the greatest choice of your life. Choosing Jesus Christ is choosing to make God your Father instead of having the devil as your father.**

Ye are of your father the devil, and the lusts of your father ye will do. He was a murderer from the beginning, and abode not in the truth, because there is no truth in him. When he speaketh a lie, he speaketh of his own: for he is a liar, and the father of it.

John 8:44

5. **Coming to Jesus Christ is making the greatest choice of your life. Choosing Jesus Christ is choosing life instead of death.**

I call heaven and earth to record this day against you, that I have set before you life and death, blessing and cursing: therefore choose life, that both thou and thy seed may live:

Deuteronomy 30:19

The Old Man and The Butterfly

There was an old man who lived in a certain village. This old man was too old to work so he went around giving advice to anybody who would listen to him. This old man was so wise that everything he said was always true and everything he said always happened.

The old man became richer and more popular as he went around from town to town giving advice. One day he went to a town where there was a little boy who heard him giving advice. The young man also heard that the old man was always right and that he never made any mistakes. But the young boy said to himself, "This man cannot always be right. It cannot be that he never makes a mistake. I am going to prove that he is not always right."

So he thought of a plan to prove that the old man was not always right – and this was his plan:

He said to himself, "I will go to the wise old man with the butterfly in my hand and I will say to the old man: 'there is a butterfly in my hand. Is it dead or alive?'."

He continued, "If the old man says the butterfly is alive, I will clench my fist and the butterfly will die. Afterwards, I will open my hand and the old man will see for the first time that he is wrong. If the old man says the butterfly is dead, I will open my fist and let the butterfly fly away. He will then see that he is wrong."

The young man was convinced that with this plan he could prove that the old man was not always right. So he caught a butterfly and went to see the old man.

"Good afternoon old man," he said, "I have an important question to ask you."

"Go ahead," said the old man, "What is your problem?"

Then the young man said, "I have a butterfly in my fist." Then he stretched out his hand. "Is it dead or alive?"

There was silence. Then the old man smiled and answered, "It depends on you."

The young man was astounded at the old man's answer because the old man was right once again. "It depends on you" was the right answer.

In the same way as the little boy decided "dead or alive" for the butterfly, God has given us the choice today. Dead or alive - it depends on you! To be saved or to perish: it depends on you! Dead or alive: it depends on you! Heaven or hell: it depends on you! God or the devil: it depends on you!

You have to choose. You must decide today whether you want to go Heaven or hell.

6. **Coming to Jesus Christ is making the greatest choice of your life. Choosing Jesus Christ is choosing Heaven as your final destination instead of hell.**

The Narrow Way and The Broad Way

Enter ye in at the strait gate: for wide is the gate, and broad is the way, that leadeth to destruction, and many there be which go in thereat: because strait is the gate, and narrow is the way, which leadeth unto life, and few there be that find it.

Matthew 7:13-14

1. **The broad way and the narrow way: Choosing Christ is to choose between walking on the broad way or the narrow way.**

If you choose the narrow way you will find life and peace.

2. **How to tell whether you are on the broad way or the narrow way is by the number of people you see on the way.**

The broad way obviously has many people and the narrow way obviously has few people on it.

3. **In this world, it is the road that has a lot of people on it which is seen as the right road.**

Whenever there is something that a lot of people choose, it is deemed to be the right thing.

That is why elections are decided by who has more votes. When more people choose a candidate it seems to make the candidate the right person. But not so with Christ! He has predicted that few people will choose Him, and He has warned that you must be among the few that will choose Him.

4. **Jesus Christ shows us that He has created a path He knows few people will ever choose and yet He warns the world to choose that unpopular way.**

When people make a drink like Coca Cola, they need many people to patronize and buy it for it to be deemed a good thing.

When people make a song or an album, they need many people to patronize it and buy it otherwise they will go bankrupt.

When people make a film they need the world to patronize it. They need many people to pay to go and watch it.

Not so with God! He does not need many people to patronize Him or support Him. He has simply shown the Way. You can take it or leave it. He knows that many will leave it because it is a narrow way with the narrow gate.

God has made a narrow way for us to come to Heaven. He does not care about the opinions of men. The right way is the way that few people will walk on. Yet still, that is the right way.

5. **I have often chosen the narrow way and I do not regret it. You may laugh at people on the narrow way, but one day you will regret it.**

I chose not to drink alcohol, smoke cigarette or take drugs or go to nightclubs as a young man. At the time, these were activities that many people my age engaged in but I do not regret not choosing it. It was a narrow way with few people on it but I am glad that I chose the narrow way.

I chose to be in the ministry and work as a pastor instead of going to America to specialise as a doctor. I do not regret this decision to serve the Lord in the ministry. It was a narrow way with very few people on it.

6. The broad way of atheism. To receive Jesus Christ is to forsake the broad way that seems right to all men.

Today, the majority of western Europeans have decided that there is no God. They do not even want to talk about the subject.

7. The broad way of homosexuality. To receive Jesus Christ is to forsake the broad way that seems right to all men.

Today, the majority of western Europeans believe that there is nothing wrong with homosexuality, even though it cannot be found in nature. This is a broad way on which the majority of Europeans are walking. It is sad to say that millions are on their way to perdition. Indeed, to come to Christ is to forsake the broad way even though the majority are walking on that road.

There is a way which seemeth right unto a man, but the end thereof are the ways of death.

Proverbs 14:12

8. Today you must enter the narrow gate by choosing Jesus Christ. Entering a narrow gate is more difficult than entering a broad gate.

It is more difficult to manoeuvre your car through a narrow gate than it is to drive it through a broad gate. It may be difficult for you to receive Jesus Christ but you will never regret it.

Wherefore as the Holy Ghost saith, to day if ye will hear his voice, harden not your hearts, as in the provocation, in the day of temptation in the wilderness:

Hebrews 3:7-8

9. **By walking on the narrow way where few walk, you will be saved from hell.**

The way of life is above to the wise, that he may depart from hell beneath.

Proverbs 15:24

SALVATION MESSAGE 49:

You Cannot Serve Two Masters...

No man can serve two masters: for either he will hate the one, and love the other; or else he will hold to the one, and despise the other. Ye cannot serve God and mammon.

Matthew 6:24

1. You cannot serve two masters: You cannot serve idols and God.

God has warned that we should not make images of stone or wood. We are not to bow down or pray to any type of idol. I once visited a town in which I found a space in the centre of the city filled with images of antelopes, leopards, fish and birds. The people in the town worshipped these idols. Yet the Word of God warns us not to make images of anything on earth (such as antelopes) or anything in the heaven above (such as birds) or anything in the water below (such as fish).

I know a town in which a solitary crab stands high in the city centre. So precious is this image that the road was diverted around it. No one dares touch that holy crab. Is it any wonder when the blessing of God is absent from such places?

Ye shall make you no idols nor graven image, neither rear you up a standing image, neither shall ye set up any image of stone in your land, to bow down unto it: for I am the LORD your God.

Leviticus 26:1

Thou shalt not make unto thee any graven image, or any likeness of any thing that is in heaven above, or that is in the earth beneath, or that is in the water under the earth:

Exodus 20:4

Thou shalt not bow down thyself to them, nor serve them: for I the LORD thy God am a jealous God, visiting the iniquity of the fathers upon the children unto the third and fourth generation of them that hate me;

Exodus 20:5

For thou shalt worship no other god: for the LORD, whose name is Jealous, is a jealous God:

Exodus 34:14

2.   **You cannot serve two masters: There is no need to fear an idol or an image because they have no power to harm you or to bless you.**

Only the living God has power to save you from evil.

The god who was urinated upon

One day, a friend of mine went to a village and needed to urinate. There was no toilet around so he had to find a place in the nearby bushes to do so. As he began passing urine, people in the village began to scream and shout pointing to his feet. He did not understand what they were saying so he continued urinating until he finished. Then he spat on the stone which he had just urinated on, zipped up his trousers and turned around to meet the frenzied locals.

"What's going on?" he asked. "What's wrong?"

The people exclaimed, "You just urinated on our god. You just spat on our god."

"What?" He asked. "Who is your god? Where is he? I didn't see any god" he explained.

The people pointed to the stone he had urinated on and said, "That is our god you just urinated on."

My bewildered friend offered his apologies to the people and hurriedly left the town.

When I heard this story, I marvelled. I thought to myself, "even a child would have complained if he was being urinated upon. Even an animal would have moved away if it was being urinated upon. If that stone was a real god, why did it not say anything at all when the warm urine of my friend was pouring upon it?" The answer is found in Jeremiah 10:3-5.

> For the customs of the people are vain: for one cutteth a tree out of the forest, the work of the hands of the workman, with the axe.
>
> They deck it with silver and with gold; they fasten it with nails and with hammers, that it move not.
>
> THEY ARE UPRIGHT AS THE PALM TREE, BUT SPEAK NOT: THEY MUST NEEDS BE BORNE, because they cannot go. Be not afraid of them; for they cannot do evil, neither also is it in them to do good.
>
> Jeremiah 10:3-5

3.   You cannot serve two masters: You cannot practice witchcraft and serve God. Witchcraft is a sin.

Thou shalt not suffer a witch to live.

Exodus 22:18

273

For rebellion is as the sin of witchcraft, and stubbornness is as iniquity and idolatry. Because thou hast rejected the word of the LORD, he hath also rejected thee from being king.

1 Samuel 15:23

And I will cut off witchcrafts out of thine hand; and thou shalt have no more soothsayers:

Micah 5:12

4. You cannot serve two masters: You cannot practice sorcery, occultism and necromancy and serve God.

There shall not be found among you any one that maketh his son or his daughter to pass through the fire, or that useth divination, or an observer of times, or an enchanter, or a witch,

Or a charmer, or a consulter with familiar spirits, or a wizard, or a necromancer. For all that do these things are an abomination unto the LORD: and because of these abominations the LORD thy God doth drive them out from before thee.

Deuteronomy 18:10-12

But the fearful, and unbelieving, and the abominable, and murderers, and whoremongers, and sorcerers, and idolaters, and all liars, shall have their part in the lake which burneth with fire and brimstone: which is the second death.

Revelation 21:8

For the idols have spoken vanity, and the diviners have seen a lie, and have told false dreams; they comfort in vain: therefore they went their way as a flock, they were troubled, because there was no shepherd.

Zechariah 10:2

But these two things shall come to thee in a moment in one day, the loss of children, and widowhood: they shall come upon thee in their perfection for the multitude of thy sorceries, and for the great abundance of thine enchantments.

Isaiah 47:9

5. You cannot serve two masters: You cannot serve money and serve God.

No man can serve two masters: for either he will hate the one, and love the other; or else he will hold to the one, and despise the other. Ye cannot serve God and mammon.

Matthew 6:24

6. You cannot serve two masters: You cannot serve other gods because there is none comparable to God.

For the LORD is a great God, and a great King above all gods.

Psalm 95:3

Bless the LORD, O my soul. O LORD my God, thou art very great; thou art clothed with honour and majesty.

Psalm 104:1

7. You cannot serve two masters: You can only serve the one God through His Son, Jesus Christ.

For there is one God, and one mediator between God and men, the man Christ Jesus; who gave himself a ransom for all, to be testified in due time.

1 Timothy 2:5-6

Jesus saith unto him, I am the way, the truth, and the life: no man cometh unto the Father, but by me.

John 14:6

Neither is there salvation in any other: for there is none other name under heaven given among men, whereby we must be saved.

Acts 4:12

SALVATION MESSAGE 50:

Are You Wise or Are You a Fool?

And he spake a parable unto them, saying, The ground of a certain rich man brought forth plentifully:

And he thought within himself, saying, What shall I do, because I have no room where to bestow my fruits?

And he said, this will I do: I will pull down my barns, and build greater; and there will I bestow all my fruits and my goods.

And I will say to my soul, Soul, thou hast much goods laid up for many years; take thine ease, eat, drink, and be merry.

BUT GOD SAID UNTO HIM, THOU FOOL, this night thy soul shall be required of thee: then whose shall those things be, which thou hast provided? So is he that layeth up treasure for himself, and is not rich toward God.

Luke 12:16-21

1. **Are you wise or are you a fool? Will you say to your soul: "You have made it in life!" "Relax and enjoy yourself!" What do you say to yourself? Are they words of pride, words of over-confidence or words of self-exaltation?**

And I will say to my soul, Soul, thou hast much goods laid up for many years; take thine ease, eat, drink, and be merry.

Luke 12:19

2. **Are you wise or are you a fool? Will you say to your soul: "You will never be demoted or humiliated."**

The pride of thine heart hath deceived thee, thou that dwellest in the clefts of the rock, whose habitation is high; that saith in his heart, WHO SHALL BRING ME DOWN TO THE GROUND?

Obadiah 1:3

3. **Are you wise or are you a fool? Will you say to your soul, "You will never be judged. You will escape."**

And as IT IS APPOINTED unto men once to die, but after this the judgment.

Hebrews 9:27

4. **Are you wise or are you a fool? Will you end up in hell? The rich man that Jesus spoke about in the story of "Lazarus and the rich man", the rich man went to hell because he was not wise and he did not know God.**

…the rich man also died, and was buried; And IN HELL HE LIFT UP HIS EYES, being in torments, and seeth Abraham afar off, and Lazarus in his bosom.

Luke 16:22-23

5. **Are you wise or are you a fool? You must say to yourself, "I know I can die at any time. I may have to stand before the judgment throne of God at any time."**

. . . there is but a step between me and death.

1 Samuel 20:3

6. **Are you wise or are you a fool? Will you receive the Blood of Jesus today? Will you be washed by the Blood or will you be foolish enough to ignore the Blood of Jesus?**

7. **Are you wise or are you a fool? Be wise and say to yourself, "Today I will put my trust in Jesus Christ and accept Him as my Saviour."**

That if thou shalt confess with thy mouth the Lord Jesus, and shalt believe in thine heart that God hath raised him from the dead, thou shalt be saved. For with the heart man believeth unto righteousness; and with the mouth confession is made unto salvation.

Romans 10:9-10

SALVATION MESSAGE 51:

One Thing Is Needful

Now it came to pass, as they went, that he entered into a certain village: and a certain woman named Martha received him into her house.

And she had a sister called Mary, which also sat at Jesus' feet, and heard his word.

But Martha was cumbered about much serving, and came to him, and said, Lord, dost thou not care that my sister hath left me to serve alone? Bid her therefore that she help me.

And Jesus answered and said unto her, Martha, Martha, thou art careful and troubled about many things:

But one thing is needful: and Mary hath chosen that good part, which shall not be taken away from her.

Luke 10:38-42

1. **Like Martha, most people are busy about many unnecessary things; whilst they neglect the one thing that is really important.**

Most people are busy about many things:

People are busy about decorating their homes;

People are busy about getting the right education for their children;

People are busy about getting food for their husbands;

People are busy about money to support their lifestyles;

People are trying to find love; people are trying to get jobs; People are trying to make friends; people are trying to be part of groups and some people are busy about going abroad.

Some people are busy about education; others are busy about having a child;

Others are also busy about getting rich.

The Professor who Could Not Swim

There was once a professor, a very learned man indeed. He was also very proud about his knowledge and achievements. One day, he went on a journey and arrived on the shores of a huge river.

There was no large ferry that he could use to cross the river. Then he noticed a young man who had a little boat he was renting nearby. "I can paddle you across if you want," the boatman said.

Reluctantly, the professor began his crossing in the little boat. As they paddled along, the professor, who looked down on the boatman, began to ask him some questions.

The Professor utterly despised the boatman and asked him, "Do you about know sociology?"

The boatman answered "no, I do not know what it is".

The Professor remarked, "10% of your life is gone".

After some minutes the professor noticed the young man eating with unwashed hands and asked him, "Do you know about bacteriology?"

The boatman said "no" and the Professor muttered, "Another10% of your life is gone."

Throughout the journey, the professor quizzed the boatman about the things he knew. He was trying to demonstrate to the boatman how ignorant he was.

"Do you know about astrology?" The boatman answered, "No I don't".

The Professor responded: "another 10% of your life is gone."

"Do you know about Physics?

Do you know about nuclear physics? Do you know about biochemistry? What about physiology? Do you know anything about parasitology?"

The boatman answered repeatedly, "no, I don't" to all his questions, to which the professor promptly replied; "Yet another 10% of your life is gone."

As they went along, there arose a great storm with mighty winds and turbulence. The waves in the river became higher and higher and the boat became more and more unstable. It was soon evident that the boat was going to capsize. Then the boatman turned to the professor and asked him, "Do you know about swimminology?

The professor answered, "No, I've never heard of it."

The boatman promptly said to the professor, "Then a hundred per cent of your life is gone!"

You see, the professor knew so many things but he did not know the one thing he needed to save his life. Jesus is the One thing that you need in your life.

2. Like Mary, the one thing that is needful is to get the wisdom and knowledge of God.

Mary sat at the feet of Jesus to receive the wisdom of God.

WISDOM IS THE PRINCIPAL THING; therefore get wisdom: and with all thy getting get understanding. Exalt her, and she shall promote thee: she shall bring thee to honour, when thou dost embrace her.

Proverbs 4:7-8

3. There is usually one thing that keeps people away from God.

Make sure that you do not allow one thing to keep you away from your salvation. Do not allow money, a habit, a woman or a man to prevent you from fulfilling your calling. It is usually one thing that keeps people from Christ whom they need!

Then Jesus beholding him loved him, and said unto him, ONE THING THOU LACKEST: go thy way, sell whatsoever thou hast, and give to the poor, and thou shalt have treasure in heaven: and COME, TAKE UP THE CROSS, AND FOLLOW ME.

Mark 10:21

4. One thing that is needful for you is to have a personal encounter with God.

Christianity is about having a personal relationship with Jesus Christ. Christianity is about seeing God and knowing God.

He answered and said, Whether he be a sinner or no, I know not: ONE THING I KNOW, that, whereas I WAS BLIND, NOW I SEE.

John 9:25

5. **One thing that is needful is for us to sacrifice so that we can have treasures in Heaven. It is time to take up your cross, deny yourself and follow Jesus.**

Now when Jesus heard these things, he said unto him, YET LACKEST THOU ONE THING: SELL ALL THAT THOU HAST, and distribute unto the poor, and thou shalt have treasure in heaven: and come, follow me.

Luke 18:22

6. **One thing that is needful is to dwell in the house of the Lord forever and to spend eternity with God. Will you dwell in the house of the Lord all the days of your life? Or will you dwell in the house of the devil all the days of your life? Choose Jesus Christ and you will dwell in the house of the Lord forever.**

ONE THING HAVE I DESIRED OF THE LORD, that will I seek after; that I may DWELL IN THE HOUSE OF THE LORD all the days of my life, to behold the beauty of the Lord, and to inquire in his temple.

Psalm 27:4

SALVATION MESSAGE 52:

The House on a Rock

Therefore whosoever heareth these sayings of mine, and doeth them, I will liken him unto a wise man, which built his house upon a rock:

And the rain descended, and the floods came, and the winds blew, and beat upon that house; and it fell not: for it was founded upon a rock.

And every one that heareth these sayings of mine, and doeth them not, shall be likened unto a foolish man, which built his house upon the sand:

And the rain descended, and the floods came, and the winds blew, and beat upon that house; and it fell: and great was the fall of it.

Matthew 7:24-27

1. **Build your house on the rock: Jesus likens your life to the building of a house.**

Except the Lord build the house, they labour in vain that build it: except the Lord keep the city, the watchman waketh but in vain

Psalms 127:1

2. **Build your house on the rock: Beware of things that are done quickly. You can do things quickly, but things done quickly are fraught with evil.**

He that hasteth to be rich hath an evil eye, and considereth not that poverty shall come upon him.

Proverbs 28:22

3. **Build your house on the rock: Beware of things that look easy. The easy way is often not the right way.**

Enter ye in at the strait gate: for wide is the gate, and broad is the way, that leadeth to destruction, and many there be which go in thereat: because strait is the gate, and narrow is the way, which leadeth unto life, and few there be that find it

Matthew 7:13-14

4. **Build your house on the rock: The same types of storms come to everybody.**

There are several types of storms. These storms come to everybody: the rich, the poor and the famous.

Man that is born of a woman is of few days, and FULL OF TROUBLE. He cometh forth like a flower, and is cut down: he fleeth also as a shadow, and continueth not.

Job 14:1-2

The same adjective "*beat vehemently*" is used to describe each person's storm.

You may be a chicken farmer and you may lose all your chickens in an epidemic. This is a kind of storm. You may be a bank manager who loses his treasured job unexpectedly. This is also a kind of storm.

You may be an investor who loses all his investments, stocks and bonds in a financial crisis. You may be a happily married person who never expected to get divorced.

286

You may lose a loved one suddenly and find yourself organizing an unexpected funeral. You may be a couple that is unable to have a child. You may hear bad news from the doctor that you are going to die soon. These are types of storms.

Indeed, there are financial storms, marital storms, storms of impending death, career storms, storms in relationships, storms of sorrow, bereavement storms, dashed expectations and disappointment, storms of divorce and storms of betrayal that beat upon everyone. Build your house on the rock.

5. **Build your house on the rock: The final and greatest storm of life is the storm of death and it also comes to everyone.**

For we must needs die, and are as water spilt on the ground, which cannot be gathered up again; neither doth God respect any person: yet doth he devise means, that his banished be not expelled from him.

2 Samuel 14:14

6. **Build your house on the rock: The storms of death will definitely come to everyone, no matter who you are.**

For I know that thou wilt bring me to death, and to the house appointed for all living.

Job 30:23

For he seeth that wise men die, likewise the fool and the brutish person perish, and leave their wealth to others.

Ps 49:10

And as it is appointed unto men once to die, but after this the judgment:

Hebrews 9:27

[4]Appointment in Accra

There was a certain Nigerian rich man who lived in the city of Lagos, the capital of Nigeria. This man had many servants, but he was particularly fond of the chief servant who was a Ghanaian and he had been with him for many years.

One day, the chief servant went to the market to buy some things for his master. And whom did he meet? He met a person called Death. Death had appeared in the market in bodily form. Death stared at the chief servant who in turn became frightened by the long stare of this stranger. He was so frightened that he abandoned his mission and forgot to buy the goods his master had sent him to buy.

When he got back home his master asked him, "Where are the things I sent you to buy?"

He told his master about how he had met Death who had appeared in a bodily form. The chief servant was truly shaken. The master quickly realized that the chief servant had been truly shaken because he had not behaved in that way before.

The chief servant begged his master saying, "I am so terrified by the way Death stared at me and I want to leave Lagos immediately. I would like to go back to Accra before tonight. I really feel that death wanted to kill me."

The master really loved his servant and so released him to leave immediately to Accra. After the chief servant left, the master decided to go to town himself and there, to his surprise, was Death in bodily form. The master was fearless and approached death, confronting and challenging him, "How dare you stare at my servant that way? Who do you think you are? What do you mean by that?"

Death stared silently at the master and then spoke. He said, "I was staring at him because I was surprised to find him in the market this morning seeing I have an appointment with him in Accra tonight."

The master was aghast. His servant was already in Accra for the appointment. He knew that there was no way his servant would escape the appointment with death.[4]

7. Build your house on the rock: When the certain storm of death comes will you be ready?

Death on a plane

Once, whilst waiting in an airport for a flight out to Malaysia, I chanced upon an amazing story of an Ethiopian Airlines plane that was hijacked and forced to crash into the sea. There were a few survivors who lived to tell the story of what had happened.

One passenger said the hijackers had taken over an Ethiopian Airlines jet that was full of passengers and commandeered the plane until it ran out of fuel. When the fuel finally ran out, the pilot announced that they had been hijacked and had run out of fuel so were going to crash.

He also added that the passengers could do whatever they wanted with the hijackers. It became clear to everyone on board that they were going to crash and the pilot guided the plane to crash into the sea.

This writer described how the cabin of the plane was filled with the stench of urine and faeces as most of the passengers urinated and defecated on themselves as the plane went down. They knew they were heading to their certain death. The plane crashed into the sea and broke up. This passenger described how water came rushing into the cabin amidst screams and cries from the passengers. It must have been a terrifying experience for all who were on board.

I often wondered what it must have been like for all these people to know that they were going to die. Most of them were terrified beyond description. That is why they urinated and defecated on themselves and the cabin was filled with such a strong smell.

What would you do, if death were staring you in the face? Would you be terrified or would you be ready to meet God? Will your house stand strong when the storm comes?

8. **Build your house on the rock: After the storm of death, you will be faced with the storm of judgment. If you build your house on the sand you will not survive; you will go to hell.**

If you build your life on Jesus Christ, you will survive the storm. If you receive Jesus Christ as your Saviour and receive His blood to wash away your sins you will survive the storm of death.

And as it is appointed unto men once to die, but after this the judgment:

Hebrews 9:27

SALVATION MESSAGE 53:

Without

All through the Bible, God shows us things that we cannot do without.

1. **WITHOUT CHRIST you cannot see God, you cannot know God and you cannot go to Heaven.** Life has many lessons, which teach you that there are some things that you cannot do without. Jesus Christ is somebody you cannot do without. The Word of God says so plainly.

I am the vine, ye are the branches: He that abideth in me, and I in him, the same bringeth forth much fruit: for WITHOUT ME YE CAN DO NOTHING.

John 15:5

That at that time ye were without Christ, being aliens from the commonwealth of Israel, and strangers from the covenants of promise, HAVING NO HOPE, AND WITHOUT GOD in the world: But now in Christ Jesus ye who sometimes were far off are made nigh by the blood of Christ.

Ephesians 2:12-13

Without a Ticket

One day a young Ghanaian man travelled to a European city with the intention of living there. The public transport in that city was made up of trams and buses. This young man began to move around this city, amazed by the efficiency of everything that seemed to function like clockwork. His greatest surprise was that everything seemed to be free. The trams were free and the buses were free. He simply sat on them and enjoyed a free ride to any part of the city that he wanted to go to.

One day, when he had been in the city for about six weeks he got onto a tram as he usually did. To his disbelief, two smartly dressed conductors got onto the tram that morning and announced that everyone should please pull out their tickets. The conductors went around from person to person and everyone seemed to produce a ticket. When they got to him he was taken aback and explained himself to the conductors.

"No one ever sold me a ticket. The tram driver never asked me for a ticket and no conductor ever came around to sell tickets to me either."

He went on, "I don't know why the others have tickets because no one ever sold one to me."

The conductors were not impressed with his story and asked him to come off the tram at the next stop. There, they showed him a metal box at the tram station and told him, "This is where you get your tickets."

"But no one ever asked me for a ticket," he protested.

"Yes", said the conductors. "Usually no one asks but occasionally we check to see if people have bought tickets."

"Anyway," they said, "Where do you come from? Do you have a passport?"

"I do," he said and produced his passport. His passport was valid and it had the right visa. But the conductors said, "Without a ticket you cannot sit on the tram. Let us please go to the police station."

At the police station he was made to pay a huge fine for being on a tram without a ticket.

After that, he was treated as a suspected African drug dealer. He was searched, hassled and made to strip completely naked.

It was a most humiliating and troubling experience for this young traveller. He had had his wallet, his food, money and even his passport but there was one thing that he needed. Without that one thing he encountered trouble.

2.   WITHOUT HOLINESS you cannot see God, you cannot know God and you cannot go to Heaven.

Follow peace with all men, and holiness, without which no man shall see the Lord:

                                                            Hebrews 12:14

Without Qualifications

When I was in university, there were some students who went for lectures in different departments and seemed to form a normal part of the student body.

After some years it was discovered that they did not have the required Advanced Level passes for entry into the university. To my amazement they were stripped of all the credentials and qualifications they acquired during the years they had spent in the university.   People who had earned degrees after years of hard work were simply stripped of those qualifications and turned into nonentities. It was as simple as that.

Without certain qualifications you cannot be in university. Is it any surprise to you that God would require certain qualifications for seeing Him?

3.   WITHOUT FAITH you cannot see God, you cannot know God and you cannot go to Heaven. No matter who you are, you need to walk by faith to see God.

But WITHOUT FAITH it is impossible to please him: for he that cometh to God must believe that he is, and that he is a rewarder of them that diligently seek him.

Hebrews 11:6

Without a Passport

One day, I got myself ready to go on another international trip to minister the Word of God. I packed my bags, my clothes, my shoes, my toiletries and everything I usually pack. Normally, I do not check to see where my passport is because it is usually in the same place.

That day, my flight happened to be in the afternoon and I had to get my passport out early. To my utter surprise my passport was not where I usually kept it. I searched my whole house from top to bottom, ransacking every nook and cranny for the missing passport.

After two hours of searching, I suddenly remembered that my passport was in the Korean Embassy. I panicked because I knew I could not travel without a passport and also the Korean Embassy was only open at certain times. Miraculously, I was able to retrieve my passport from the Korean Embassy just minutes before they closed. God had delivered me from aborting an important trip that I could not make *without* a passport.

Your journey to Heaven will be aborted *without* faith. You cannot access God and you cannot go on a journey to Heaven *without* faith.

4.   **WITHOUT THE SHEDDING OF THE BLOOD OF JESUS you cannot see God, you cannot know God and you cannot go to Heaven.**

And almost all things are by the law purged with blood; and WITHOUT SHEDDING OF BLOOD is no remission.

Hebrews 9:22

Without a Visa

One day, I invited a French-speaking preacher to Ghana. This preacher got himself a ticket, packed his bags and got on a flight to Accra, Ghana. We were expecting a powerful visitation through his ministry.

When he arrived at the airport, he duly presented his passport to the immigration officers.

"You do not have a visa," they told him.

He stuttered, "I'm sure I do," taking his passport from the immigration officer.

This was his second trip to Ghana but somehow he had forgotten to get another visa.

"I am sorry," said the immigration officer, "You cannot come to Ghana without a visa."

An argument ensued as this European preacher tried to bulldoze his way into the country. But the immigration officials would have none of it (they probably remembered the numerous

Africans who are sent back from the shores of Europe for the same reasons). To his amazement, this European preacher was put back on the very plane he came on and within one hour he was on the flight back to his country.

He had his bags, his Bible, his itinerary, his passport and his money.

But *without a visa* he simply could not enter the country. Without the Blood of Jesus you simply cannot enter Heaven.

SALVATION MESSAGE 54:

Remember Lot's Wife

Remember Lot's wife.

Luke 17:32

1.   To remember Lot's wife is to remember that Lot's wife had a great opportunity to be saved.

Lot and his wife lived in Sodom.   Lot's wife had the opportunity to avoid death and to live with a righteous man. Salvation came to the house of Lot that day just as salvation is coming to your house today.

> And when the morning arose, then the angels hastened Lot, saying, Arise, take thy wife, and thy two daughters, which are here; lest thou be consumed in the iniquity of the city.
>
> And while he lingered, the men laid hold upon his hand, and upon the hand of his wife, and upon the hand of his two daughters; the Lord being merciful unto him: and they brought him forth, and set him without the city.

Genesis 19:15-16

And delivered righteous Lot, who was oppressed by the filthy conduct of the wicked;

2 Peter 2:7 (NKJV)

2.   To remember Lot's wife is to remember how God has sent people to help you and to minister to you.

God sent angels to help Lot and his wife to come out of Sodom.

And there came two angels to Sodom at even; and Lot sat in the gate of Sodom: and Lot seeing them rose up to meet them; and he bowed himself with his face toward the ground;

Genesis 19:1

I HAVE SENT ALSO UNTO YOU ALL MY SERVANTS THE PROPHETS, rising up early and sending them, saying, Return ye now every man from his evil way, and amend your doings, and go not after other gods to serve them, and ye shall dwell in the land which I have given to you and to your fathers: but ye have not inclined your ear, nor hearkened unto me.

Jeremiah 35:15

3.   To remember Lot's wife is to remember that you must forsake the sins of this world.

Lot's wife did not forsake Sodom. The sins of Sodom were pride, fullness of bread and idleness. That is why God sent judgment to Sodom.

Behold, this was THE INIQUITY OF THY SISTER SODOM, pride, fulness of bread, and abundance of idleness was in her and in her daughters, neither did she strengthen the hand of the poor and needy. And they were haughty, and committed abomination before me: therefore I took them away as I saw good.

Ezekiel 16:49-50

4. To remember Lot's wife is to remember that you will lose your salvation if you love this present world.

Sodom represents the world and Lot's wife could not help turning back to look at what she loved. Her heart was in Sodom that is why she looked back. To remember Lot's wife is to remember not to give your heart to this world.

LOVE NOT THE WORLD, neither the things that are in the world. If any man love the world, the love of the Father is not in him.

1 John 2:15

For the grace of God that bringeth salvation hath appeared to all men, teaching us that, denying ungodliness and worldly lusts, we should live soberly, righteously, and godly, in this present world;

Titus 2:11-12

5. To remember Lot's wife is to remember that if you turn back you will be destroyed. Anyone who rejects God is destroyed.

But his wife looked back from behind him, and she became a pillar of salt.

Genesis 19:26

But WE ARE NOT OF THEM WHO DRAW BACK UNTO PERDITION; but of them that believe to the saving of the soul.

Hebrews 10:39

Because I have called, and ye refused; I have stretched out my hand, and no man regarded; but ye have set at nought all my counsel, and would none of my reproof:

I also will laugh at your calamity; I will mock when your fear cometh;

Proverbs 1:24-26

SALVATION MESSAGE 55:

The Wise Virgins

Then shall the kingdom of heaven be likened unto ten virgins, which took their lamps, and went forth to meet the bridegroom. And five of them were wise, and five were foolish.

They that were foolish took their lamps, and took no oil with them: But the wise took oil in their vessels with their lamps.

While the bridegroom tarried, they all slumbered and slept. And at midnight there was a cry made, Behold, the bridegroom cometh; go ye out to meet him.

Then all those virgins arose, and trimmed their lamps.

And the foolish said unto the wise, give us of your oil; for our lamps are gone out. But the wise answered, saying, not so; lest there be not enough for us and you: but go ye rather to them that sell, and buy for yourselves.

And while they went to buy, the bridegroom came; and they that were ready went in with him to the marriage: and the door was shut.

Afterward came also the other virgins, saying, Lord, Lord, open to us. But he answered and said, Verily I say unto you, I know you not.

Watch therefore, for ye know neither the day nor the hour wherein the Son of man cometh.

Matthew 25:1-13

1. Be a wise virgin: Like the ten virgins, you have been invited to a great and happy wedding feast.

Your invitation to Christ is like the invitation to a wedding feast.

Coming to Christ is not a bad and nasty experience. It is more painful and costly to reject Jesus Christ.

Being born again will be the greatest and happiest experience of your life. The day you are born again is greater than your birthday, your graduation or your wedding day.

Then said he unto him, A certain man made a great supper, and bade many:

Luke 14:16

2. Be a wise virgin: Out of the ten virgins invited to the wedding feast only the wise were admitted. So also, out of the billions invited to Christ only the wise will be admitted to Heaven.

If thou be wise, thou shalt be wise for thyself: but if thou scornest, thou alone shalt bear it.

Proverbs 9:12

It takes wisdom to receive Jesus Christ. The fool says in his heart, "There is no God." Out of the billions invited some are foolish enough to reject the invitation. When Jesus was born wise men went to seek Him. Today, it is still wise men who seek Jesus.

The devil is waiting to push you into hell. Without wisdom you will not escape from hell. The wisdom you need today is the wisdom of humbling yourself before the cross of Jesus Christ. Only those who are wise enough to seek Jesus Christ today will be saved.

3. **Just as the ten virgins had to meet certain requirements in order to attend the wedding, you will have to meet certain requirements to be able to go to Heaven.**

The simple requirement for the wedding was to have lamps with oil. There are also requirements for heaven.

a. You need to acknowledge that you are a sinner: "For all have sinned, and come short of the glory of God."

Romans 3:23

b. You need to acknowledge that the wages of sin is death: "For the wages of sin is death; but the gift of God is eternal life through Jesus Christ our Lord".

Romans 6:23

c. You need to know that God loves you and does not want you to perish: "For God so loved the world, that he gave his only begotten Son, that whosoever believeth in him should not perish, but have everlasting life."

John 3:16

d. You need to have your sins washed by the blood of Jesus: "If we confess our sins, he is faithful and just to forgive us our sins, and to cleanse us from all unrighteousness."

1 John 1:9

e. You need to receive Christ: "But as many as received him, to them gave he power to become the sons of God, even to them that believe on his name."

John 1:12

f. You need to confess Jesus Christ as your Lord and Saviour: "That if thou shalt confess with thy mouth the Lord Jesus, and shalt believe in thine heart that God hath raised him from the dead, thou shalt be saved. For with the heart man believeth unto righteousness; and with the mouth confession is made unto salvation."

Romans 10:9-10

4. Just as the ten virgins were surprised at the time the bridegroom came, many people will be surprised at the time the Son of God will come.

My first few days in Medical School were challenging, to say the least. I looked ahead and saw only seven long, dreary years. I wondered when I would ever finish school and become a doctor.

One day, I turned around, looked across to my colleague and asked her whether we were in the right school. I simply could not imagine that seven years would come to pass. And yet today, as I write this book, it has been more than thirty years since I sat in the classroom asking my friend whether we were in the right place. Indeed, our lives will be over before we realise what has happened.

I heard Billy Graham speak about the one thing that had really surprised him in his life. He said one of the greatest surprises of his life was "the brevity of life".

The bridegroom, in the parable of the Ten Virgins, took a long time but he eventually came. The coming of Christ may take a long time but it will come. The Day of Judgment may take a long time in coming but it will eventually come. The end of your life may take a long time to come but it will eventually come. The day of your death may take a long time to come but it will eventually come. The coming of the Lord is scheduled for a time that no one expects. Do not forget that the bridegroom came at midnight!

For the vision is yet for an appointed time, but at the end it shall speak, and not lie: though it tarry, wait for it; because it will surely come, it will not tarry.

Habakkuk 2:3

The Lord is not slack concerning his promise, as some men count slackness; but is longsuffering to us-ward, not willing that any should perish, but that all should come to repentance.

2 Peter 3:9

SECTION 8:

SALVATION AND
THE NEW LIFE

The New Creation

Therefore if any man be in Christ, he is a new creature: old things are passed away; behold, all things are become new.

2 Corinthians 5:17

1. **Man is a spirit, has a soul and lives in a body.**

And the very God of peace sanctify you wholly; and I pray God your whole spirit and soul and body be preserved blameless unto the coming of our Lord Jesus Christ.

1 Thessalonians 5:23

2. **The spirit of an unsaved man is dead and desperately wicked.**

The heart is deceitful above all things, and desperately wicked: who can know it?

Jeremiah 17:9

3. The spirit of a saved man is righteous and truly holy.

And that ye put on the new man, which after God is created in righteousness and true holiness.

2 Corinthians 5:17

4. After you are born again, your spirit is a new born baby and it must grow.

As newborn babes, desire the sincere milk of the word, that ye may grow thereby:

1 Peter 2:2

5. After you are saved, your mind is still the same; it must be renewed.

And be not conformed to this world: but be ye transformed by the renewing of your mind, that ye may prove what is that good, and acceptable, and perfect, will of God.

Romans 12:2

6. After you are saved, your body is still the same; you must keep it under control.

But I keep under my body, and bring it into subjection: lest that by any means, when I have preached to others, I myself should be a castaway.

1 Corinthians 9:27

The Man Whose Flesh Was Not Born Again

One day, I visited a friend of mine; a hardened sinner who was not interested in being born again. The Holy Spirit led me to witness to him about Christ; and for the first time, he listened. When I finished, he asked me, "What must I do?" I led him in the sinner's prayer, and he said afterwards, "Dag, thank you very much. I feel I am a changed person." Then I decided to lead him to receive the baptism of the Holy Spirit. I laid hands on him and to my surprise he received the Holy Spirit, speaking in tongues fluently. Suddenly something else happened. When I touched him, he was "slain in the Spirit" and fell on his bed. He spoke in tongues for some time. An hour later, I decided to leave.

Approximately five hours later, I returned to his apartment to see him. When I got there, I paused at the door before going in. What did I hear? My new convert was fornicating in the bedroom with his girlfriend! Oh dear! So soon after a wonderful salvation experience and the Holy Ghost baptism! I was aghast! I asked myself, "Was this man really born again? Does being born again have any effect on a person?" The answer is: "Yes, it does!" The reality was that my friend's body was still the same and capable of committing all the sins of the flesh. As a baby Christian, he had yielded his flesh to all the old sins. His flesh had once again engaged itself in sin, because it had not been affected by the "born-again experience".

Though you are born again, your flesh is still the same. Never forget this! Keep it under control, or else it will lead you into sin.

7. **After you are born again, your mind is still open to all kinds of thoughts; you must learn to think on the right things.**

Finally, brethren, whatsoever things are true, whatsoever things are honest, whatsoever things are just, whatsoever things are pure, whatsoever things are lovely, whatsoever things are of good report; if there be any virtue, and if there be any praise, think on these things.

Philippians 4:8

Born Again

There was a man of the Pharisees, named Nicodemus, a ruler of the Jews:

The same came to Jesus by night, and said unto him, Rabbi, we know that thou art a teacher come from God: for no man can do these miracles that thou doest, except God be with him.

Jesus answered and said unto him, Verily, verily, I say unto thee, except a man be born again, he cannot see the kingdom of God.

Nicodemus saith unto him, how can a man be born when he is old? Can he enter the second time into his mother's womb, and be born?

Jesus answered, Verily, verily, I say unto thee, Except a man be born of water and of the Spirit, he cannot enter into the kingdom of God.

That which is born of the flesh is flesh; and that which is born of the Spirit is spirit.

Marvel not that I said unto thee, ye must be born again.

John 3:1-7

Why You Must Be Born Again

1. You must be born again because the first time you were born, you were born in sin.

Why do you have to write an exam again? Because it did not work out well the first time you did it.

Have mercy upon me, O God, according to thy lovingkindness: according unto the multitude of thy tender mercies blot out my transgressions.

Wash me throughly from mine iniquity, and cleanse me from my sin.

For I acknowledge my transgressions: and my sin is ever before me.

Against thee, thee only, have I sinned, and done this evil in thy sight: that thou mightest be justified when thou speakest, and be clear when thou judgest.

Behold, I WAS SHAPEN IN INIQUITY; AND IN SIN DID MY MOTHER CONCEIVE ME.

Psalm 51:1-5

2. You must be born again because you are dead. Death has fallen on all men because of their sins.

The whole world lives in sin and wickedness. Americans, Iraqis, Ghanaians, Canadians and South Africans live in the fallen state of sinful man. Evil can be found in beautiful places like Switzerland. Amidst the beautiful mountains and lakes, can be found all the sins of mankind like prostitution, murder, drug addiction and suicide.

But God, who is rich in mercy, for his great love wherewith he loved us, even WHEN WE WERE DEAD IN SINS, hath quickened us together with Christ, (by grace ye are saved;) And hath raised us up together, and made us sit together in heavenly places in Christ Jesus:

Ephesians 2:4-6

3. **You must be born again because when Adam sinned he introduced death into the whole world.**

Wherefore, as BY ONE MAN SIN ENTERED INTO THE WORLD, and death by sin; and so death passed upon all men, for that all have sinned:"

Romans 5:12

4. **You must be born again because death has spread to the whole world since Adam introduced sin into the world.**

Wherefore, as by one man sin entered into the world, and death by sin; and SO DEATH PASSED UPON ALL MEN, for that all have sinned:

Romans 5:12

5. **You must be born again because although death was introduced by one man, Adam, the free gift of life has been re-introduced by one man, Jesus Christ.**

Therefore as by the offence of one judgment came upon all men to condemnation; even so BY THE RIGHTEOUSNESS OF ONE THE FREE GIFT CAME UPON ALL MEN unto justification of life.

For as by one man's disobedience many were made sinners, so by the obedience of one shall many be made righteous.

Romans 5:18-19

6. **You must be born again by hearing and receiving the incorruptible Word of God.**

Being born again, not of corruptible seed, but of incorruptible, by the word of God, which liveth and abideth for ever.

1 Peter 1:23

7. **You can be born again by believing in Jesus Christ's death, the shedding of His blood, His burial and His resurrection.**

But AS MANY AS RECEIVED HIM, to them gave he power to become the sons of God, even to them that believe on his name:

John 1:12

Abundant Life

The thief cometh not, but for to steal, and to kill, and to destroy: I am come that they might have life, and that they might have it more abundantly.

I am the good shepherd: the good shepherd giveth his life for the sheep.

John 10:10-11

… For this purpose the Son of God was manifested, that he might destroy the works of the devil.

1 John 3:8

1. Who has destroyed our perfect world? Who destroyed the righteousness of our lives? Who made men become sinful and evil? A thief called satan!

And the Lord God said unto the woman, What is this that thou hast done? And the woman said, THE SERPENT BEGUILED ME, and I did eat.

Genesis 3:13

Adam and Eve were living happily in the Garden of Eden. Adam was prosperous and never sick or unhappy with his work. He would return from work whistling with joy. They did not quarrel, there was no sickness, there was no funeral to attend and there was no cemetery.

One day, a thief came to the garden in the form of a serpent. The serpent started to talk to the woman who was relaxing in the garden.

"Did God say you should not eat of this fruit?" the serpent asked Eve.

"I think so," the woman responded.

The serpent continued, "This is the best fruit. Take it and eat it. God knows this is something sweet and He does not want you to enjoy it."

She took the fruit and ate it. Immediately, she was full of sin and noticed that she was naked.

Then she went to her husband and offered the fruit to him. He also ate and immediately became a sinner.

When God came to see them, Adam was hiding because he had sinned.

God asked Eve, "What is this that you have done?"

From that day sin, curses, sickness and death came into the world.

Adam was cursed to suffer on earth, to die and to be buried in the ground because of his sin.

Eve was also cursed because of her sin.

Unto the woman he said, I will greatly multiply thy sorrow and thy conception; in sorrow thou shalt bring forth children; and thy desire shall be to thy husband, and he shall rule over thee.

Genesis 3:16

Adam and Eve gave birth to Cain and Abel. Cain killed Abel and so murder and death also came into the world.

One day, whilst visiting a church in Asia, I had the opportunity to minister to a businessmen's fellowship. I was picked up from my hotel by a top businessman who was part of the fellowship. As we drove to the church he told me how he had become a regular church attendee.

"I used to do all sorts of things on Sunday mornings instead of going to church. But something happened to me that changed everything," he told me.

He continued, "One Sunday morning, instead of going to church, I went swimming in a river by a popular waterfall. I was with many other people swimming under the waterfall when suddenly a snake, which had been carried by the river and the waterfall, fell on me. It was an extremely venomous viper and it bit me. I was rushed to the hospital where I went into a coma and was in intensive care for over six weeks, teetering between life and death. The skin on half my body peeled off. I very nearly died," he told me. "Now, I am always in church on Sunday mornings. I don't go swimming on Sundays any more."

I thought about this man and how his life almost ended through one bite of a serpent. The bite of the serpent sent this man into a critical condition, where he teetered between life and death.

This is exactly what has happened to mankind. One bite from the serpent has changed everything. The entire human race has been sent into emergency mode with many critical problems, diseases, tragedies, calamities and sorrows.

Perhaps, this is the only explanation for the state of the human race, which is constantly balancing itself between life and extinction.

2. **Who has destroyed the peace of the nations and brought war and conflict to every corner of this earth? A thief called satan!**

And when the thousand years are expired, SATAN shall be loosed out of his prison,

And shall go out to deceive the nations which are in the four quarters of the earth, Gog and Magog, TO GATHER THEM TOGETHER TO BATTLE: the number of whom is as the sand of the sea.

Revelation 20:7-8

3. **Who has destroyed and stolen the health of the human race and brought sickness to this world? A thief called satan!**

And ought not this woman, being a daughter of Abraham, WHOM SATAN HATH BOUND, lo, these eighteen years, be loosed from this bond on the sabbath day?

Luke 13:16

4. **Who has destroyed our prosperity and stolen our riches? A thief called satan!**

Then Satan answered the Lord, and said, Doth Job fear God for nought?

Hast not thou made an hedge about him, and about his house, and about all that he hath on every side? thou hast blessed the work of his hands, and his substance is increased in the land.

But put forth thine hand now, and touch all that he hath, and he will curse thee to thy face.

And the Lord said unto Satan, Behold, all that he hath is in thy power; only upon himself put not forth thine hand. So Satan went forth from the presence of the Lord.

And there came a messenger unto Job, and said, The oxen were plowing, and the asses feeding beside them: And the Sabeans fell upon them, and took them away; yea, they have slain the servants with the edge of the sword; and I only am escaped alone to tell thee.

While he was yet speaking, there came also another, and said, The fire of God is fallen from heaven, and hath burned up the sheep, and the servants, and consumed them; and I only am escaped alone to tell thee.

While he was yet speaking, there came also another, and said, The Chaldeans made out three bands, and fell upon the camels, and have carried them away, yea, and slain the servants with the edge of the sword; and I only am escaped alone to tell thee.

Job 1:9-12, 14-17

5. Who has destroyed our family lives? A thief called satan!

And the Lord said unto Satan, Behold, all that he hath is in thy power; only upon himself put not forth thine hand. So Satan went forth from the presence of the Lord.

While he was yet speaking, there came also another, and said, Thy sons and thy daughters were eating and drinking wine in their eldest brother's house:

And, behold, there came a great wind from the wilderness, and smote the four corners of the house, and it fell upon the young men, and they are dead; and I only am escaped alone to tell thee.

Job 1:12, 18-19

6. **Who has destroyed our peace of mind? A thief called satan!**

And lest I should be exalted above measure through the abundance of the revelations, there was given to me a thorn in the flesh, THE MESSENGER OF SATAN TO BUFFET ME, lest I should be exalted above measure.

2 Corinthians 12:7

7. **Unless you catch the thief who destroys and kills, he will continue to destroy your life.**

You will need help to catch the thief who is destroying you.

I once had a thief in the church who stole equipment, money, mobile phones, food, and laptops. I knew that if the thief was not caught, the stealing would continue and we would continue to suffer. So I called a friend and asked if he could help me to catch this thief and stop the suffering in the church. My friend agreed to help me. After I caught the thief, our money was no longer stolen.

There is a thief who has stolen your health and you must catch him today. There is a thief who has stolen your peace of mind and you must catch him today.

There is a thief who has stolen your money and you must catch him today. There is a thief who wants to take you to hell and you must catch him today.

8. **God loved us so much that He sent His Son to catch and destroy the thief who was destroying us.**

Jesus did not descend into the earth with a parachute. He was born of a virgin. Jesus Christ came to catch, stop and destroy the thief.

… For this purpose the Son of God was manifested, that he might destroy the works of the devil.

1 John 3:8

9. Jesus is the Good Shepherd who lays His life down to save the sheep.

Jesus Christ destroyed the power of the thief over us through the cross and the blood that He shed for us.

Jesus gives us life through His blood that He shed on the cross. Only the blood of Jesus can wash away our sins.

And almost all things are by the law purged with blood; and without shedding of blood is no remission.

Hebrews 9:22

10. Jesus Christ is the Good Shepherd who takes away our diseases and infirmities.

Middle eastern shepherds rub their sheep with oil so that flies are driven away from the sheep. Jesus Christ, is the Good Shepherd who rubs us with oil to keep the demons away from us.

Surely he hath borne our griefs, and carried our sorrows: yet we did esteem him stricken, smitten of God, and afflicted. But he was wounded for our transgressions, he was bruised for our iniquities: the chastisement of our peace was upon him; and with his stripes we are healed. All we like sheep have gone astray; we have turned every one to his own way; and the Lord hath laid on him the iniquity of us all.

Isaiah 53:4-6

SECTION 9:

SALVATION AND JESUS CHRIST

Why Many People Believe in Jesus Christ

Then cried Jesus in the temple as he taught, saying, ye both know me, and ye know whence I am: and I am not come of myself, but he that sent me is true, whom ye know not.

But I know him: for I am from him, and he hath sent me.

Then they sought to take him: but no man laid hands on him, because his hour was not yet come.

And MANY of the PEOPLE BELIEVED ON HIM, and said, when Christ cometh, will he do more miracles than these which this man hath done?

John 7:28-31

1. **Many people believe in Jesus because of His sayings and His preaching. Jesus Christ said amazing things.**

   a. He said, "I am the Way…"

   b. He said, "I am the Truth..."

   c. He said, "I am the Life..."

d.   He said, "I am the true Light."

e.   He said, "I am the Good Shepherd."

f.   He said, "I am the Resurrection."

g.   He said, "I am the Door."

2.   Many people believe in Jesus because of His miracles. He had miracles in every department.

He was a healer in the eye department – Blind Bartimaeus

He was a healer in the gynaecology department – the woman with the issue of blood.

He was a healer in the ear, nose and throat department – the deaf and dumb boy.

He was a healer in the orthopaedics department – the lame man who was lowered from the roof.

He was a healer in the paediatric department – the Syrophoenician woman's child.

He was a healer in the pathology department –

a.   Jairus' Daughter: freshly dead

b.   Widow of Nain's son: on the way to the cemetery

c.   Lazarus: dead for 4 days and buried

3.   Many people believe in Jesus because He rose from the dead.   People want to follow a living person and not a dead person.

We know that Jesus rose from the dead because He was seen by His disciples after He rose from the dead.

We know that Jesus rose from the dead because He was seen by over five hundred people when He rose from the dead.

We know that Jesus rose from the dead because His disciples were transformed after seeing their living Saviour.

The Girl Who Followed the Living Husband

There was a certain lady who was only 26 years old when her husband died suddenly. She was very sad and cried everyday. At the funeral I took her to see her husband's body. When she saw her husband's body she was terrified because it had changed so much.

Two years later, she came to introduce to me a young man who wanted to marry her. I accepted him and he married her and took her to Europe. On their wedding day, I saw this lady wearing a white dress. She was looking beautiful. She came to my office to see me with her husband. As she left I remembered something. Do you want to know what I remembered? I remembered the dead body that she was crying over. She certainly did not want to follow her dead husband.

This made me realize that no one wants to follow a dead person. Everybody wants to follow a living person. This is why many people believe in Jesus, because He is alive. People do not want to follow a dead leader or a dead saviour.

4.   Many people believe in Jesus because of His blood.

Jesus Christ took away the sins of the whole world. He died and went to hell and rose from the dead for us.

Jesus Christ went to hell. He took the keys of hell and opened the doors of all the prisons. It took Him three days to open the prisons and set free all the Chinese, all the Germans, all the Nigerians, all the Ghanaians, all the Americans, all the Australians, all the Koreans, all the Indians – everybody! Jesus Christ then went to Heaven and presented His blood.

Forasmuch as ye know that ye were not redeemed with corruptible things, as silver and gold, from your vain conversation received by tradition from your fathers; But with the precious blood of Christ, as of a lamb without blemish and without spot:

1 Peter 1:18-19

Why Many People Believe that Jesus is the Son of God

Jesus said that He was the Son of God. Many people believe that Jesus is indeed the Son of God because of the amazing things He did.

You cannot make claims without supporting them with actions. If you say you are a doctor you must be able to prove it.

Any Doctor on Board?

Once, I was on a flight when an announcement was made in request for anyone who was a doctor. There was a man who had stopped breathing and they wanted a doctor to help. At that moment, anyone who claimed to be a doctor would have to know what to do. He would have to be able to resuscitate the dead or dying man. He would have to know how to reactivate the person's heart and help him to breathe.

On another occasion, I was on a flight when a pregnant woman went into labour. Again they called for a doctor. This time, the doctor would have to know how to deliver a baby, deliver the placenta, cut the cord and ensure that the baby breathed normally and that both mother and baby were safe.

Indeed, this is why some doctors would not own up that they are doctors when an announcement is made. All their medical knowledge and skills would be tested if they did.

Jesus Christ claimed to be the Son of God. That was one of the most daring statements for anybody to make. He would have to prove beyond all reasonable doubt that He was the Son of God. And He did! Many things that He did attested to this reality. At the end of the day, many came to believe that the Son of God had visited the earth.

He healed the sick, He spoke great words, He walked on water, He fed thousands and He raised the dead. What more can you expect of the Son of God? This is why many people believe that Jesus Christ is the Son of God.

1. Many people believed that Jesus was the Son of God because of the great words that He spoke.

Jesus said many amazing things and claimed to be many amazing things. For example He said that He was the Way, the Truth and the Life. He claimed to be the only way to God the Father.

Jesus saith unto him, I am the way, the truth, and the life: no man cometh unto the Father, but by me.

John 14:6

2. Many people believed that Jesus Christ was the Son of God because of the miracles that He did.

Now when he was in Jerusalem at the passover, in the feast day, many believed in his name, when they saw the miracles which he did.

John 2:23

3.   Many people believed that Jesus was the Son of God because He was instantly recognized by evil spirits who had lived on the earth for years.

And they went into Capernaum; and straightway on the sabbath day he entered into the synagogue, and taught.

And they were astonished at his doctrine: for he taught them as one that had authority, and not as the scribes.

And there was in their synagogue a man with an unclean spirit; and he cried out, Saying, Let us alone; what have we to do with thee, thou Jesus of Nazareth? Art thou come to destroy us? I KNOW THEE WHO THOU ART, THE HOLY ONE OF GOD.

Mark 1:21-24

4.   Many people believed that Jesus was the Son of God because He walked on water.

And straightway Jesus constrained his disciples to get into a ship, and to go before him unto the other side, while he sent the multitudes away.

And when he had sent the multitudes away, he went up into a mountain apart to pray: and when the evening was come, he was there alone.

But the ship was now in the midst of the sea, tossed with waves: for the wind was contrary.

And in the fourth watch of the night Jesus went unto them, WALKING ON THE SEA.

Matthew 14:22-25

5.   Many people believed that Jesus was the Son of God because He calmed storms with His words.

And, behold, there arose a great tempest in the sea, insomuch that the ship was covered with the waves: but he was asleep.

And his disciples came to him, and awoke him, saying, Lord, save us: we perish.

And he saith unto them, Why are ye fearful, O ye of little faith? Then he arose, and REBUKED THE WINDS AND THE SEA; AND THERE WAS A GREAT CALM.

Matthew 8:24-26

6.   Many people believed that Jesus was the Son of God because He fed five thousand people in one day.

And when it was evening, his disciples came to him, saying, This is a desert place, and the time is now past; send the multitude away, that they may go into the villages, and buy themselves victuals.

But Jesus said unto them, They need not depart; give ye them to eat.

And they say unto him, We have here but five loaves, and two fishes.

He said, Bring them hither to me.

And he commanded the multitude to sit down on the grass, and took the five loaves, and the two fishes, and looking up to heaven, he blessed, and brake, and gave the loaves to his disciples, and the disciples to the multitude.

And they did all eat, and were filled: and they took up of the fragments that remained twelve baskets full.

And THEY THAT HAD EATEN WERE ABOUT FIVE THOUSAND MEN, beside women and children.

Matthew 14:15-21

7.   Many people believed that Jesus was the Son of God because He raised the dead.

And it came to pass the day after, that he went into a city called Nain; and many of his disciples went with him, and much people.

Now when he came nigh to the gate of the city, behold, there was a dead man carried out, the only son of his mother, and she was a widow: and much people of the city was with her.

And when the Lord saw her, he had compassion on her, and said unto her, Weep not.

And he came and touched the bier: and they that bare him stood still. And he said, Young man, I say unto thee, Arise.

And HE THAT WAS DEAD SAT UP, AND BEGAN TO SPEAK. And he delivered him to his mother.

Luke 7:11-15

8.   **Many people believed that Jesus was the Son of God because He was crucified on a cross and rose from the dead as He predicted.**

And they bring him unto the place Golgotha, which is, being interpreted, The place of a skull.

And they gave him to drink wine mingled with myrrh: but he received it not.

And when they had crucified him, they parted his garments, casting lots upon them, what every man should take.

And it was the third hour, and they crucified him.

Mark 15:22-25

And as they thus spake, JESUS HIMSELF STOOD IN THE MIDST OF THEM, AND SAITH UNTO THEM, PEACE BE UNTO YOU.

BUT THEY WERE TERRIFIED AND AFFRIGHTED, and supposed that they had seen a spirit.

And he said unto them, Why are ye troubled? and why do thoughts arise in your hearts?

Behold my hands and my feet, that it is I myself: handle me, and see; for a spirit hath not flesh and bones, as ye see me have.

Luke 24:36-39

9. You must believe in Jesus Christ and receive Him as the Son of God and the Saviour of the world.

You must ask Him to wash you and cleanse you with His blood that was shed for you on Calvary's cross.

Jesus Christ, the Same Yesterday, Today and Forever

Jesus Christ the same yesterday, and to day, and for ever.

Hebrews 13:8

1. **Jesus Christ is the same: Even though men change so much Jesus Christ never changes. He is the same today and forever.**

I once visited an old man with some little children. The old man stretched out his hand to embrace the children but they ran away from him. We soon forgot about the children and began chatting. After a while, he told me, "Old age is not an easy experience."

"Why do you say that?" I asked.

He said, "I used to be a very handsome man. Can you see my picture over there?"

He continued, "When you grow old you change so much that even children are afraid of you."

When he said that, I thought of how much human beings change as the years go by. If Jesus Christ is the same yesterday, today and forever then He is certainly not a man because He never changes.

One day a relative of mine died and it was time for his funeral. His body was laid in state for the wake keeping and the funeral was successfully conducted. Because he was a lawyer, a large group of lawyers gathered around his body to honour him. They made several speeches over his dead body and recounted his good deeds.

A few weeks after the funeral, another family approached the family of this lawyer to inform them that it was suspected that they had buried the wrong person. Indeed, there had been a swap of the bodies and the person they had buried was not a lawyer at all. He was a poor man from a poor family but his body had been mistaken for the lawyer's. This poor man had received all the praise and honour that was due the lawyer.

How was this amazing swap possible? How was it possible that the widow and relatives who were sitting by the body did not recognize that it was not the body of their loved one? This had happened because dead bodies change so much that the relatives assumed that their beloved lawyer had changed because he had been so long in the mortuary. Human beings change so much when they die. They are simply not the same that is why we agree to bury our loved ones away and out of our sight forever. But Jesus Christ does not change. He is the same yesterday, today and forever!

2.   Jesus Christ is the same: Jesus Christ is still DOING the same things that He used to do.

He is healing your diseases and your sicknesses just as He healed the diseases and sicknesses of many people.

You Have Not Changed!

One day I had a telephone call from someone I knew in school. As we talked for some time he said, "Dag, you have not changed!"

And I asked him why he said I had not changed. He said, "The way you talk has not changed and the way you laugh has not changed and the things you like have not changed."

I mused over my good old friend's comment and realized that he had given me an important revelation about Hebrews 13:8. When you say that someone has not changed, it means that he does the things he used to do and says the things he used to say. That is what my friend meant when he said I had not changed.

God has not changed and therefore His words have not changed, the things He does have not changed and His expectations of us have not changed!

3.   Jesus Christ is the same: Jesus Christ is still HEALING

a.   JESUS IS THE HEALER OF THE BLIND

-    As He healed blind Bartimaeus (Mark 10:46-52)

-    As He healed the blind man by the pool of Siloam (John 9:1-17)

-    As He healed the blind man who saw men as trees (Mark 8:22-26)

-    As he healed the two blind men who followed Him to Jairus' house (Matthew 9:27-31)

b.   JESUS IS THE HEALER OF WOMEN WITH GYNECOLOGICAL PROBLEMS

-    As He healed the woman with the issue of blood. (Mark 5:25-34)

c.   JESUS IS THE HEALER OF MAD MEN

-    As He healed the mad man of Gadara. (Mark 5:1-16)

d. JESUS IS THE HEALER OF THE PARALYZED

- Just as He healed the paralytic who was led down the roof (Mark 2:1-12)

- As He healed the man with the withered hand (Matthew 12:9-13)

e. JESUS IS THE HEALER OF THE DEAF AND DUMB

- As He healed the dumb man (Matthew 9:32-33)

- As He cast out the dumb spirit (Luke 11:14-15)

- As He healed the deaf and dumb man (Mark 7:31-37)

f. JESUS IS THE HEALER OF LONG-STANDING ILLNESSES

- As He healed the woman who had been bent over for eighteen years (Luke 13:11-17)

- The man who had been ill for thirty-eight years. (John 5:2-9)

g. JESUS IS THE HEALER OF EPILEPTICS

- As He healed the epileptic boy (Matthew 17:14-18).

h. JESUS IS THE HEALER OF LEPERS

- As He healed the ten lepers (Luke 17:12-19)

- As He healed the leper (Matthew 8:1-4)

i. JESUS IS THE HEALER OF LARGE CROWDS

- As He healed the large crowd in Luke 6:17-19

j. JESUS IS THE HEALER OF CHILDREN

- As He healed the Syro-Phoenician woman's Daughter (Matthew 15:21-28)

- As He healed the nobleman's son (John 4:46-54)

k. JESUS IS THE HEALER OF PEOPLE'S SERVANTS

- As He healed the centurion's servant (Luke 7:1-10)

l. JESUS IS THE HEALER OF FAMILY MEMBERS

- As He healed Peter's mother-in-law (Luke 4:38-39)

m. JESUS RAISES THE DEAD

- As He raised the widow of Nain's son from the dead (Luke 7:11-15)

- As He raised Jairus' daughter from the dead (Mark 5:22-24, 35-42)

- As He raised Lazarus from the dead (John 11:1-47)

4. Jesus Christ is the same: Jesus Christ is still SAYING the same things that He used to say.

a. He is still saying, "I am the way, the truth and the life" (John 14:6)

b. He is still saying, "I am the door" (John 10:9)

c. He is still saying, "I am the resurrection" (John 11:25)

d. He is still saying, "I am the good shepherd" (John 10:11)

5. Jesus Christ is the same: Jesus Christ's blood is still the same.

a. The Blood of Jesus will never lose its power because the Blood of Jesus is not like the blood of bulls and goats. It remains the same and it has the same power to save and to wash away sins.

Forasmuch as ye know that ye were not redeemed with corruptible things, as silver and gold, from your vain conversation received by tradition from your fathers; But with the precious blood of Christ, as of a lamb without blemish and without spot:

1 Peter 1:18-19

b. The Blood of Jesus still has power to forgive and to cleanse you from your sins.

But if we walk in the light, as he is in the light, we have fellowship one with another, and the blood of Jesus Christ his Son cleanseth us from all sin.

1 John 1:7

c. The Blood of Jesus still has the power to redeem you.

In whom we have redemption through his blood, the forgiveness of sins, according to the riches of his grace;

Ephesians 1:7

Are You Lost?

For the Son of man is come to seek and to save that which was lost.

Luke 19:10

The Bible talks about four things that are lost: the lost coin, the lost sheep, the lost son and the lost world.

To be lost means to be adrift, to be castaway, to be down the drain, to go astray, to be irrecoverable, to be wayward, to be off course and to be found nowhere. These are not nice descriptions of the fallen state of man. That is why Jesus Christ came to the world to save lost coins, lost sheep, lost sons and a lost world.

1.   **You may be a lost coin.** Your life may be lost in hell through carelessness and failing to take the Word of God seriously.

Either what woman having TEN PIECES OF SILVER, IF SHE LOSE ONE PIECE, doth not light a candle, and sweep the house, and seek diligently till she find it?

And when she hath found it, she calleth her friends and her neighbours together, saying, Rejoice with me; for I have found the piece which I had lost. Likewise, I say unto you, there is joy in the presence of the angels of God over one sinner that repenteth.

Luke 15:8-10

2.   You may be a lost sheep.

Your life may be lost because you have wandered away from the paths of righteousness, having neither shepherd nor saviour in your life. You need Jesus Christ the Good Shepherd.

What man of you, having an hundred SHEEP, if he lose one of them, doth not leave the ninety and nine in the wilderness, AND GO AFTER THAT WHICH IS LOST, until he find it?

And when he hath found it, he layeth it on his shoulders, rejoicing.

And when he cometh home, he calleth together his friends and neighbours, saying unto them, Rejoice with me; for I have found my sheep which was lost.

I say unto you, that likewise joy shall be in heaven over one sinner that repenteth, more than over ninety and nine just persons, which need no repentance.

Luke 15:4-7

3.   You may be a lost son.

You may be a lost son because you are rebellious and misguided. You do not want to do anything the same way your father did. You want to be different and you may pay for that by going to hell.

But the father said to his servants, Bring forth the best robe, and put it on him; and put a ring on his hand, and shoes on his feet:

And bring hither the fatted calf, and kill it; and let us eat, and be merry:

For this MY SON was dead, and is alive again; HE WAS LOST, AND IS FOUND. And they began to be merry.

Luke 15:22-24

4. You may be following a world that is lost.

People are lost because they are blind and cannot see Heaven and hell. The broad way is teeming with multitudes that are rushing headlong into the lake of fire. The broad way is filled with people who have no hope and no answers to the complicated problems of this world. They are waiting for a good shepherd to come and lead them away from their destructions.

But if our gospel be hid, it is hid to them that are lost:

2 Corinthians 4:3

5. Repent and come to Jesus Christ so that you do not go to hell.

It is never too late to follow the Shepherd out of the darkness of this lost world, into the glorious light of the gospel of Jesus Christ.

I Am the Way, the Truth and the Life

And whither I go ye know, and the way ye know. Thomas saith unto him, Lord, we know not whither thou goest; and how can we know the way?

Jesus saith unto him, I am the way, the truth, and the life: no man cometh unto the Father, but by me.

John 14:4-6

1. **Jesus is the Way, the Truth and the Life: There is a way that seems right unto man; these are the ways of men and the ways of death.**

There is a way which seemeth right unto a man, but the end thereof are the ways of death.

Proverbs 14:12

2. **Jesus is the Way, the Truth and the Life: The way of working hard and heaping up riches is not the way to Heaven or to God.**

There is one alone, and there is not a second; yea, he hath neither child nor brother: yet is there no end of all his labour; neither is his eye satisfied with riches; neither saith he, For whom do I labour, and bereave my soul of good? This is also vanity, yea, it is a sore travail.

Ecclesiastes 4:8

3. Jesus is the Way, the Truth and the Life: A way of pleasure is not the way to Heaven or to God.

Therefore hear now this, THOU THAT ART GIVEN TO PLEASURES, that dwellest carelessly, that sayest in thine heart, I am, and none else beside me; I shall not sit as a widow, neither shall I know the loss of children: but these two things shall come to thee in a moment in one day, the loss of children, and widowhood: they shall come upon thee in their perfection for the multitude of thy sorceries, and for the great abundance of thine enchantments.

Isaiah 47:8-9

4. Jesus is the Way, the Truth and the Life: The way of occultism is not the way to Heaven or to God.

There shall not be found among you any one that maketh his son or his daughter to pass through the fire, or that useth divination, or an observer of times, or an enchanter, or a witch, Or a charmer, or a consulter with familiar spirits, or a wizard, or a necromancer.

Deuteronomy 18:10-11

5. Jesus is the Way, the Truth and the Life: The way of idol worship is not the way to Heaven.

Ye shall make you no idols nor graven image, neither rear you up a standing image, neither shall ye set up any image of stone in your land, to bow down unto it: for I am the LORD your God.

Leviticus 26:1

Thou shalt not make unto thee any graven image, or any likeness of any thing that is in heaven above, or that is in the earth beneath, or that is in the water under the earth:

Exodus 20:4

They shall be turned back, they shall be greatly ashamed, that trust in graven images, that say to the molten images, ye are our gods.

Isaiah 42:17

The Lizards and the Goddess of Mercy

One day I met a lady who told me an amazing story. She and her husband ran a business to control pests of all sorts. They had special methods of tackling termites, flies, lizards, wall geckos, mosquitoes, rats, mice and cockroaches. You name the pest and they would get rid of it!

One day, an elderly lady walked into the office with a special problem.

This elderly client said, "I have a very big problem."

She began, "I work in a large temple in which there are a number of gods and goddesses."

She continued, "Some of the gods are very large and tall, almost the height of a two-storey block building."

The pest control manageress was wondering what this client from the temple would want from her as a pest control expert.

Then she explained, "Some of our gods have not been answering the prayers that are being offered to them in the temple and we are worried about it."

"Why are they not answering the prayers that are being offered to them?" asked the pest control manageress. She answered, "We feel that they cannot hear the prayers that are being offered to them."

"Hear?" the manager asked, "Did you say they cannot hear?"

"Yes", the client continued. "There are many lizards in the temple which have been going into the ears of the gods and goddesses and we feel that it is because of these lizards that are in their ears that they cannot hear our prayers."

So I asked the pest control manageress, "Did you go to kill the lizards that had entered the goddess' ears?"

"Yes," she exclaimed, " And there were many of them."

As I thought over this amazing story I realized how true the Word of God is. How can a piece of wood be a god? The Bible says they cannot hear, they cannot speak, they cannot move. Why should you worship a dead piece of wood? There is only one God and His name is Jehovah.

6. **Jesus is the Way, the Truth and the Life: The way of being religious is not the way to Heaven. Following traditions and singing hymns without knowing God is not the way to Heaven.**

This people draweth nigh unto me with their mouth, and honoureth me with their lips; but their heart is far from me.

Matthew 15:8

7. **Jesus is the Way, the Truth and the Life: The way of following other religions is not the way to Heaven. False religions offer many other ways that are not true.**

Neither is there salvation in any other: for there is none other name under heaven given among men, whereby we must be saved.

Acts 4:12

8. **Jesus is the Way, the Truth and the Life: The way of doing good works is not the way to Heaven. Good works will not take you to Heaven. The only way to Heaven is through the Blood of Jesus!**

But we are all as an unclean thing, and all our righteousnesses are as filthy rags; and we all do fade as a leaf; and our iniquities, like the wind, have taken us away.

Isaiah 64:6

For by grace are ye saved through faith; and that not of yourselves: it is the gift of God: not of works, lest any man should boast.

Ephesians 2:8-9

9. **Jesus is the Way, the Truth and the Life: No one comes to the Father except through Jesus.**

"No one" includes presidents, mothers, friends, brothers and teachers. Come to Jesus today, come to the cross and humble yourself before God. Be washed by the Blood of Jesus and gain access to the throne of Heaven.

Jesus saith unto him, I am the way, the truth, and the life: no man cometh unto the Father, but by me.

John 14:6

Jesus is the First and the Last

And when I saw him, I fell at his feet as dead. And he laid his right hand upon me, saying unto me, Fear not; I AM THE FIRST AND THE LAST:

Revelation 1:17

1. **Jesus is the First and the Last Saviour; there will be no other saviour. There was no other saviour. There is no other saviour. There shall be no other saviour.**

Neither is there salvation in any other: for there is none other name under heaven given among men, whereby we must be saved.

Acts 4:12

For there is one God, and one mediator between God and men, the man Christ Jesus;

1 Timothy 2:5

The First and the Last Train

I was once at a train station deep in the heart of France. I desperately needed to get a train to take me to Switzerland, where my grandmother lived. I had run out of money and needed to get home again. When I inquired at the station I found out that the only train that was going in my direction had already left. I grew even more desperate, knowing that I was in big trouble. Indeed, I had to beg absolute strangers for lifts from France, all the way through Germany into Switzerland.

I have been at many train stations where I have been told, "This is the only train that leaves this station and it leaves once a day"; and because it is the first and the last train, you are going to be stuck there in the cold, at the mercy of the elements of the weather if you miss it. As I continued to live in Europe I came to appreciate what it meant when there was only one train going somewhere. If you missed it you were doomed. You could not afford to miss it!

How important it is to catch the train, the plane or the bus when it is the first and the last!

Jesus Christ is the First and the Last Saviour of the world.

He is the First and the Last Lover of this world.

He is the First and Last Son of God!

He is the First and the Last Shepherd! He is the First and the Last Way to God! If you miss Him you are doomed to dwell in darkness and eternal hell and damnation.

2. Jesus is the First and the Last Saviour; there will be no other saviour. Jesus is the first and last person God will send to this world.

For God so loved the world, that he gave his only begotten Son, that whosoever believeth in him should not perish, but have everlasting life.

John 3:16

Many people claimed to have come to save the world but were unable to do so.

a. Many African presidents claimed that they were saving their nations through coup d'états, revolutions, democratic changes and political reforms. The only thing that has happened is that they have left Africa poorer and more destitute.

b. Hitler claimed to be a saviour of Germany with his Nazi party. By the time he left power, fifty million people were dead.

c. Stalin claimed to be a saviour of the Soviet Union. But he starved Russia and killed millions of ordinary people. Stalin killed even more people than Hitler.

3. **Jesus is the First and the Last Saviour; there will be no other saviour. Jesus is the First and the Last person who died on the cross and shed His blood for us.**

No one else's life or blood can save mankind. There is power in the blood of Jesus. The blood of Jesus is the blood of the Lamb of God and it is precious.

Martin Luther King died for the freedom and liberty of black people in America. Many years after, black people in America are still the poorest, the least educated, they live in the poorest housing and have the poorest health conditions out of all the American communities. No one's life or blood could save this world.

Jesus Christ died on the cross to shed His blood for the world. It is only through the blood of the cross that you can be saved.

And having made peace through the blood of his cross, by him to reconcile all things unto himself; by him, I say, whether they be things in earth, or things in heaven.

Colossians 1:20

In whom WE HAVE REDEMPTION THROUGH HIS BLOOD, the forgiveness of sins, according to the riches of his grace;

Ephesians 1:7

But if we walk in the light, as he is in the light, we have fellowship one with another, and THE BLOOD OF JESUS CHRIST HIS SON CLEANSETH US FROM ALL SIN.

1 John 1:7

4.   Jesus is the First and the Last Saviour; there will be no other saviour. Jesus Christ is the One who has the keys of death and hell.

Therefore it is only Jesus Christ who can keep you out of hell. If you miss Jesus Christ, you would have missed your opportunity to go to Heaven.

Jesus has the keys and so controls the access to Heaven. Jesus is the only One who has the ability to keep you from going into your deserved punishment of going to hell.

Christ in You, the Hope of Glory

To whom God would make known what is the riches of the glory of this mystery among the Gentiles; which is Christ in you, the hope of glory:

Colossians 1:27

1. **Christ is your Hope of Glory: People hope in their businesses, their houses, their cars and their money. But it is Christ who is your Hope of Glory.**

People put their hope in their uncles and their fathers, but they may not take care of them in return. Some also put their hope in their mothers who may abandon them. Some hope in their education whilst others hope in their wealth. Yet others put their hope in their jobs and others have hopes of going to America. But none of these things that men hope in can save us. Jesus Christ is the only hope for this world.

Wilt thou set thine eyes upon that which is not? for riches certainly make themselves wings; they fly away as an eagle toward heaven.

Proverbs 23:5

An horse is a vain thing for safety: neither shall he deliver any by his great strength.

Psalms 33:17

2. **Christ is your Hope of Glory: People put their hope in man but that is a mistake. It is Christ who is your Hope of Glory.**

It is better to take refuge in the Lord than to trust in man.

Psalms 118:8 (NASB)

Some trust in chariots, and some in horses: but we will remember the name of the LORD our God.

Psalms 20:7

3. **Christ is your Hope of Glory: People put their hope in politicians to give us all a good life. But Jesus is our only Hope for an abundant life.**

Even the disciples thought that Jesus was bringing a political solution to their problem. They asked Jesus: "Lord, wilt thou at this time restore again the kingdom to Israel?" (Acts 1:6) This was a request for political change. But Jesus did not come to bring political changes.

All over the world, people hoped that political change would bring solutions to the many problems of their lives. African nations hoped that independence would bring freedom, justice and prosperity. But instead, independence has brought bondage, injustice and poverty.

Ghana has undergone different types of political change. Ghana has gone through many political upheavals. From colonialism to independence to coup d'etats, to house-cleaning exercises, to revolutions and more democratic reforms. None of these situations have brought the glory that people so desire. The truth is simple, "Christ in us is the Hope of glory!"

Europe, which has developed its democratic systems perfectly, has equally given birth to other evils and depravities in their society. Civil rights movements in America have certainly not eradicated poverty from the black community. Independence from the evil apartheid system has certainly not taken away all the problems of the black people in South Africa.

Jesus Christ is the One who can give us the abundant life that we so desire. Christ is our only Hope of Glory! "The thief cometh not, but for to steal, and to kill, and to destroy: I am come that they might have life, and that they might have it more abundantly" (John 10:10).

The Lying Politicians

I once heard an interesting account of an election campaign in an African country we shall call "Duburungana". There were two main political parties and both of them were campaigning hard to win the presidential elections that year.

The campaigning was done by travelling to the different towns and villages to hold rallies and to ask people to vote for them. Some of the towns and villages were, to say the least, very remote and were only visited during election years. The villagers had become accustomed to seeing electioneering politicians visit them once every four years. These politicians would make promises to them and then would not show up again till the next election. As a result the villagers had lost all faith in politicians.

One day, something terrible happened during the Duburungana national campaign. A large convoy of Nissan patrols, Toyota Land Cruisers and other smaller cars were involved in a terrible accident near one of these remote towns. Several people were killed and others were seriously injured.

It took several days before the police and other institutional authorities arrived from the city to the accident scene. Unfortunately, there were no telephones and there was no electricity in that town. There were also no hospitals or mortuaries in that neglected town.

When the information about the accident finally reached them, it took forever for the medical team to get there, as there were no roads to these villages. Upon arrival, the teams of police and health care personnel asked, "Where are the victims of the accident?"

"Everyone is dead, and everyone is buried," the villagers answered.

The police asked, "Did everyone die in the accident?"

"Yes, of course everyone died in the accident! What do you take us for? Do you think we would bury people who were alive?"

The police and the health teams were baffled.

Then the villagers explained further, "We have no light here, we have no hospital, we have no electricity, we have no mortuary and we have nowhere to keep dead bodies so we buried them."

There was silence from the team that had come from the city. They could not believe their ears. "Everyone dead?"

Then they asked the villagers again, "Did everyone really die?"

The villagers retorted, "Of course everybody was dead. That is why we buried them. We even buried those who claimed that they were not dead because we knew they were lying since they were politicians."

The villagers had grown to believe that politicians only tell lies and never the truth. So they did not believe the politicians when they claimed to be alive after the accident.

This is how low the trust placed in man and his political systems have fallen.

4. **Christ is your Hope of Glory: Christ is our Hope of healing and prosperity. Only Christ can give us the prosperity and the healing that we want.**

The Spirit of the Lord is upon me, because he hath anointed me to preach the gospel to the poor; he hath sent me to heal the brokenhearted, to preach deliverance to the captives, and recovering of sight to the blind, to set at liberty them that are bruised,

Luke 4:18

5. **Christ is your Hope of Glory: Christ is our Hope for salvation and Heaven.**

Neither is there salvation in any other: for there is none other name under heaven given among men, whereby we must be saved.

Acts 4:12

In my Father's house are many mansions: if it were not so, I would have told you. I go to prepare a place for you. And if I go and prepare a place for you, I will come again, and receive you unto myself; that where I am, there ye may be also.

John 14:2-3

SALVATION MESSAGE 66:

Who is Jesus?

When Jesus came into the coasts of Caesarea Philippi, he asked his disciples, saying, Whom do men say that I the SON OF MAN am?

And they said, Some say that thou art John the Baptist: some, Elias; and others, Jeremias, or one of the prophets.

He saith unto them, But whom say ye that I am?

And Simon Peter answered and said, Thou art the Christ, the Son of the living God.

And Jesus answered and said unto him, Blessed art thou, Simon Barjona: for flesh and blood hath not revealed it unto thee, but my Father which is in Heaven.

Matthew 16:13-17

1. **Who is Jesus? Jesus was the Son of man.** Because He was the Son of man, He can be touched with the feeling of our infirmity.

When Jesus came into the coasts of Caesarea Philippi, he asked his disciples, saying, whom do men say that I the SON OF MAN am?

Matthew 16:13

The Lift

I once had a church member who gave a lift to a young lady. Half way through the journey, the passenger disappeared from the car and could not be found anymore. The church member was terrified, to say the least.

She searched everywhere but her passenger had vanished into thin air. I was called to attend to this petrified church member.

This shows that some of the so-called human beings are actually not human beings at all. They may be spirit beings or entities, which are illegally moving around on earth.

Jesus Christ emphasized that He was the Son of Man because He wanted everyone to know that He was legally present on earth and had not come by any illegitimate channel. He had been born into this world like every other human being.

2.   Who is Jesus? Jesus is a Great Prophet.

Many people knew that Jesus was a Prophet because of His supernatural abilities. The woman of Samaria knew and recognized that Jesus was a Prophet because He knew that she had had five husbands and was not married to the man she was currently with. When he raised the dead man in the city of Nain the Bible says that they glorified God and said a great Prophet had arisen in the city.

And there came a fear on all: and they glorified God, saying, That a great prophet is risen up among us; and, That God hath visited his people.

Luke 7:16

Jesus saith unto her, Go, call thy husband, and come hither. The woman answered and said, I have no husband. Jesus said unto her, Thou hast well said, I have no husband: For thou hast had five husbands; and he whom thou now hast is not thy husband: in that saidst thou truly.

The woman saith unto him, Sir, I perceive that thou art a prophet.

John 4:16-19

3. Who is Jesus? Jesus is the Way the Truth and the Life.

Jesus is the Way because no sinner can enter into Heaven without going through Him.

Jesus is the Way because His blood is the way to go to Heaven. It was His blood that was shed on Calvary. His blood is what makes a way for murderers, thieves, fornicators and liars to go to Heaven.

Jesus saith unto him, I AM THE WAY, the truth, and the life: no man cometh unto the Father, but by me.

John 14:6

4. Who is Jesus? Jesus is the Son of God.

This means that the blood that Jesus shed was not ordinary blood. It was the blood of the Son of God. The blood of bulls, the blood of angels, the blood of any man could not pay the price for so many people. Jesus was the Son of God that is why His blood was powerful. It was enough to pay the price for the lives of over 20 million Ghanaians, 150 million Nigerians, 1.2 billion Chinese people, and 1.1 billion Indians to mention a few! Normal blood expires and loses its power. The blood of Jesus is the blood of the Son of God so it can never expire. Receive the blood of Jesus today!

5. Who is Jesus? Jesus is the Light of the World.

Light is a symbol of spiritual truth; it is the light that sets you free from the darkness of occultism, idol worship and witchcraft.

Then spake Jesus again unto them, saying, I am the light of the world: he that followeth me shall not walk in darkness, but shall have the light of life.

John 8:12

When we follow Jesus He takes darkness away from our lives.

6. Who is Jesus? Jesus is the Resurrection and the Life of this world.

Jesus said unto her, I am the resurrection, and the life: he that believeth in me, though he were dead, yet shall he live.

John 11:25

7. Who is Jesus? Jesus is the Good Shepherd. He died on the cross for you. He loves you; He guides you and He cares for you.

I am the good shepherd: the good shepherd giveth his life for the sheep.

John 10:11

8. Who is Jesus? Jesus is the Saviour of the world. Come to Jesus and receive Salvation.

And said unto the woman, Now we believe, not because of thy saying: for we have heard him ourselves, and know that this is indeed the Christ, the Saviour of the world.

John 4:42

SALVATION MESSAGE 67:

What Do You Think of Jesus?

And there was much murmuring among the people concerning him: for some said, He is a good man: others said, Nay; but he deceiveth the people.

Howbeit no man spake openly of him for fear of the Jews.

Now about the midst of the feast Jesus went up into the temple, and taught.

And the Jews marvelled, saying, How knoweth this man letters, having never learned?

Jesus answered them, and said, My doctrine is not mine, but his that sent me.

If any man will do his will, he shall know of the doctrine, whether it be of God, or whether I speak of myself.

He that speaketh of himself seeketh his own glory: but he that seeketh his glory that sent him, the same is true, and no unrighteousness is in him. Did not Moses give you the law, and yet none of you keepeth the law? Why go ye about to kill me?

The people answered and said, Thou hast a devil: who goeth about to kill thee?

Jesus answered and said unto them, I have done one work, and ye all marvel.

Moses therefore gave unto you circumcision; (not because it is of Moses, but of the fathers;) and ye on the sabbath day circumcise a man.

If a man on the sabbath day receive circumcision, that the law of Moses should not be broken; are ye angry at me, because I have made a man every whit whole on the sabbath day?

Judge not according to the appearance, but judge righteous judgment. Then said some of them of Jerusalem, Is not this he, whom they seek to kill?

But, lo, he speaketh boldly, and they say nothing unto him. Do the rulers know indeed that this is the very Christ?

Howbeit we know this man whence he is: but when Christ cometh, no man knoweth whence he is.

Then cried Jesus in the temple as he taught, saying, Ye both know me, and ye know whence I am: and I am not come of myself, but he that sent me is true, whom ye know not.

But I know him: for I am from him, and he hath sent me.

Then they sought to take him: but no man laid hands on him, because his hour was not yet come.

And many of the people believed on him, and said, When Christ cometh, will he do more miracles than these which this man hath done?

John 7:12-31

1.   What do you think about Jesus? People have different opinions about Jesus Christ.

And there was much murmuring among the people concerning him: for some said, He is a good man: others said, Nay; but he deceiveth the people.

John 7:12

2. What do you think about Jesus? Some people think Jesus was just a good man.

Jesus Christ was more than a good man. His birth, life and crucifixion were prophesied in over one hundred places in the Old Testament with remarkable accuracy. The combined weight of these prophecies alone is enough to prove that Jesus was the Messiah. This is unlike any other religious leader, whose coming was not foretold.

> And there was much murmuring among the people concerning him: for some said, HE IS A GOOD MAN...
>
> John 7:12

3. What do you think about Jesus? Some people think he was a deceiver.

Jesus was not a deceiver. The life, the mission and the death of other religious leaders reveal their earthly and worldly origins. Jesus Christ was different. Jesus Christ was the Messiah. He was born miraculously to a virgin. This is in contrast to other claimants who had nothing miraculous about their birth. He rose from the dead after three days unlike other religious leaders of this world who remain dead and rotten in their graves. Jesus is the only One who can say, "I was dead and behold I am alive for ever and ever."

> And there was much murmuring among the people concerning him: for some said, He is a good man: others said, Nay; but HE DECEIVETH THE PEOPLE.
>
> John 7:12

4. What do you think about Jesus? Some people saw him as a wise man.

But Jesus Christ was more than a teacher. Unlike other people, His death did not come without warning, without plan and without forethought. The death of Jesus was anticipated and ordained by God for a purpose.

And the Jews marvelled, saying, HOW KNOWETH THIS
MAN LETTERS, having never learned?

John 7:15

5. What do you think about Jesus? Some people think he was demon-possessed.

But how could Jesus Christ have been demon-possessed?
We all know the signs of demon possession. Jesus Christ never
sinned. He lived a perfect life. This cannot be said about other
people who claim to be messengers of God.

Jesus Christ never killed anybody in His life.

He never married anyone nor did He mistreat any woman.
Jesus Christ never had sexual relations with any woman, man or
child. Jesus Christ never murdered anyone.

Jesus never attacked anyone in His house. Jesus Christ never
invaded anyone's city. Jesus Christ never looted and pillaged
any town or city. He never stole anything from anyone. But
some people thought He had a devil.

The people answered and said, THOU HAST A DEVIL:
who goeth about to kill thee?

John 7:20

6. What do you think about Jesus? Some people see Him as a doer of miraculous signs.

Jesus did many miracles. He also commanded His disciples
to heal the sick, raise the dead and cleanse those who had leprosy.
Jesus Christ is recorded to have performed over thirty miracles
and John writes that Jesus did many other things as well.

And many of the people believed on him, and said, When
Christ cometh, will he do MORE MIRACLES THAN
THESE which this man hath done?

John 7:31

And there are also many other things which Jesus did, the which, if they should be written every one, I suppose that even the world itself could not contain the books that should be written. Amen.

John 21:25

7. What do you think about Jesus? Some people see Him as the prophet.

But Jesus was more than a prophet. Jesus Christ is the central figure of Christianity. His life and ministry separate Him eternally from any past or present religious leader.

Many of the people therefore, when they heard this saying, said, Of a truth THIS IS THE PROPHET. Others said, this is the Christ. But some said, shall Christ come out of Galilee?

John 7:40-41

8. What do you think about Jesus? Who do you say He is? Peter answered, "You are the Saviour".

In order to be saved you must have a personal revelation about who Jesus Christ is to you. He may be different things to different people. But who is He to you? You must receive Him as the only Mediator between God and man. You must receive Him as your Saviour. Jesus Christ became a Saviour to Peter.

He saith unto them, But whom say ye that I am? And Simon Peter answered and said, Thou art the Christ, the Son of the living God.

Matthew 16:15-16

9.   **What do you think about Jesus? Jesus is the Mediator between God and man.**

For there is one God, and one mediator between God and men, the man Christ Jesus;

1 Timothy 2:5

Neither is there salvation in any other: for there is none other name under heaven given among men, whereby we must be saved.

Acts 4:12

Jesus saith unto him, I am the way, the truth, and the life: no man cometh unto the Father, but by me.

John 14:6

Why We Preach Christ

Therefore they that were scattered abroad went every where preaching the word.

Then Philip went down to the city of Samaria, and PREACHED CHRIST unto them.

And the people with one accord gave heed unto those things which Philip spake, hearing and seeing the miracles which he did.

For unclean spirits, crying with loud voice, came out of many that were possessed with them: and many taken with palsies, and that were lame, were healed.

And there was great joy in that city.

Acts 8:4-8

1. Why do we preach Christ? Philip went to Samaria and preached Christ to them. Why did Philip preach about Christ?

Philip could have preached about how to provide water for Samaria. Obviously, Samaria did not have pipe-borne water at the time.

Philip could have preached about how to get electricity into Samaria. Obviously Samaria did not have electricity.

Evangelist Philip could have spoken about building universities.

Evangelist Philip could have talked about how to have happy marriages.

Evangelist Philip could have told them bed time stories or other fairy tales.

So why then did he preach about Christ?

2. Why do we preach Christ? We preach about Christ because Christ is the Hope of our Glory.

To whom God would make known what is the riches of the glory of this mystery among the Gentiles; which is Christ in you, THE HOPE OF GLORY:

Colossians 1:27

3. Why do we preach Christ? We preach about Christ because Christ is a Healer.

That it might be fulfilled which was spoken by Esaias the prophet, saying, HIMSELF TOOK OUR INFIRMITIES, AND BARE OUR SICKNESSES.

Matthew 8:17

4. Why do we preach Christ? We preach about Christ because Christ is the way to Heaven.

Jesus saith unto him, I am the way, the truth, and the life: no man cometh unto the Father, but by me.

John 14:6

5. **Why do we preach Christ? We preach about Christ because Christ is the truth about God.**

Jesus saith unto him, I am the way, the truth, and the life: no man cometh unto the Father, but by me.

John 14:6

6. **Why do we preach Christ? We preach about Christ because Christ is the door to Heaven.**

Then said Jesus unto them again, verily, verily, I say unto you, I am the door of the sheep.

John 10:7

7. **Why do we preach Christ? We preach about Christ because Jesus Christ gives light and life.**

Then spake Jesus again unto them, saying, I am the light of the world: he that followeth me shall not walk in darkness, but shall have the light of life.

John 8:12

In him was life; and the life was the light of men.

John 1:4

He that hath the Son hath life; and he that hath not the Son of God hath not life.

1 John 5:12

8. **Why do we preach Christ? We preach about Christ because Christ died for our sins.**

But God commendeth his love toward us, in that, while we were yet sinners, Christ died for us.

Romans 5:8

SALVATION MESSAGE 69:

The Bread of Life

Our fathers did eat manna in the desert; as it is written, He gave them bread from heaven to eat.

Then Jesus said unto them, Verily, verily, I say unto you, Moses gave you not that bread from heaven; but my Father giveth you the true bread from heaven.

For the bread of God is he which cometh down from heaven, and giveth life unto the world.

Then said they unto him, Lord, evermore give us this bread.

And Jesus said unto them, I AM THE BREAD OF LIFE: he that cometh to me shall never hunger; and he that believeth on me shall never thirst.

John 6:31-35

1. **Jesus is the Bread of Life and men should seek Him for fulfilment. Yet men are seeking fulfilment, satisfaction and accomplishment in all the wrong places.**

Yes, we are all hungry. Men are always seeking to satisfy their hunger in the wrong way. To be hungry means to desire something that will satisfy you. To hunger is to have a need for something. To hunger is to have a wish that needs to be satisfied. To be hungry is to have a passionate desire for something. To hunger is to have a yearning. To hunger is to have a longing or a craving for something.

All men do have a hunger and craving within them. They are looking for their Creator and their Maker. Unfortunately, most people are seeking to satisfy this longing in the wrong way. They are seeking to fulfil their needs in the wrong places. Indeed, blessed are those who hunger and thirst after the right thing, which is righteousness, for they shall truly be filled and satisfied.

Ho, every one that thirsteth, come ye to the waters, and he that hath no money; come ye, buy, and eat; yea, come, buy wine and milk without money and without price.

Wherefore do ye spend money for that which is not bread? and your labour for that which satisfieth not? hearken diligently unto me, and eat ye that which is good, and let your soul delight itself in fatness.

Incline your ear, and come unto me: hear, and your soul shall live; and I will make an everlasting covenant with you, even the sure mercies of David.

Isaiah 55:1-3

2. **Jesus is the Bread of Life and men should seek Him for fulfilment. Yet men are seeking fulfilment, satisfaction and accomplishment by SEEKING MONEY AND WEALTH.**

Sadly, the money they are seeking for will not give them the satisfaction and fulfilment they need.

You have planted much but harvested little. You have food to eat, but not enough to fill you up. You have wine to drink, but not enough to satisfy your thirst. You have clothing to wear, but not enough to keep you warm. Your wages disappear as though you were putting them in pockets filled with holes!

"This is what the LORD Almighty says: Consider how things are going for you!" "Now go up into the hills, bring down timber, and rebuild my house. Then I will take pleasure in it and be honored, says the LORD."

Haggai 1:6-8 (NLT)

He that loveth silver shall not be satisfied with silver; nor he that loveth abundance with increase: this is also vanity.

Ecclesiastes 5:10

3. **Jesus is the Bread of Life and men should seek Him for fulfilment. Yet men are seeking fulfilment, satisfaction and accomplishment by SEEKING KNOWLEDGE.**

EVER LEARNING, and never able to come to the knowledge of the truth.

2 Timothy 3:7

For in much wisdom is much grief: and he that INCREASETH KNOWLEDGE increaseth sorrow.

Ecclesiastes 1:18

And further, by these, my son, be admonished: of making many books there is no end; and MUCH STUDY is a weariness of the flesh.

Ecclesiastes 12:12

4. **Jesus is the Bread of Life and men should seek Him for fulfilment. Yet men are seeking fulfilment, satisfaction and accomplishment by giving themselves to sin and pleasure. THE LIFE OF PLEASURE they seek will not give them the satisfaction and fulfilment they want.**

For the time already past is sufficient for you to have carried out the desire of the Gentiles, having pursued a course of sensuality, lusts, drunkenness, carousals, drinking parties and abominable idolatries.

And in all this, they are surprised that you do not run with them into the same excess of dissipation, and they malign you; but they shall give account to Him who is ready to judge the living and the dead.

1 Peter 4:3-5 (NASB)

5. Jesus is the Bread of Life and men should seek Him for fulfilment. Yet men are seeking fulfilment and satisfaction by DRINKING THEMSELVES TO DEATH.

The alcohol they drink will only destroy their lives.

Who hath woe? Who hath sorrow? Who hath contentions? Who hath babbling? Who hath wounds without cause? Who hath redness of eyes? They that tarry long at the wine; they that go to seek mixed wine. Look not thou upon the wine when it is red, when it giveth his colour in the cup, when it moveth itself aright.

Proverbs 23:29-31

Woe unto them that rise up early in the morning, that they may follow strong drink; that continue until night, till wine inflame them!

Isaiah 5:11

6. Jesus is the Bread of Life and men should seek Him for fulfilment. Yet men are seeking fulfilment and satisfaction by having NUMEROUS AFFAIRS WITH WOMEN.

Unfortunately, instead of these sexual desires leading to satisfaction, they often lead to wounds, destruction and dishonour.

But whoso committeth adultery with a woman lacketh understanding: he that doeth it destroyeth his own soul.

A wound and dishonour shall he get; and his reproach shall not be wiped away.

Proverbs 6:32-33

7.   Jesus is the Bread of Life and men should seek Him for fulfilment. Yet men are seeking fulfilment, through HOMOSEXUALITY. But homosexuality will lead to more curses and more destruction.

For this cause God gave them up unto vile affections: for even their women did change the natural use into that which is against nature: And likewise also the men, leaving the natural use of the woman, burned in their lust one toward another; men with men working that which is unseemly, and receiving in themselves that recompence of their error which was meet.

Romans 1:26-27

8.   Jesus is the Bread of Life and men should seek Him for fulfilment. Yet men are seeking fulfilment, satisfaction and accomplishment by WORKING THEMSELVES TO DEATH.

But fulfilment can only be found in Christ.

There is one alone, and there is not a second; yea, he hath neither child nor brother: yet is there no end of all his labour; neither is his eye satisfied with riches; neither saith he, For whom do I labour, and bereave my soul of good? This is also vanity, yea, it is a sore travail.

Ecclesiastes 4:8

9.   Jesus Christ is the Bread of Life, which was broken for us on the Cross of Calvary. This is how the body of Christ was broken for us:

a. *He was whipped for us:* "And they smote him on the head with a reed…" (Mark 15:19).

b. *He was spat upon for us:* "… and did spit upon him …" (Mark 15:19).

c. *His hands and legs were pierced with nails:* "…they pierced my hands and my feet…" (Psalm 22:16).

d. *His head was pierced with thorns:* "And they clothed him with purple, and platted a crown of thorns, and put it about his head," (Mark 15:17).

e. *He was beaten and wounded for us:* "But he was wounded for our transgressions, he was bruised for our iniquities: the chastisement of our peace was upon him; and with his stripes we are healed" (Isaiah 53:5).

f. *His side was pierced for us:* "But one of the soldiers with a spear pierced his side, and forthwith came there out blood and water" (John 19:34).

10. Receive the broken Body of Christ and have eternal life:

Whoso eateth my flesh, and drinketh my blood, hath eternal life; and I will raise him up at the last day.

John 6:54

Resurrection Power

1. **Resurrection Power: Jesus Christ demonstrated resurrection power by raising Jairus' daughter from the dead.** Jairus' daughter had just died when He raised her from the dead.

And when he was come in, he saith unto them, why make ye this ado, and weep? The damsel is not dead, but sleepeth.

And they laughed him to scorn. But when he had put them all out, he taketh the father and the mother of the damsel, and them that were with him, and entereth in where the damsel was lying.

And he took the damsel by the hand, and said unto her, Talitha cumi; which is, being interpreted, Damsel, I say unto thee, arise.

And straightway the damsel arose, and walked; for she was of the age of twelve years. And they were astonished with a great astonishment.

Mark 5:39-42

2. **Resurrection Power: Jesus Christ demonstrated resurrection power by stopping a funeral procession that was on its way to the burial grounds and raising the dead person.**

In this case, the dead person whom Jesus raised had been dead for some time and was on the way to being buried.

> Now when he came nigh to the gate of the city, behold, there was a dead man carried out, the only son of his mother, and she was a widow: and much people of the city was with her.
>
> And when the Lord saw her, he had compassion on her, and said unto her, Weep not.
>
> And he came and touched the bier: and they that bare him stood still. And he said, Young man, I say unto thee, Arise.
>
> And he that was dead sat up, and began to speak. And he delivered him to his mother.

Luke 7:12-15

3. **Resurrection Power: Jesus Christ demonstrated resurrection power by raising a decomposing, stinking Lazarus from the dead.**

In this case, the dead person whom Jesus raised had been dead, buried and decomposed for four days.

> Jesus said, Take ye away the stone. Martha, the sister of him that was dead, saith unto him, Lord, by this time HE STINKETH: for he hath been dead four days.

John 11:39

He Stinketh

When I was in the medical school, one of my colleagues committed suicide in his room. Somehow, no one noticed that he had not been around for some days. People began to notice a smell in the hostel; and initially, everyone thought a rat had died in the hostel. However the smell became very strong after some time. The source of the smell was traced to his room and so they called out his name at his door. After some time it was realized that he had not been seen for some time. So, someone climbed into his room from the balcony and there, was his body - swollen, smelling and decomposing after four days of death.

This is the kind of condition that Lazarus was in when Jesus raised him from the dead. Jesus performed a true and powerful miracle that demonstrated that He was indeed the Son of God.

4. **Resurrection Power: Resurrection power is the greatest power that any man can ever have because it combines three types of power.**

a. **The power to call back a dead spirit from the regions of the dead.** When Jesus raised the dead he exercised the power to call back the spirit of a person from the dead.

b. **The power to heal sick bodies.** When Jesus raised the dead He exercised the power to heal the person of the sickness from which he had died. If the resurrection power had not healed the person he would have died again from the sickness.

c. **The power to restore decomposed bodies.** When Jesus raised the dead He exercised the power to restore a decomposed body to normalcy.

5. **Resurrection Power: Jesus Christ demonstrated resurrection power by fearlessly giving up His life on the cross and promising to rise from the dead after three days.** Jesus exercised resurrection power and died on the cross to save us from our sins. Because He knew He could exercise resurrection power, He died fearlessly for us on the cross and shed His blood for the whole world.

Therefore doth my Father love me, because I lay down my life, that I might take it again. No man taketh it from me, but I lay it down of myself. I have power to lay it down, and I HAVE POWER TO TAKE IT AGAIN. This commandment have I received of my Father.

John 10:17-18

6. **Resurrection Power: Jesus Christ demonstrated resurrection power by actually rising from the dead after three days.** That is why we believe in Him and that is why we follow Him. We do not follow people who are dead because they cannot help us.

And with great power gave the apostles WITNESS OF THE RESURRECTION of the Lord Jesus: and great grace was upon them all.

Acts 4:33

The Widow

One day a young lady lost her husband in a tragic way. She was devastated and so were the pastors. I counselled and prayed with her, hoping for healing from the Lord from this desolation. One day, I asked her to take off her wedding ring. She was shocked. I asked her to give it to me and I said to her, "It is over." She was even more shocked.

I explained to her, "Your marriage is over. You cannot remain committed to a dead person and you cannot follow a dead person."

If Jesus Christ were dead like anyone else, we would not be able to follow Him. I feel sorry for religions whose leaders are dead men. We have a Living Saviour and that is why we are confident to preach about Him and follow Him.

7. **Resurrection Power: Jesus Christ will use His resurrection power to raise you from the dead and take you to Heaven.** You must believe in Jesus Christ because He is alive.

Jesus said unto her, I am the resurrection, and the life: he that believeth in me, though he were dead, yet shall he live: and whosoever liveth and believeth in me shall never die. Believest thou this?

John 11:25-26

The True Light

In the beginning was the Word, and the Word was with God, and the Word was God.

The same was in the beginning with God.

All things were made by him; and without him was not any thing made that was made.

In him was life; and the life was the light of men.

And the light shineth in darkness; and the darkness comprehended it not.

There was a man sent from God, whose name was John.

The same came for a witness, to bear witness of the Light, that all men through him might believe.

He was not that Light, but was sent to bear witness of that Light. That was the true Light, which lighteth every man that cometh into the world.

He was in the world, and the world was made by him, and the world knew him not.

He came unto his own, and his own received him not.

But as many as received him, to them gave he power to become the sons of God, even to them that believe on his name:

John 1:1-12

1. You must respect Jesus Christ because He was there at the beginning.

In the beginning was the Word, and the Word was with God, and the Word was God. The same was in the beginning with God.

John 1:1-2

Jesus Christ was there in the beginning of the world.

You cannot go to Ghana and disrespect Kwame Nkrumah. Ghanaians respect him greatly because he was there from the beginning, from the inception of the nation Ghana in 1957.

2. Everything in the world was made by Him and through Him.

All things were made by him; and without him was not any thing made that was made.

John 1:3

Everything in the world was made by Jesus Christ. Ghana's first president was Kwame Nkrumah. In Ghana, virtually everything was built by Kwame Nkrumah and through him; the motorway, the harbours, the airport and many of the secondary schools in the country were all built by him. This is why Kwame Nkrumah is such a great figure in Ghana. That is why he is respected.

3. The life of Jesus Christ produced a very bright light and that light which comes from Jesus Christ is the light that men need to live in this world.

In him was life; and the life was the light of men. And the light shineth in darkness; and the darkness comprehended it not.

John 1:4-5

4.   Just as John the Baptist was not the light but came preaching about the light, likewise every preacher is not the light but comes to preach about the light.

There was a man sent from God, whose name was John.

The same came for a witness, to bear witness of the Light, that all men through him might believe. He was not that Light, but was sent to bear witness of that Light.

John 1:6-8

5.   Jesus Christ is the True Light. He is the correct light and the right light.

That was the true Light, which lighteth every man that cometh into the world.

John 1:9

There are many lights that can be seen on the shore. Amongst all these lights is one that comes from the lighthouse. That light directs the ship away from the rocks. If you follow the wrong light your ship will hit the rocks and sink. It is important that you follow Jesus Christ because He is the True Light.

False Money And False Light

One day, I went into a shop in Holland. When I was paying for an item, the lady at the till scrutinized the dollar bill I gave her for a long time. She did not want to accept my money.

However, after some time, she was forced to accept it.

When I asked her why she was scrutinizing my money so closely, she explained that a lot of false hundred dollar bills had

379

been released into the market so she did not want to make the mistake of receiving false money. If she made the mistake of receiving counterfeit dollars, she would pay dearly for all them.

Similarly, you must be afraid of following a false light. If you follow the wrong light, you will pay dearly with your life.

Jesus Christ knew that there would be other people who would claim to be lights. That is why He said that He was the True Light and that is why John the Baptist said that he was not the light.

6. Jesus Christ is the True Light. Follow Him and you will end up in Heaven.

Then spake Jesus again unto them, saying, I am the light of the world: he that followeth me shall not walk in darkness, but shall have the light of life.

John 8:12

How Jesus Destroyed the Serpent

...For this purpose the Son of God was manifested, that he might destroy the works of the devil.

1 John 3:8

And the great dragon was cast out, THAT OLD SERPENT, called the Devil, and Satan, which deceiveth the whole world: he was CAST OUT into the earth, and his angels were cast out with him. And I heard a loud voice saying in heaven, Now is come salvation, and strength, and the kingdom of our God, and the power of his Christ: for the accuser of our brethren is cast down, which accused them before our God day and night.

And THEY OVERCAME HIM BY THE BLOOD OF THE LAMB, and by the word of their testimony; and they loved not their lives unto the death.

Revelation 12:9-11

Now the serpent was more subtil than any beast of the field which the Lord God had made. And he said unto the woman, Yea, hath God said, ye shall not eat of every tree of the garden?

And the woman said unto the serpent, We may eat of the fruit of the trees of the garden: but of the fruit of the tree which is in the midst of the garden, God hath said, Ye shall not eat of it, neither shall ye touch it, lest ye die.

And the serpent said unto the woman, Ye shall not surely die: for God doth know that in the day ye eat thereof, then your eyes shall be opened, and ye shall be as gods, knowing good and evil.

And when the woman saw that the tree was good for food, and that it was pleasant to the eyes, and a tree to be desired to make one wise, she took of the fruit thereof, and did eat, and gave also unto her husband with her; and he did eat.

And the eyes of them both were opened, and they knew that they were naked; and they sewed fig leaves together, and made themselves aprons.

And they heard the voice of the Lord God walking in the garden in the cool of the day: and Adam and his wife hid themselves from the presence of the Lord God amongst the trees of the garden.

And the Lord God called unto Adam, and said unto him, where art thou? And he said, I heard thy voice in the garden, and I was afraid, because I was naked; and I hid myself.

And he said, Who told thee that thou wast naked? Hast thou eaten of the tree, whereof I commanded thee that thou shouldest not eat?

Genesis 3:1-11

1. Man's problems began when the serpent came into the Garden.

Man has been "bitten" by the serpent. This bite has caused the human race to go into shock and crisis. The wars, the conflicts, the lack of political systems, poverty, the lack of education and the lack of development, are all signs of the critical condition that the human race is in.

2. **The serpent is a very dangerous and deadly animal and is able to kill even lions, human beings and other animals much larger than itself.**

3. **How does a serpent kill? The serpent kills and takes away life in many different and ingenious ways.** For example:

   a. Vipers kill by causing bleeding.

   b. Cobras kill by paralyzing the nerves.

   Likewise, the "serpent's bite" also has the entire human race perishing in many different ingenious ways through drugs, wars, murder, smoking, alcohol and disease.

4. **You can overcome and neutralize a serpent by WISDOM. Jesus Christ is wiser than the serpent.** Human beings are wiser than snakes.

   That is why we can catch snakes with traps and keep them in zoos. Snake catchers are able to trap deadly snakes and keep them in containers through wisdom. Certain animals, like the mongoose, are faster and smarter than snakes. Many snakes have been eaten in Jamaica, where mongooses live freely.

   Jesus is wiser and faster than any serpent. The wisdom of the princes of this world could not match the wisdom of Christ. If they had known the wisdom of God, they would not have crucified the Son of God. God outwitted the principalities, devils and evil powers.

   For it is written, I will destroy the wisdom of the wise, and will bring to nothing the understanding of the prudent. Where is the wise? where is the scribe? where is the disputer of this world? hath not God made foolish the wisdom of this world?

   1 Corinthians 1:19-20

Howbeit we speak wisdom among them that are perfect: yet not the wisdom of this world, nor of the princes of this world, that come to nought:

But we speak the wisdom of God in a mystery, even the hidden wisdom, which God ordained before the world unto our glory: Which none of the princes of this world knew: for had they known it, they would not have crucified the Lord of glory.

1 Corinthians 2:6-8

5. You can overcome and neutralize a serpent by having the anti-venom serum or potion or liquid, which neutralizes the effect of the venom of the snake.

Jesus' blood is the serum or liquid or potion that neutralized the effect of satan's poison.

And the great dragon was cast out, THAT OLD SERPENT, called the Devil, and Satan, which deceiveth the whole world: he was CAST OUT into the earth, and his angels were cast out with him.

And I heard a loud voice saying in heaven, Now is come salvation, and strength, and the kingdom of our God, and the power of his Christ: for the accuser of our brethren is cast down, which accused them before our God day and night. And THEY OVERCAME HIM BY THE BLOOD OF THE LAMB, and by the word of their testimony; and they loved not their lives unto the death.

Revelation 12:9-11

6. The blood of Jesus is like polyvalent anti-venom, which can neutralize the effects of the most deadly and frightening snakes in one dose.

A powerful polyvalent anti-venom can neutralize the venom from several snakes in one dose. For instance, there exists polyvalent anti-venom that can neutralize the effect of the green mamba, the black mamba, the cape cobra, the Gaboon viper, the snouted Egyptian cobra, the Mozambique spitting cobra, the puff adder, the forest cobra and the green Jameson mamba.

This is how the blood of Jesus is! With one dose of the blood of Jesus, multiple, diverse problems caused by that old serpent, satan, the devil are neutralized.

7. **Receive the Word of God (the wisdom of God) and the blood of Jesus (the anti venom) and be saved today.**

SECTION 10:

SALVATION AND THE KINGDOM OF GOD

SALVATION MESSAGE 73:

Seek Ye First the Kingdom of God

But seek ye first the kingdom of God, and his righteousness; and all these things shall be added unto you.

Matthew 6:33

There was a man of the Pharisees, named Nicodemus, a ruler of the Jews: The same came to Jesus by night, and said unto him, Rabbi, we know that thou art a teacher come from God: for no man can do these miracles that thou doest, except God be with him.

Jesus answered and said unto him, Verily, verily, I say unto thee, Except a man be born again, he cannot see the kingdom of God.

Nicodemus saith unto him, How can a man be born when he is old? can he enter the second time into his mother's womb, and be born?

Jesus answered, Verily, verily, I say unto thee, Except a man be born of water and of the Spirit, he cannot enter into the kingdom of God.

John 3:1-5

1. **Seek ye first the kingdom of God: Everybody belongs to a natural kingdom and is proud to belong to those kingdoms such as Ghana, Nigeria, the United Kingdom or the United States of America.** But everybody also belongs to one or the other of two spiritual kingdoms: the kingdom of darkness or the Kingdom of Light.

Who hath delivered us from the power of darkness, and hath translated us into the kingdom of his dear Son:

Colossians 1:13

The Ghanaian with the German passport

I once arrived at the airport in Ghana and saw a fellow Ghanaian who had been in Germany for many years. This man was very happy that he had come back having acquired German citizenship. At the airport there were four lines for Ghanaians, ECOWAS Nationals, Foreign Nationals and Diplomats. This man happily went to the Foreign Nationals desk and displayed his German passport.

He was so proud to belong to the German kingdom and not the Ghanaian kingdom. One day, it will not be the natural kingdom that will be important but the spiritual kingdom to which you belong.

Do you belong to the right spiritual kingdom?

2. **Seek ye first the kingdom of God: People seek to become citizens of the rich kingdoms of this world. But you must seek to belong to the Kingdom of God.**

Many times I have seen Ghanaians who live in Europe return home wielding European and American passports. They are so proud of these passports and of the fact that they belong to another earthly kingdom. Which spiritual kingdom do you belong to? Of what use is it, if you belong to the American or British kingdom and end up in hell?

Jesus answered, My kingdom is not of this world: if my kingdom were of this world, then would my servants fight, that I should not be delivered to the Jews: but now is my kingdom not from hence.

John 18:36

The Stowaway Story

I once met a Ghanaian man who had sought with all his heart to become a European citizen. He had been a stowaway on a number of occasions and even been thrown into the sea by a captain of a ship. On that occasion he swam to the shore and discovered he had only reached as far as Liberia. He made his way back to Ghana and stowed away again. This time he hid in the engine room of a ship and was not discovered. This attempt at stowing away was successful, and when the ship docked, he found out that he was in Holland. He came out of the ship and entered the country. He proudly showed his passport to me and said he was a Dutch citizen and had married a white lady.

Even though this man was ready to die in the ocean to become a citizen of Holland, he was not prepared to come to church when I invited him the very next day.

As you can see he was more concerned about belonging to a rich natural kingdom than belonging to the Kingdom of God.

3. **Seek ye first the Kingdom of God: You must seek first to become a member of the Kingdom of God because if you are not a member of the Kingdom of God you will not enter Heaven.** You cannot force your way into a spiritual kingdom.

Entering the Kingdom

People are able to enter countries using false identities because immigration officers are sometimes unable to differentiate between persons of an ethnicity different to theirs; for example it said that all Africans look alike or all Chinese look alike. As a result many people are being admitted into a country using the same passport, simply because, to the immigration officers from another ethnic group cannot tell them apart. Such deceptions will not work for you to get into the Kingdom of God.

4. **Seek ye first the Kingdom of God: When you become a part of the new Kingdom you receive and experience new things.** When you go into a new country you come across new things like their shops, bridges and buildings.

When you become a member of the Kingdom of God, you experience nice things like Love, Joy and Peace in the Holy Ghost.

> For the kingdom of God is not meat and drink; but righteousness, and peace, and joy in the Holy Ghost.
>
> Romans 14:17

5. **Seek ye first the Kingdom of God: When the Kingdom of God comes there are miracles and there is power. When you go to certain nations, you benefit from amenities such as constant electric power and nuclear power.**

> But go rather to the lost sheep of the house of Israel. And as ye go, preach, saying, the kingdom of heaven is at hand.
>
> Heal the sick, cleanse the lepers, raise the dead, cast out devils: freely ye have received, freely give.
>
> Matthew 10:6-8

SALVATION MESSAGE 74:

The Kingdom of Heaven is Like a Mustard Seed

Another parable put he forth unto them, saying, The kingdom of heaven is like to a grain of mustard seed, which a man took, and sowed in his field: which indeed is the least of all seeds: but when it is grown, it is the greatest among herbs, and becometh a tree, so that the birds of the air come and lodge in the branches thereof.

Matthew 13:31-32

But God hath chosen the foolish things of the world to confound the wise; and God hath chosen the weak things of the world to confound the things which are mighty; And base things of the world, and things which are despised, hath God chosen, yea, and things which are not, to bring to nought things that are: That no flesh should glory in his presence.

1 Corinthians 1:27-29

Most small things are despised. Be careful that you do not despise something because it is small. God has chosen the small mustard seed of the Word of God to accomplish His will. The Word of God, faith and the blood of Jesus may all look like minor things to you. But that is what God has chosen to accomplish His will. The mustard seeds of the Kingdom of God must be recognized for what they are - blessings that have come forth to humanity.

1. **The Kingdom of Heaven is like a small mustard seed: God has chosen the foolishness of preaching to save the world.** God could have chosen wisdom or could even have paid huge sums of money to cause salvation to come to mankind. But He chose the foolishness of preaching to save them that believe.

> For after that in the wisdom of God the world by wisdom knew not God, it pleased God by the FOOLISHNESS OF PREACHING to save them that believe.
>
> 1 Corinthians 1:21

2. **The Kingdom of Heaven is like a small mustard seed: God has chosen the message of the gospel of Christ to save the world.** The message of the gospel is the best message for the whole world. There is no better news than the good news that we are redeemed and washed by the blood of Jesus through our faith in Him. That is why Paul said he was not ashamed of the gospel of Christ.

> For I am not ashamed of the gospel of Christ: for it is the power of God unto salvation to every one that believeth; to the Jew first, and also to the Greek. For therein is the righteousness of God revealed from faith to faith: as it is written, The just shall live by faith.
>
> Romans 1:16-17

3. **The Kingdom of Heaven is like a small mustard seed: God has chosen the foolishness of the cross to win the world.** The cross of Jesus Christ presents the weakness and humanity of Jesus Christ to the world. The cross does not present Jesus as victorious or powerful. And yet it is this cross, which looks so unimportant and insignificant, that our salvation depends on. This is what God has chosen to save the world.

For the preaching of the cross is to them that perish foolishness; but unto us which are saved it is the power of God. For it is written, I will destroy the wisdom of the wise, and will bring to nothing the understanding of the prudent.

1 Corinthians 1:18-19

4.   **The Kingdom of Heaven is like a small mustard seed: God has chosen the shedding of the Blood of Jesus as His method of forgiveness.** How can blood wash away sins? How can the five litres of blood that were in Jesus' body wash away the sins of billions of people? And yet this is what God has chosen to wash away the sins of the world. You must accept these apparently insignificant things in order to be saved.

And almost all things are by the law purged with blood; and without shedding of blood is no remission.

Hebrews 9:22

Do You Have True Riches?

Again, the kingdom of heaven is like unto treasure hid in a field; the which when a man hath found, he hideth, and for joy thereof goeth and selleth all that he hath, and buyeth that field.

Matthew 13:44

1. **Do you have true riches? Heavenly treasures are greater than the treasures of the earth. Most people only acquire treasures on earth. But it is time to find the treasures of the Kingdom of God.**

If therefore ye have not been faithful in the unrighteous mammon, who will commit to your trust the true riches?

Luke 16:11

I counsel thee to buy of me gold tried in the fire, that thou mayest be rich; and white raiment, that thou mayest be clothed, and that the shame of thy nakedness do not appear; and anoint thine eyes with eyesalve, that thou mayest see.

Revelation 3:18

2. **Do you have true riches? Heavenly treasures are like all treasures because they are often hidden from the untrained eye. Heaven is hidden. Salvation through Jesus Christ is not so easy to see. Abundant life is hidden. It is not apparent to the casual browser.**

Verily thou art A GOD THAT HIDEST THYSELF, O God of Israel, the Saviour.

Isaiah 45:15

⁶The Twins

One day a lady became pregnant and went to the hospital for her routine ante-natal visit. It was discovered that she was carrying twins in her womb. One of them was a boy and the other was a girl. As the pregnancy progressed she could feel a lot of movement and she knew that there was a lot of tension within her.

There was actually, a very strong argument going on between the twins.

The twin sister and brother were talking to each other in the womb.

The sister said to the brother, "Do you believe that there is life after birth?"

Her brother answered, "Of course not. There is nothing like life after birth."

He continued, "No, no, this is all there is to our existence."

The sister protested, "But this is a dark and difficult place."

Her brother continued, "It is dark, but this is where we will be forever. You have to hold on to the cord because that is where we get food from."

But the baby girl insisted: "There must be something more than this dark place, there must be someplace else where there is light and freedom to move. I believe we are going to have a place where there is more space, more freedom and more happiness." However she could not convince her twin brother.

On another day, the sister said, "Do you believe that there is such a thing as a 'mother'?"

Her twin brother now became furious: " 'A mother, a mother', what are you talking about? I have never seen a mother and neither have you. Who put that idea in your head? As I told you, this place is all we have so let's be content."

But his sister insisted, "I believe there is such a thing as a mother. I believe we will see our mother soon."

Her twin brother was too angry to respond. He muttered under his breath, "This girl is crazy. How can you believe in something you can't see?"

Finally, the little sister said: "Don't you feel this pressure sometimes? It's really unpleasant and sometimes even painful."

"Yes," he answered, "What is special about that?"

"Well," the sister said, "I think this pressure exists to get us ready for another place, much more beautiful than this, where we will see our mother face to face! Don't you think that's exciting?"

Her exasperated brother said, "You are full of delusions."[6]

Eventually, the twins were born and they found out that:

1. There is life after birth.

2. There existed a real mother and a real father. They lived in their mother even though they did not know their mother.

3. All the pressures and darkness they had experienced in the womb were simply to prepare them for real life on earth.

One day, you will die and go out of this world. You will discover that:

1. There is life after death.

2. There existed a real God. That you lived in the world that was made by God but you did not even know Him. "He was in the world, and the world was made by him, and the world knew him not" (John 1:10).

3. All the pressures and darkness you experienced on the earth were simply to prepare you for real life in Heaven.

3. Do you have true riches? Heavenly treasures are so valuable that you must give up everything to get them.

BUY THE TRUTH, and sell it not; also wisdom, and instruction, and understanding.

Proverbs 23:23

Ho, every one that thirsteth, come ye to the waters, and he that hath no money; come ye, buy, and eat; yea, come, buy wine and milk without money and without price.

Isaiah 55:1

4. Do you have true riches? Heavenly treasures are precious things that God has given to us. The riches of His grace and goodness towards us are some of the greatest treasures given to mankind.

In whom we have redemption through his blood, the forgiveness of sins, according to the RICHES OF HIS GRACE;

Ephesians 1:7

That in the ages to come he might shew the exceeding RICHES OF HIS GRACE in his kindness toward us through Christ Jesus.

Ephesians 2:7

Or despisest thou the RICHES OF HIS GOODNESS
and forbearance and longsuffering; not knowing that the
goodness of God leadeth thee to repentance?

Romans 2:4

5. **Do you have true riches? Heavenly treasures are
    precious things that God has given to us. Our faith in
    Jesus Christ is one of the greatest treasures given to
    humankind.**

    Simon Peter, a servant and an apostle of Jesus Christ, to
    them that have obtained like PRECIOUS FAITH with us
    through the righteousness of God and our Saviour Jesus
    Christ:

2 Peter 1:1

6. **Do you have true riches? Heavenly treasures are
    precious things that God has given to us. The precious
    Blood of Jesus is one of the greatest treasures given to
    humankind.** One of the greatest treasures is the blood of
    Jesus, which is far more precious than silver or gold.

    Forasmuch as ye know that ye were not redeemed with
    corruptible things, as silver and gold, from your vain
    conversation received by tradition from your fathers;
    But with the PRECIOUS BLOOD of Christ, as of a lamb
    without blemish and without spot:

1 Peter 1:18-19

7. **Do you have true riches? Heavenly treasure is being
    offered to you today. Pay the price today and receive
    the riches of Christ and salvation.**

    Yea doubtless, and I count all things but loss for the
    excellency of the knowledge of Christ Jesus my Lord: for
    whom I have suffered the loss of all things, and do count
    them but dung, that I may win Christ,

Philippians 3:8

SALVATION MESSAGE 76:

The Great Feast

And sent his servant at supper time to say to them that were bidden, Come; for all things are now ready.

And they all with one consent began to make excuse. The first said unto him, I have bought a piece of ground, and I must needs go and see it: I pray thee have me excused.

And another said, I have bought five yoke of oxen, and I go to prove them: I pray thee have me excused.

And another said, I have married a wife, and therefore I cannot come.

So that servant came, and shewed his lord these things. Then the master of the house being angry said to his servant, Go out quickly into the streets and lanes of the city, and bring in hither the poor, and the maimed, and the halt, and the blind.

And the servant said, Lord, it is done as thou hast commanded, and yet there is room.

And the lord said unto the servant, Go out into the highways and hedges, and compel them to come in, that my house may be filled.

For I say unto you, that none of those men which were bidden shall taste of my supper.

Luke 14:17-24

1.   The great feast: God has invited us to a great feast.

God has given us a great privilege of dining with Him in honour. This is the greatest feast for all mankind. Our invitation to Christ and Christianity is an invitation to a great feast.

COME UNTO ME, all ye that labour and are heavy laden, and I will give you rest.

Matthew 11:28

And the Spirit and the bride say, COME. And let him that heareth say, Come. And let him that is athirst come. And whosoever will, let him take the water of life freely.

Revelation 22:17

COME, and let us return unto the LORD: for he hath torn, and he will heal us; he hath smitten, and he will bind us up.

Hosea 6:1

2.   The great feast: At the great feast, you will enjoy the milk of the Word. This milk will help you to develop and grow properly so that you can meet all the challenges of this life.

As newborn babes, desire the sincere MILK OF THE WORD, that ye may grow thereby:

1 Peter 2:2

3.   The great feast: At the great feast, you will enjoy the Bread of Life. You will be satisfied and you will be full when you meet Jesus Christ. You will not need any other kind of experience to satisfy you.

THIS IS THE BREAD which cometh down from heaven, that a man may eat thereof, and not die. I am the living bread which came down from heaven: if any man eat of this bread, he shall live for ever: and the bread that I will give is my flesh, which I will give for the life of the world.

John 6:50-51

4. **The great feast: At the great feast, you will enjoy the meat of the Word.** At this feast, you will have the pleasure of enjoying the tasty meat of the Word.

But STRONG MEAT belongeth to them that are of full age, even those who by reason of use have their senses exercised to discern both good and evil.

Hebrews 5:14

5. **The great feast: At the great feast you will enjoy the water of the Word and the Holy Spirit.**

But whosoever DRINKETH OF THE WATER that I shall give him shall never thirst; but the water that I shall give him shall be in him a well of water springing up into everlasting life.

John 4:14

…Come. And let him that is athirst come. And whosoever will, let him take the water of life freely.

Revelation 22:17

6. **The great feast: At the great feast you will enjoy the fruit of the Spirit.** Because of the fruit of the Spirit that you will receive you will have a better life. You will have the joy, love, peace and faith which cannot be found anywhere in the world.

But THE FRUIT of the Spirit is love, joy, peace, longsuffering, gentleness, goodness, faith, meekness, temperance: against such there is no law.

Galatians 5:22-23

7. The great feast: At the great feast you will enjoy a feast of healings and miracles.

Coming to the feast opens you up to God's powerful healing. It is a well-known fact that most diseases are caused by what we eat. By receiving the body and the blood of Jesus, you receive life and health into your body. Actually, those who partook of the body and the blood of Jesus in an unworthy way (as mentioned in 1 Corinthians 11:29-30) became sick and even died. There is truly healing power for all those who partake of His body.

a.   JESUS IS THE HEALER OF THE BLIND

- As He healed blind Bartimaeus (Mark 10:46-52)

- As He healed the blind man by the pool of Siloam (John 9:1-17)

- As He healed the blind man who saw men as trees (Mark 8:22-26)

- As He healed the two blind men who followed Him to Jairus' house (Matthew 9:27-31)

b.   JESUS IS THE HEALER OF WOMEN WITH GYNAECOLOGICAL PROBLEMS

- As He healed the woman with the issue of blood (Mark 5:25-34)

c.   JESUS IS THE HEALER OF MAD MEN

- As He healed the mad man of Gadara (Mark 5:1-16)

d.   JESUS IS THE HEALER OF THE PARALYZED

- As He healed the paralytic who was led down the roof (Mark 2:1-12)

- As He healed the man with the withered hand (Matthew 12:9-13)

e.   JESUS IS THE HEALER OF THE DEAF AND DUMB

- As He healed the dumb man (Matthew 9:32-33)

- As He cast out the dumb spirit (Luke 11:14-15)

- As He healed the deaf and dumb man (Mark 7:31-37)

f.   JESUS IS THE HEALER OF LONG-STANDING ILLNESSES

- As He healed the woman who had been bent over for eighteen years (Luke 13:11-17)

- As He healed the man who had been ill for thirty-eight years (John 5:2-9)

g.   JESUS IS THE HEALER OF EPILEPTICS

- As He healed the epileptic boy (Matthew 17:14-18)

h.   JESUS IS THE HEALER OF LEPERS

- As He healed the ten lepers (Luke 17:12-19)

- As He healed the leper (Matthew 8:1-4)

i.   JESUS IS THE HEALER OF LARGE CROWDS

- As He healed the large crowd (Luke 6:17-19)

j.   JESUS IS THE HEALER OF CHILDREN

- As He healed the Syro-Phoenician woman's daughter (Matthew 15:21-28)

- As He healed the nobleman's son (John 4:46-54)

k.   JESUS IS THE HEALER OF SERVANTS

- As He healed the centurion's servant (Luke 7:1-10)

l.   JESUS IS THE HEALER OF FAMILY MEMBERS

- As He healed Peter's mother-in-law (Luke 4:38-39)

m.   JESUS IS THE RAISER OF THE DEAD

- As He raised the widow of Nain's son from the dead (Luke 7:11-15)

- As He raised Jairus' daughter from the dead (Mark 5:22-24, 35-42)

- As He raised Lazarus from the dead (John 11:1-47)

8.   **At the great feast you will enjoy the wine, which is the Blood of Jesus.** The greatest thing you will receive at this feast is the Blood of Jesus to wash away your sins and make you a new person. Accept the invitation to this great feast.

Whoso eateth my flesh, and drinketh my blood, hath eternal life; and I will raise him up at the last day.

John 6:54

SECTION 11:

SALVATION AND THE ANOINTING

Jesus is Anointed for You!
(The Spirit of the Lord
is Upon Me)

The Spirit of the Lord is upon me, because he hath anointed me to preach the gospel to the poor, he hath sent me to heal the brokenhearted, to preach deliverance to the captives, and recovering or sight to the blind, to set at liberty them that are bruised.

Luke 4:18

1.   **Jesus is anointed for you: God the Father, God the Son and God the Holy Spirit decided to save the world.**

For God so loved the world, that he gave his only begotten Son, that whosoever believeth in him should not perish, but have everlasting life.

John 3:16

2.   **Jesus is anointed for you: God the Father, God the Son and God the Holy Spirit agreed that Jesus should take the lead and be born through a virgin.**

But when the fulness of the time was come, God sent forth his Son, made of a woman, made under the law, …

Galatians 4:4

3. **Jesus is anointed for you: God the Father, God the Son and God the Holy Spirit agreed that the Holy Spirit would join Jesus at the right time on earth.** The Holy Spirit teamed up with Jesus in the River Jordan.

And Jesus, when he was baptized, went up straightway out of the water: and, lo, the heavens were opened unto him, and he saw the Spirit of God descending like a dove, and lighting upon him:

Matthew 3:16

4. **Jesus is anointed for you: After Jesus was anointed with the Holy Spirit everything changed.** Miracles began to happen and people were healed.

How God anointed Jesus of Nazareth with the Holy Ghost and with power: who went about doing good, and healing all that were oppressed of the devil; for God was with him.

Acts 10:38

5. **Jesus is anointed for you: Before the Holy Spirit came Jesus was only known as a carpenter.**

Is not this the carpenter, the son of Mary, the brother of James, and Joses, and of Juda, and Simon? and are not his sisters here with us? And they were offended at him.

Mark 6:3

6. **Jesus is anointed for you: At the River Jordan the Holy Spirit came.** He whispered to Jesus and said, "I am here now, things are going to begin to happen."

407

And it came to pass in those days, that Jesus came from Nazareth of Galilee, and was baptized of John in Jordan. And straightway coming up out of the water, he saw the heavens opened, and the Spirit like a dove descending upon him: And there came a voice from heaven, saying, Thou art my beloved Son, in whom I am well pleased.

Mark 1:9-11

How God anointed Jesus of Nazareth with the Holy Ghost and with power: who went about doing good, and healing all that were oppressed of the devil; for God was with him.

Acts 10:38

7. **Jesus is anointed for you: Jesus went to the synagogue and preached.** His very first message was to inform the people that He was anointed for them. He informed them that the Holy Spirit had arrived and that things were going to happen. He told them that He was anointed to do many great things.

The Spirit of the Lord is upon me, because he hath anointed me to preach the gospel to the poor; he hath sent me to heal the brokenhearted, to preach deliverance to the captives, and recovering of sight to the blind, to set at liberty them that are bruised,

Luke 4:18

8. **Jesus is anointed for you: From the time the Holy Spirit arrived, miracles began to happen in Jesus' ministry.**

And great multitudes came unto him, having with them those that were lame, blind, dumb, maimed, and many others, and cast them down at Jesus' feet; and he healed them:

Matthew 15:30

But so much the more went there a fame abroad of him: and great multitudes came together to hear, and to be healed by him of their infirmities.

Luke 5:15

But when Jesus knew it, he withdrew himself from thence: and great multitudes followed him, and he healed them all;

Matthew 12:15

9. **Jesus is anointed for you: Jesus Christ is anointed to shed His blood for you so that you can be saved.** Jesus Christ shed His blood for us through the help of the eternal Spirit. He was anointed to shed His blood for you through the eternal Spirit. Receive Jesus today!

How much more shall the blood of Christ, who THROUGH THE ETERNAL SPIRIT OFFERED HIMSELF without spot to God, purge your conscience from dead works to serve the living God?

Hebrews 9:14

Jesus Will Do You Good

How God anointed Jesus of Nazareth with the Holy Ghost and with power: who went about doing good, and healing all that were oppressed of the devil; for God was with him.

Acts 10:38

1.   Jesus will do you good: Jesus will heal you. Healing is the good thing that Jesus will do for you. Jesus will do something good for you as He did to the many people that he encountered. Look at all the good healings that Jesus did for many people that He encountered. He will do the same for you.

i.   Jesus will do something good for you as He did to blind Bartimaeus (Mark 10:46-52).

ii.   Jesus will do something good for you as He did to the blind man by the pool of Siloam (John 9:1-17).

iii. Jesus will do something good for you as He did to the blind man who saw men as trees (Mark 8:22-26).

iv.   Jesus will do something good for you as He did to the two blind men who followed Him from Jairus' house (Matthew 9:27-31).

v.   Jesus will do something good for you as He did to the woman with the issue of blood (Mark 5:25-34).

vi.   Jesus will do something good for you as He did to the mad man of Gadara (Mark 5:1-16).

vii. Jesus will do something good for you as He did to the paralytic who was let down through the roof (Mark 2:1-12).

viii. Jesus will do something good for you as He did to the man with the withered hand (Matthew 12:9-13).

ix.   Jesus will do something good for you as He did to the dumb man who was brought to him when he left Jairus' house (Matthew 9:32-33).

x.   Jesus will do something good for you as he did to the man from whom He cast out the dumb spirit (Luke 11:14-15).

xi.   Jesus will do something good for you as he did to the deaf and dumb man whom He healed by spitting and touching his tongue (Mark 7:31-37).

xii. Jesus will do something good for you as He did to the woman who had been bent over for eighteen years (Luke 13:11-17).

xiii. Jesus will do something good for you as he did to the man who had been ill for thirty-eight years (John 5:2-9).

xiv. Jesus will do something good for you as He did to the epileptic boy (Matthew 17:14-18).

xv.   Jesus will do something good for you as He did to the ten lepers (Luke 17:12-19).

xvi.   Jesus will do something good for you as He did to the leper when He came down from the mountain (Matthew 8:1-4).

xvii.   Jesus will do something good for you as He did to the large crowd after He had appointed his twelve disciples (Luke 6:17-19).

xviii. Jesus will do something good for you as He did to the Syro-Phoenician woman's daughter (Matthew 15:21-28).

xix.   Jesus will do something good for you as He did to the nobleman's son (John 4:46-54).

xx.   Jesus will do something good for you as He did to the centurion's servant (Luke 7:1-10).

xxi.   Jesus will do something good for you as He did to Peter's mother-in-law (Luke 4:38-39)

xxii.   Jesus will do something good for you as He did to the widow of Nain's son (Luke 7:11-15).

xxiii. Jesus will do something good for you as He did to Jairus' daughter whom He raised from the dead (Mark 5:22-24, 35-42)

xxiv.   Jesus will do something good for you as He did to Lazarus when He raised him from the dead (John 11:1-47)

2.   Jesus will do you good: Jesus will forgive you for your sins. Forgiveness is the good thing that Jesus will do for you. Jesus will do something good for you by forgiving you of your sins. Look at how He forgave the sinners that He encountered.

i.   Jesus forgave the woman who was caught in adultery. Jesus will forgive you for your sins as He did to the woman who was caught in adultery (John 8:1-11).

ii.   Jesus forgave the paralytic of his sins. Jesus will forgive you for your sins as He did to the paralytic who was dropped down through the roof (Mark 2:1-5).

3.   **Jesus will do you good: Jesus will save you. Salvation is the good thing that Jesus will do for you. Jesus has done something good for you by paying the price for your salvation with His blood.**

Forasmuch as ye know that ye were not redeemed with corruptible things, as silver and gold, from your vain conversation received by tradition from your fathers; But with the precious blood of Christ, as of a lamb without blemish and without spot:

1 Peter 1:18-19

4.   **Jesus will do you good: Jesus has shed His blood for you. Jesus has done something good for you by shedding His blood for your salvation.**

And one of the elders answered, saying unto me, What are these which are arrayed in white robes? and whence came they? And I said unto him, Sir, thou knowest. And he said to me, These are they which came out of great tribulation, and have washed their robes, and made them white in the blood of the Lamb.

Revelation 7:13-14

413

Jesus, the Saviour and the Healer

1. JESUS CHRIST IS THE SAVIOUR OF THE WORLD.

For unto you is born this day in the city of David A SAVIOUR, which is Christ the Lord.

Luke 2:11

And we have seen and do testify that the Father sent the Son to be THE SAVIOUR of the world.

1 John 4:14

The God of our fathers raised up Jesus, whom ye slew and hanged on a tree. Him hath God exalted with his right hand to be a Prince and A SAVIOUR, for to give repentance to Israel, and forgiveness of sins.

Acts 5:30-31

2. WHAT DID JESUS COME TO SAVE US FROM? JESUS CAME TO SAVE US FROM OUR SINS.

Jesus did not come to save us from a lack of electricity.

Jesus did not come to save us from a lack of education.

Jesus did not come to save us from a lack of schools.

Jesus did not come to save us from a lack of roads.

Jesus did not come to save us from a lack of hospitals.

Jesus did not come to save us from a lack of good water.

When Jesus came to this world, there was no electricity in Jerusalem.

When Jesus came to this world, there were probably no good roads in Jerusalem.

When Jesus came to this world, there were no universities in Jerusalem.

But Jesus Christ did not correct any of these things.

So what did Jesus come to save us from? He came to save us from our sins!

But while he thought on these things, behold, the angel of the Lord appeared unto him in a dream, saying, Joseph, thou son of David, fear not to take unto thee Mary thy wife: for that which is conceived in her is of the Holy Ghost.

And she shall bring forth a son, and thou shalt call his name JESUS: for HE SHALL SAVE HIS PEOPLE FROM THEIR SINS.

Matthew 1:20-21

3. JESUS THE SAVIOUR IS ABLE TO SAVE US FROM OUR SINS BECAUSE OF THE POWER IN HIS BLOOD.

a. Christ died on the cross and shed His Blood so we could have FORGIVENESS FOR ALL OUR SINS through His blood. Thank God for the blood of Jesus!

> In whom we have redemption through his blood, THE FORGIVENESS OF SINS, according to the riches of his grace;

> Ephesians 1:7

b. Christ Jesus the Saviour, shed His blood on the cross so that we could be cleansed from our sins through the blood of Jesus.

> But if we walk in the light, as he is in the light, we have fellowship one with another, and the blood of Jesus Christ his Son CLEANSETH US FROM ALL SIN.

> 1 John 1:7

c. Every one of us is a sinner and we deserve to be punished for our sins. The punishment for all our sins is death.

> For all have sinned, and come short of the glory of God;

> Romans 3:23

> For the wages of sin is death; but the gift of God is eternal life through Jesus Christ our Lord.

> Romans 6:23

> How many of us have told a lie before? All of us!

> How many of us have stolen something before? All of us!

> How many of us have murdered someone before? All of us because if you hate your brother you are a murderer.

> How many of us have committed fornication before? All of us because if you look at a woman lustfully, you have already committed fornication with her.

> It is clear that we are all sinners.

4. JESUS CHRIST IS ALSO THE HEALER OF THE WORLD.

When the even was come, they brought unto him many that were possessed with devils: and he cast out the spirits with his word, and HEALED ALL THAT WERE SICK: That it might be fulfilled which was spoken by Esaias the prophet, saying, Himself took our infirmities, and bare our sicknesses.

Matthew 8:16-17

a. JESUS IS THE HEALER OF THE BLIND.

1. As He healed blind Bartimaeus (Mark 10:46-52)

2. As He healed the blind man by the pool of Siloam (John 9:1-17)

3. As He healed the blind man who saw men as trees (Mark 8:22-26)

4. As he did to the two blind men who followed Him to Jairus' house (Matthew 9:27-31)

b. JESUS IS THE HEALER OF WOMEN WITH GYNAECOLOGICAL PROBLEMS.

1. As He healed the woman with the issue of blood (Mark 5:25-34)

c. JESUS IS THE HEALER OF MAD MEN.

1. As He healed the mad man of Gadara (Mark 5:1-16)

d. JESUS IS THE HEALER OF THE PARALYZED.

1. As He healed the paralytic who was led down the roof (Mark 2:1-12)

e.   JESUS IS THE HEALER OF THE DEAF AND DUMB.

1. As He healed the dumb man (Matthew 9:32-33)

2. As He cast out the dumb spirit (Luke 11:14)

3. As He healed the deaf and dumb man (Mark 7:31-37)

f.   JESUS IS THE HEALER OF LONG-STANDING ILLNESSES.

1. As He healed the woman who had been bent over for eighteen years (Luke 13:11-17)

2. As He healed the man who had been ill for thirty-eight years (John 5:2-9)

g.   JESUS IS THE HEALER OF EPILEPTICS.

1. As He healed the epileptic boy (Matthew 17:14-18)

h.   JESUS IS THE HEALER OF LEPERS.

1. Just as He healed the ten lepers (Luke 17:12-19)

2. Just as He healed the leper (Matthew 8:1-4)

i.   JESUS IS THE HEALER OF LARGE CROWDS.

1. As He healed the large crowd in (Luke 6:17-19)

j.   JESUS IS THE HEALER OF CHILDREN.

1. As He healed the Syro-Phoenician woman's daughter (Matthew 15:21-28)

2. As He healed the nobleman's son (John 4:46-54)

k.   JESUS IS THE HEALER OF SERVANTS.

1. As He healed the centurion's servant (Luke 7:1-10)

l.   JESUS IS THE HEALER OF FAMILY MEMBERS.

  1. As He healed Peter's mother-in-law (Luke 4:38-39)

m.   JESUS RAISES THE DEAD.

  1. As He raised the widow of Nain's son from the dead
      (Luke 7:11-15)

  2. As He raised Jairus' daughter from the dead
      (Mark 5:22-24, 35-42)

  3. As He raised Lazarus from the dead (John 11:1-47)

SECTION 12:

SALVATION AND MIRACLES

The Greatest Miracle
(The Greatest Miracle is the Miracle of Salvation)

HOW SHALL WE ESCAPE, IF WE NEGLECT SO GREAT SALVATION; which at the first began to be spoken by the Lord, and was confirmed unto us by them that heard him;

Hebrews 2:3

1. **Salvation is the greatest miracle because it is a great miracle to be forgiven.**

There was a man who came home and found his wife in bed with another man. When he reported this to the pastors, every one of them expected that he would divorce his wife. To everyone's amazement, he did not divorce his wife but rather took her back and asked her to please not do that again. This was a big surprise to the entire church family. It was indeed a great miracle for the husband to forgive his wife, even after catching her in the very act. This is what it means for your sins to be red as scarlet and made to be as white as snow. That was a miracle of forgiveness.

Come now, and let us reason together, saith the Lord:
THOUGH YOUR SINS BE AS SCARLET, THEY
SHALL BE AS WHITE AS SNOW; THOUGH THEY BE
RED LIKE CRIMSON, THEY SHALL BE AS WOOL.

Isaiah 1:18

2.   Salvation is the greatest miracle because it is always a miracle for your sins to be wiped away.

It is a miracle for there to be no record of your sins anymore.
It is as if you never sinned. In our world today, the records of past
criminal convictions are never wiped away. There are always
forms to fill which call up for our past sins and mistakes. It is
indeed a great blessing to have our sins washed away without any
record!   Through the blood of Jesus your sins will be washed
away - though they were red like crimson they become white as
wool.

Come now, and let us reason together, saith the Lord:
THOUGH YOUR SINS BE AS SCARLET, THEY
SHALL BE AS WHITE AS SNOW; THOUGH THEY BE
RED LIKE CRIMSON, THEY SHALL BE AS WOOL.

Isaiah 1:18

3.   Salvation is the greatest miracle because it is always a miracle for someone to love a person who has many problems.

In our world today, it is a miracle for someone with serious
deformities to find a spouse. I once saw a man who had fallen in
love with a crippled lady. It was a miracle for him to marry her
because she could not do anything to help herself. It is unusual to
find someone who will marry a person with physical deformities
and obvious handicaps? This is the question you must ask Jesus
Christ. Why would He come towards us and even desire people
with such complex failings? But God has demonstrated His love
towards us in a miraculous way. While we were yet sinners, full
of evil, full of wickedness and full of defects He loved us.

But God commendeth his love toward us, in that, while we were yet sinners, Christ died for us.

Romans 5:8

4.   Salvation is the greatest miracle because it is always a miracle for someone to be released from prison.

I once met a prisoner who touched my heart. This man was a convicted murderer. He was in prison for life because he had murdered his own son. But his fervency, zeal and prayer life touched me so much that I wanted him to be released from prison. Try as I could, I could not think of any way to get him out of prison. The prison gates were heavily guarded and there were armed solders everywhere, so I quickly discarded the option of helping him escape. I thought about getting a presidential pardon for this man. But I did not know the president, nor did I know anyone who knew the president. As I left the prison that day, I looked at this prayerful prisoner and thought to myself, "It is going to take a miracle to get you out of here." Indeed, it took a miracle to release the souls of this world from the prison of sin. To be saved is to be set free from captivity. Today, if salvation has come to you, the great miracle of being set free from prison has happened to you.

The Spirit of the Lord is upon me, because he hath anointed me to preach the gospel to the poor; he hath sent me to heal the brokenhearted, TO PREACH DELIVERANCE TO THE CAPTIVES, and recovering of sight to the blind, to set at liberty them that are bruised,

Luke 4:18

5.   Salvation is the greatest miracle because it is always a great miracle for light to come to darkness.

It is a great miracle for light to come into a person's life. The appearance of light is a miracle. When light shines into the darkness, a great miracle has taken place. For lights (electrical power) to come on in a country, there must be a dam or a massive power plant. Great technology, scientific discoveries and lots of money must be deployed to bring light into a country. That is why there is no electrical power and no light in many countries today. It takes a miracle for light to come on. If salvation has appeared to you, a great light has shone into the darkness of your soul. God has shown mercy to you and has done a great miracle in your life.

> THE PEOPLE THAT WALKED IN DARKNESS HAVE SEEN A GREAT LIGHT: they that dwell in the land of the shadow of death, upon them hath the light shined.
>
> Isaiah 9:2

6.   Salvation is the greatest miracle because it is a great miracle for you to go to Heaven.

Even in this world there are places that you will never go to. Will you ever walk in the Kremlin, in the White House or in the Head of State's bedroom? Not likely! It will take a miracle for you to ever walk in the Oval Office of the White House. Heaven is even greater than the Oval Office! It will take a greater miracle for you to walk on those streets of gold.

So today, if God is giving you entrance into Heaven, a great miracle is taking place. Think about how bad, how full of sin and how full of evil you are. For somebody like you to be welcomed into Heaven is a great miracle indeed.

> And one of the elders answered, saying unto me, WHAT ARE THESE WHICH ARE ARRAYED IN WHITE ROBES? AND WHENCE CAME THEY?
>
> And I said unto him, Sir, thou knowest. And he said to me, these are they which came out of great tribulation, and have washed their robes, and made them white in the blood of the Lamb.
>
> Revelation 7:13-14

7. Salvation is the greatest miracle because it is a great miracle for you to meet Jesus Christ, the Son of God.

Finding salvation is finding Jesus Christ. There are certain people you may never meet in your life. You may never meet the President of China or the Prime Minister of England. For some of us, to meet any of these people would be a great miracle indeed.

To meet Jesus Christ is an even greater miracle. To be saved is to be married to Christ. You would never have thought that you could be married to Christ. Even on earth, you cannot easily marry a prince; and it would be such a miracle to be married to one - to live with him, stay with him, bathe with him and eat with him.

Today, God is giving you the great privilege of coming close to the Prince of Peace and the Lord of Lords.

Wherefore, my brethren, ye also are become dead to the law by the body of Christ; THAT YE SHOULD BE MARRIED TO ANOTHER, EVEN TO HIM who is raised from the dead, that we should bring forth fruit unto God.

Romans 7:4

Jesus and Jairus' Daughter
(Fear Not, Only Believe)

And, behold, there cometh one of the rulers of the synagogue, Jairus by name; and when he saw him, he fell at his feet,

And besought him greatly, saying, My little daughter lieth at the point of death: I pray thee, come and lay thy hands on her, that she may be healed; and she shall live.

While he yet spake, there came from the ruler of the synagogue's house certain which said, Thy daughter is dead: why troublest thou the Master any further?

As soon as Jesus heard the word that was spoken, he saith unto the ruler of the synagogue, BE NOT AFRAID, ONLY BELIEVE.

And he suffered no man to follow him, save Peter, and James, and John the brother of James.

And he cometh to the house of the ruler of the synagogue, and seeth the tumult, and them that wept and wailed greatly.

And when he was come in, he saith unto them, why make ye this ado, and weep? The damsel is not dead, but sleepeth. And they laughed him to scorn. But when he had put them all out, he taketh the father and the mother of the damsel, and them that were with him, and entereth in where the damsel was lying. And he took the damsel by the hand, and said unto her, Talitha cumi; which is, being interpreted, Damsel, I say unto thee, arise.

And straightway the damsel arose, and walked; for she was of the age of twelve years. And they were astonished with a great astonishment And he charged them straitly that no man should know it; and commanded that something should be given her to eat.

Mark 5:22-23, 35-43

1. Jesus was asked by Jairus to come all the way to his house to lay hands on his daughter.

And, behold, there cometh one of the rulers of the synagogue, Jairus by name; and when he saw him, he fell at his feet, And besought him greatly, saying, My little daughter lieth at the point of death: I pray thee, come and LAY THY HANDS on her, that she may be healed; and she shall live.

Mark 5:22-23

2. When Jairus' daughter died, Jairus was asked not to disturb Jesus any further.

While he yet spake, there came from the ruler of the synagogue's house certain which said, Thy daughter is dead: why troublest thou the Master any further?

Mark 5:35

3. Jesus immediately said, "Be not afraid, only believe." The devil always comes with fear and fearful things. Jesus always comes with be not afraid, fear not. Watch out for prophets who always bring prophecies of fear and doom.

As soon as Jesus heard the word that was spoken, he saith unto the ruler of the synagogue, BE NOT AFRAID, ONLY BELIEVE.

Mark 5:36

4. **Jesus did this great miracle in front of a few people. Many of the greatest miracles of our Lord were done in private and not in public.**

And he suffered no man to follow him, save Peter, and James, and John the brother of James.

Mark 5:37

5. **The house of Jairus was the scene of mourning.**

And he cometh to the house of the ruler of the synagogue, and seeth the tumult, and them that wept and wailed greatly.

Mark 5:38

6. **Many doctors are afraid of certain diseases that are not in their field of medicine. But Jesus was not afraid of any disease, or death. That is why He fearlessly went into Jairus' house.**

And when he was come in, he saith unto them, WHY MAKE YE THIS ADO, and weep? The damsel is not dead, but sleepeth. And they laughed him to scorn. But when he had put them all out, he taketh the father and the mother of the damsel, and them that were with him, and entereth in where the damsel was lying.

Mark 5:39-40

7. **Jesus spoke to the dead girl and she immediately rose up from the dead.**

And he took the damsel by the hand, and said unto her, Talitha cumi; which is, being interpreted, Damsel, I say unto thee, arise. And straightway the damsel arose, and walked; for she was of the age of twelve years. And they were astonished with a great astonishment.

Mark 5: 41-42

8. Jesus asked that she should be given some of her favourite food.

And He gave them strict orders that no one should know about this, and He said that something should be given her to eat.

Mark 5:43 (NASB)

9. The miracle healing of Jairus' daughter demonstrates the love of God, the compassion of Jesus Christ, the greatness of Jesus Christ and the power of the Holy Spirit.

… For this purpose the Son of God was manifested, that he might destroy the works of the devil.

1 John 3:8

For God so loved the world, that he gave his only begotten Son, that whosoever believeth in him should not perish, but have everlasting life.

John 3:16

10. Every time Jesus raised somebody from the dead, He demonstrated the greatest kind of power because, as shown below with Jairus' daughter, raising of the dead is three miracles in one:

i. The first miracle was the calling forth of the spirit of Jairus' daughter from heaven or hell, wherever it was.

ii. The second miracle was the restoration of a decomposing body to normalcy.

iii. The third miracle was the healing of Jairus' daughter's body of the disease of which she died. If she were not healed of

429

the disease from which she died, she would have died again when her spirit returned into her body.

11. **"Fear not, only believe" were the words of Jesus to reassure and to help Jairus to receive his salvation and his daughter's healing.**

12. **Jesus said, "Fear not, only believe" because believing is very important.**

When you die, only what you believed will be important.

Once you die, only what you have believed will be important.

When you are entering Singapore, they may check to see if you have excess chewing gum.

When you are entering Malaysia they may check to see if you have drugs. They may even announce on the plane that there is a death penalty for those carrying hard drugs.

When you enter any country they will check to see if you have a valid passport and visa.

When you are entering South Africa, you may be asked to show your Yellow Fever vaccination card.

To enter Heaven, you will not be checked for drugs, chewing gum, visas, passports or proof of a Yellow Fever vaccination. Heaven will require none of these. Heaven will want to know what you believed! Heaven will only demand faith in Jesus Christ. That is the demand of Heaven. That is why Jesus said, "Fear not ONLY BELIEVE."

Do you believe in Jesus Christ as Saviour? Have you received Him into your heart?

But as many as received him, to them gave he the right to become children of God, even TO THOSE WHO BELIEVE IN HIS NAME,

John 1:12 (NASB)

SALVATION MESSAGE 82:

Jesus and the Woman with the Issue of Blood
(Your Faith Has Made You Whole)

And a certain woman, which had an issue of blood twelve years,

And had suffered many things of many physicians, and had spent all that she had, and was nothing bettered, but rather grew worse,

When she had heard of Jesus, came in the press behind, and touched his garment.

For she said, If I may touch but his clothes, I shall be whole.

And straightway the fountain of her blood was dried up; and she felt in her body that she was healed of that plague.

And Jesus, immediately knowing in himself that virtue had gone out of him, turned him about in the press, and said, Who touched my clothes?

And his disciples said unto him, Thou seest the multitude thronging thee, and sayest thou, Who touched me?

And he looked round about to see her that had done this thing.

But the woman fearing and trembling, knowing what was done in her, came and fell down before him, and told him all the truth. And he said unto her, Daughter, THY FAITH HATH MADE THEE WHOLE; go in peace, and be whole of thy plague.

Mark 5:25-34

1. **This woman had been bleeding for twelve years. A woman is normally supposed to bleed for three to five days. This woman probably was smelling because blood starts to smell after some time.**

And a certain woman, which had an issue of BLOOD TWELVE YEARS,

Mark 5:25

2. **This woman was financially broke because she had spent all her money on many physicians and doctors. She must also have been dizzy because she was suffering from blood loss and anaemia. This woman was not feeling any better despite all the medical tests and procedures she had undergone.**

And had suffered many things of many physicians, and had SPENT ALL THAT SHE HAD, and was nothing bettered, but rather grew worse,

Mark 5:26

3. **When she heard of Jesus she immediately had faith and made a confession within herself. Faith comes by hearing. She knew that in the Old Testament the garments of the priests were anointed. Therefore, she knew that when if she could just touch the hem of His garment, the anointing would flow into her.**

When SHE HAD HEARD of Jesus, came in the press behind, and touched his garment.

Mark 5:27

4.   You can have what you say! You will have what you say! This woman said if she touched His garments she would be made whole. And she had what she said.

FOR SHE SAID, If I may touch but his clothes, I shall be whole.

Mark 5:28

5.   Many other people touched Jesus that night but none of them got healed. This shows that there are different types of touches. A touch of love! A touch of lust! A touch of comfort and a touch of faith! This woman had a touch of faith!

For she said, IF I MAY TOUCH but his clothes, I shall be whole.

Mark 5:28

6.   The power of God is something that can be felt. Jesus felt the power of God going out of Him and the woman also felt the power of God entering her.

And straightway the fountain of her blood was dried up; and SHE FELT in her body that she was healed of that plague.

Mark 5:29

And Jesus, immediately knowing in himself that virtue had gone out of him, turned him about in the press, and said, Who touched my clothes?

Mark 5:30

7.   Some of the people around a man of God may not be sensitive to the anointing.

And HIS DISCIPLES SAID unto him, Thou seest the multitude thronging thee, and sayest thou, who touched me?

Mark 5:31

8. Jesus looked around Himself for the one who had touched Him.

And he looked round about to see her that had done this thing.

Mark 5:32

9. The lady confessed that she had touched Him with faith.

But the woman fearing and trembling, knowing what was done in her, came and fell down before him, and told him all the truth.

Mark 5:33

10. Jesus explained to the lady that it was her faith that had made her whole.

And he said unto her, Daughter, THY FAITH HATH MADE THEE WHOLE; go in peace, and be whole of thy plague.

Mark 5:34

11. The miracle healing of the woman with the issue of blood demonstrates the love of God, the compassion of Jesus Christ, the greatness of Jesus Christ and the power of the Holy Spirit.

… For this purpose the Son of God was manifested, that he might destroy the works of the devil.

1 John 3:8

For God so loved the world, that he gave his only begotten Son, that whosoever believeth in him should not perish, but have everlasting life.

John 3:16

12. At the time of your death, only your faith will be important.

But as many as received him, to them gave he the power to become the sons of God, even TO THEM THAT BELIEVE ON HIS NAME:

John 1:12

1. You must have faith in the blood of Jesus.

2. You must have faith in the resurrection of Jesus.

3. Your faith in the death of Jesus Christ on the cross will make you whole.

Jesus and Blind Bartimaeus
(Thou Son of David, Have Mercy on Me!)

And they came to Jericho: and as he went out of Jericho with his disciples and a great number of people, blind Bartimaeus, the son of Timaeus, sat by the highway side begging.

And when he heard that it was Jesus of Nazareth, he began to cry out, and say, Jesus, thou SON OF DAVID, HAVE MERCY ON ME.

And many charged him that he should hold his peace: but he cried the more a great deal, Thou Son of David, have mercy on me.

And Jesus stood still, and commanded him to be called. And they call the blind man, saying unto him, be of good comfort, rise; he calleth thee.

And he, casting away his garment, rose, and came to Jesus.

And Jesus answered and said unto him, what wilt thou that I should do unto thee? The blind man said unto him, Lord, that I might receive my sight.

And Jesus said unto him, Go thy way; thy faith hath made thee whole. And immediately he received his sight, and followed Jesus in the way.

Mark 10:46-52

1. **Blind Bartimaeus was blind from birth. Blindness from birth is a very difficult medical condition to cure. Famous people all over the world have had this condition and are unable to be cured with modern medical science.**

And they came to Jericho: and as he went out of Jericho with his disciples and a great number of people, BLIND BARTIMAEUS, the son of Timaeus, sat by the highway side begging.

Mark 10:46

2. **When blind Bartimaeus heard the unusual sound of many people passing by, he realized it was his only chance to be seen to by Jesus.**

And when he heard that it was Jesus of Nazareth, he began to cry out, and say, Jesus, thou SON OF DAVID, HAVE MERCY ON ME.

Mark 10:47

3. **Many people tried to drown out his cries and suppress him but he could not be suppressed. He knew that was his one and only chance.** He called upon the mercy of God and not upon his rights as a Jew or a righteous person. When you call upon the mercy of God, there is no legal reason for the love of God to be withheld from you.

And many charged him that he should hold his peace: but he cried the more a great deal, Thou Son of David, have mercy on me.

Mark 10:48

4. **Jesus called for him to come. Jesus is calling for you today.**

And Jesus stood still, and commanded him to BE CALLED. And they call the blind man, saying unto him, be of good comfort, rise; he calleth thee. And he, casting away his garment, rose, and came to Jesus.

Mark 10:49-50

5. **Jesus asked him what he wanted. He said that he wanted his sight. He could have asked for money. He could have asked for clothes. But he asked for his miracle healing.**

And Jesus answered and said unto him, WHAT WILT THOU that I should do unto thee? The blind man said unto him, Lord, that I might receive my sight.

Mark 10:51

6. **Jesus gave him what he asked for. Today, Jesus will give you what you ask for.**

And Jesus said unto him, Go thy way; thy faith hath made thee whole. And immediately he received his sight, and followed Jesus in the way.

Mark 10:52

7. **The miracle healing of blind Bartimaeus demonstrates the love of God, the compassion of Jesus Christ, the greatness of Jesus Christ and the power of the Holy Spirit.**

… For this purpose the Son of God was manifested, that he might destroy the works of the devil.

1 John 3:8

For God so loved the world, that he gave his only begotten Son, that whosoever believeth in him should not perish, but have everlasting life.

John 3:16

8. **"Thou Son of David, have mercy on me" was the cry of Bartimaeus to Jesus which led to his salvation and healing. Call on Jesus today and ask for His mercy. Ask Him to wash away your sins and you will be saved.**

    a. God will have mercy on you today because He sent His Son to die on the cross to save you from your sins.

    b. Receive the mercy of God, which comes to you through the blood of Jesus.

Jesus and the Blind Man Who Saw Men as Trees
(He Touched Me)

And he cometh to Bethsaida; and they bring a blind man unto him, and besought him to touch him.

And he took the blind man by the hand, and led him out of the town; and When he had spit on his eyes, and PUT HIS HANDS UPON HIM, he asked him if he saw ought.

And he looked up, and said, I see men as trees, walking.

After that HE PUT HIS HANDS AGAIN UPON HIS EYES, and made him look up: and he was restored, and saw every man clearly. And he sent him away to his house, saying, neither go into the town, nor tell it to any in the town.

And Jesus went out, and his disciples, into the towns of Caesarea Philippi: and by the way he asked his disciples, saying unto them, Whom do men say that I am?

Mark 8:22-27

1. **When people ask for prayer and come for it themselves, it shows that they have faith and that they will be healed.**

And he cometh to Bethsaida; and they bring a blind man unto him, and besought him to touch him.

Mark 8:22

2. **Through the laying on of hands, many diseases are forced to leave.**

And he took the blind man by the hand, and led him out of the town; and When he had spit on his eyes, and PUT HIS HANDS UPON HIM, he asked him if he saw ought.

Mark 8:23

3. **Sometimes people do not get healed after the first prayer so they need another prayer.**

And he looked up, and said, I see men as trees, walking. After that HE PUT HIS HANDS AGAIN UPON HIS EYES, and made him look up: and he was restored, and saw every man clearly.

Mark 8:24-25

4. **God is not struggling to prove anything to you. That is why Jesus told him not to tell anybody about the miracle. Unfortunately, when people are healed partially, they come under pressure to say they are healed totally.**

And he sent him away to his house, saying, neither go into the town, nor tell it to any in the town.

Mark 8:26

5. **The miracle healing of the blind man who saw men as trees demonstrates the love of God, the compassion of Jesus Christ, the greatness of Jesus Christ and the power of the Holy Spirit.**

… For this purpose the Son of God was manifested, that he might destroy the works of the devil.

1 John 3:8

For God so loved the world, that he gave his only begotten Son, that whosoever believeth in him should not perish, but have everlasting life.

John 3:16

6. **Every touch of Jesus in your life will heal you and set you free.**

    a. When Jesus touches your body your body will be healed.

    b. When Jesus touches your soul your mind and soul will change.

    c. When Jesus touches your heart you will be born again.

7. **Receive the touch of the blood of Jesus so that your sins will be washed away and you will be born again.**

SALVATION MESSAGE 85:

Jesus and the Epileptic Boy
(All Things Are Possible
to Him That Believeth)

And one of the multitude answered and said, Master, I have brought unto thee my son, which hath a dumb spirit;

And wheresoever he taketh him, he teareth him: and he foameth, and gnasheth with his teeth, and pineth away: and I spake to thy disciples that they should cast him out; and they could not.

He answereth him, and saith, O faithless generation, how long shall I be with you? how long shall I suffer you? bring him unto me.

And they brought him unto him: and when he saw him, straightway the spirit tare him; and he fell on the ground, and wallowed foaming.

And he asked his father, How long is it ago since this came unto him? And he said, of a child.

And ofttimes it hath cast him into the fire, and into the waters, to destroy him: but if thou canst do any thing, have compassion on us, and help us. Jesus said unto him, If thou canst believe, ALL THINGS ARE POSSIBLE TO HIM THAT BELIEVETH.

And straightway the father of the child cried out, and said with tears, Lord, I believe; help thou mine unbelief.

When Jesus saw that the people came running together, he rebuked the foul spirit, saying unto him, Thou dumb and deaf spirit, I charge thee, come out of him, and enter no more into him. And the spirit cried, and rent him sore, and came out of him: and he was as one dead; insomuch that many said, He is dead. But Jesus took him by the hand, and lifted him up; and he arose.

Mark 9:17-27

1. **Many conditions are caused by evil spirits. The dumb condition of this young man was caused by evil spirits.**

And one of the multitude answered and said, Master, I have brought unto thee my son, which hath a DUMB SPIRIT;

Mark 9:17

2. **Evil spirits cause people to fall to the ground to roll around and scream. This is a common phenomenon where evil spirits inhabit people.**

And wheresoever he taketh him, HE TEARETH HIM: and he foameth, and gnasheth with his teeth, and pineth away: and I spake to thy disciples that they should cast him out; and they could not.

Mark 9:18

3. **Jesus wanted us to learn how to cast out devils without Him being physically present.**

He answereth him, and saith, O faithless generation, how long shall I be with you? how long shall I suffer you? bring him unto me.

Mark 9:19

4. **Demons begin to manifest when they encounter the presence of the power of God. That is why the boy started reacting when he saw Jesus. The main characteristic manifestations that indicate the presence of demon activity are:**

a. The person is literally torn apart by the demon

b. Falling to the ground

c. Wallowing or rolling on the ground

d. Foaming at the mouth or vomiting

And they brought him unto him: and WHEN HE SAW HIM, straightway the SPIRIT TARE HIM; and he fell on the ground, and wallowed foaming.

Mark 9:20

The reason why demonized people foam at the mouth is that spirits usually come in and go out of people through their mouths. A number of people who have had the experience of going out and coming back into their bodies (through near death experiences, for example) they describe how they entered back into their bodies through their mouths. Likewise, the mouth seems to be the portal for the entry and departure of demons.

5. **As is the case of this boy, many people are possessed with evil spirits from childhood. Evil spirits enter children's lives through television, sexual molestation and family witchcraft practices.**

And he asked his father, How long is it ago since this came unto him? And he said, OF A CHILD.

Mark 9:21

6. **Many people are both believers and unbelievers. In one breath the man said he believed. In another breath**

he said, "Please help my unbelief." God is merciful. And He helps us even though we have unbelief.

And straightway the father of the child cried out, and said with tears, Lord, I BELIEVE; HELP THOU MINE UNBELIEF. When Jesus saw that the people came running together, he rebuked the foul spirit, saying unto him, Thou dumb and deaf spirit, I charge thee, come out of him, and enter no more into him.

Mark 9:24-25

5.   When evil spirits come out of people, they become still and they look as though they are dead or asleep. This is the sign that they have been delivered.

And the spirit cried, and rent him sore, and came out of him: and HE WAS AS ONE DEAD; insomuch that many said, He is dead.

But Jesus took him by the hand, and lifted him up; and he arose.

Mark 9:26-27

6.   The miracle healing of the epileptic boy demonstrates the love of God, the compassion of Jesus Christ, the greatness of Jesus Christ and the power of the Holy Spirit.

… For this purpose the Son of God was manifested, that he might DESTROY THE WORKS OF THE DEVIL.

1 John 3:8

For God so loved the world, that he gave his only begotten Son, that whosoever believeth in him should not perish, but have everlasting life.

John 3:16

7.   "…all things are possible to him that believeth" (Mark 9:23) were the words of Jesus to reassure and to help the man to receive his salvation and healing.

8.   The devil wanted to destroy the boy and cast him into the fire (Mark 9:22). This is the plan of the devil for you; to destroy you and cast you into the fires of hell.

The devil wants to take us into the fires of hell. But Jesus has come to set us free so that we wouldn't have to go into the lake of fire.

Receive Jesus Christ as your Saviour. He will wash you with his blood and you will escape the fire of hell.

Jesus and the Paralytic
(Your Sins Are Forgiven)

And, behold, men brought in a bed a man which was taken with a palsy: and they sought means to bring him in, and to lay him before him.

And when they could not find by what way they might bring him in because of the multitude, they went upon the housetop, and let him down through the tiling with his couch into the midst before Jesus.

And when he saw their faith, he said unto him, MAN, THY SINS ARE FORGIVEN THEE.

And the scribes and the Pharisees began to reason, saying, Who is this which speaketh blasphemies? Who can forgive sins, but God alone?

But when Jesus perceived their thoughts, he answering said unto them, What reason ye in your hearts?

Whether is easier, to say, Thy sins be forgiven thee; or to say, Rise up and walk?

But that ye may know that the Son of man hath power upon earth to forgive sins, (he said unto the sick of the palsy,) I say unto thee, Arise, and take up thy couch, and go into thine house.

And immediately he rose up before them, and took up that whereon he lay, and departed to his own house, glorifying God.

Luke 5:18-25

1.   **This paralytic man's friends knew how to break into a house and so they were probably thieves. Their evil ways were quite obvious and that was why Jesus said, "Thy sins are forgiven thee."**

And, behold, men brought in a bed a man which was taken with a palsy: and they sought means to bring him in, and to lay him before him.

And when they could not find by what way they might bring him in because of the multitude, they WENT UPON THE HOUSETOP, and let him down through the tiling with his couch into the midst before Jesus.

Luke 5:18-19

2.   **Jesus healed this man by forgiving him of his sins. This is because sin leads to death. One of the agents of death is disease.**

And when he saw their faith, he said unto him, MAN, THY SINS ARE FORGIVEN THEE.

Luke 5:20

Then when lust hath conceived, it bringeth forth sin: and sin, when it is finished, bringeth forth death.

James 1:15

3.   **Many diseases are caused by sin. That is why Jesus forgave them for their sins.**

And when he saw their faith, he said unto him, Man, thy sins are forgiven thee.

Luke 5:20

4. Even in the presence of the power of God there are people who are always criticizing and finding fault.

And the scribes and the Pharisees began to reason, saying, Who is this which speaketh blasphemies? Who can forgive sins, but God alone?

But when Jesus PERCEIVED THEIR THOUGHTS, he answering said unto them, What reason ye in your hearts?

Whether is easier, to say, Thy sins be forgiven thee; or to say, Rise up and walk?

Luke 5:21-23

5. Jesus ministered the power of healing by telling the man what to do. When you obey the voice of the man of God, healing will come to you.

But that ye may know that the Son of man hath power upon earth to forgive sins, (he said unto the sick of the palsy,) I SAY UNTO THEE, ARISE, and take up thy couch, and go into thine house.

And immediately he rose up before them, and took up that whereon he lay, and departed to his own house, glorifying God.

Luke 5:24-25

6. The miracle healing of the paralytic demonstrates the love of God, the compassion of Jesus Christ, the greatness of Jesus Christ and the power of the Holy Spirit.

… For this purpose the Son of God was manifested, that he might destroy the works of the devil.

1 John 3:8

For God so loved the world, that he gave his only begotten Son, that whosoever believeth in him should not perish, but have everlasting life.

John 3:16

7.   Today, God is saying to you, "Your sins are forgiven."

Your sins of lying, stealing, killing, jealousy and fornication are all forgiven if you receive Jesus today. Jesus will forgive you of your sins. That is why He came.

8.   Receive Jesus and have your sins washed away by the powerful blood of Jesus.

Jesus and the Woman Who Was Bent Over
(Woman, Thou Art Loosed!)

And he was teaching in one of the synagogues on the Sabbath.

And, behold, there was a woman which had a spirit of infirmity eighteen years, and was bowed together, and could in no wise lift up herself.

And when Jesus saw her, he called her to him, and said unto her, Woman, THOU ART LOOSED FROM THINE INFIRMITY.

And he laid his hands on her: and immediately she was made straight, and glorified God.

Luke 13:10-13

1. **The teaching of the Word of God is a good atmosphere for the hearts of people to be prepared for miracles.**

And HE WAS TEACHING in one of the synagogues on the Sabbath.

Luke 13:10

2. **An evil spirit of infirmity caused this woman to suffer from a type of scoliosis. Evil spirits are very wicked and they love to deform, disfigure and disgrace people. Evil spirits can affect you physically. The evil spirit bent the woman's back. The woman could not lift herself up.**

And, behold, there was a woman which had a spirit of infirmity eighteen years, and was BOWED TOGETHER, and could in no wise lift up herself.

Luke 13:11

3. **Jesus ministered to her by declaring that she was healed. Declarations from the man of God are a powerful way of being blessed. Tonight you are loosed from every infirmity!**

And when Jesus saw her, he called her to him, and said unto her, Woman, THOU ART LOOSED FROM THINE INFIRMITY.

Luke 13:12

4. **Jesus continued to minister to her by laying His hands on her. Sometimes, different methods of healing are combined to bring about a miracle. In this case, a proclamation of faith was combined with the laying on of hands.**

And HE LAID HIS HANDS ON HER: and immediately she was made straight, and glorified God.

Luke 13:13

5. **No one could prevent the joy and the dancing that came from this woman as she glorified God.**

And he laid his hands on her: and immediately she was made straight, and GLORIFIED GOD.

Luke 13:13

453

6.   The miracle healing of the woman who was bent over demonstrates the love of God, the compassion of Jesus Christ, the greatness of Jesus Christ and the power of the Holy Spirit.

… For this purpose the Son of God was manifested, that he might destroy the works of the devil.

1 John 3:8

For God so loved the world, that he gave his only begotten Son, that whosoever believeth in him should not perish, but have everlasting life.

John 3:16

7.   "Woman, thou art loosed" were the words of Jesus to reassure and to help the woman to receive her salvation and healing.

   a. You need to be loosed from the sins that are threatening to take you to hell.

   b. Through the blood of Jesus your sins will be washed away and you will receive salvation.

8.   Allow Jesus to loose you from your sins through the Blood of Jesus Christ. If you are not loosed from your sins, you will go to hell. Through the blood of Jesus you can receive salvation.

SALVATION MESSAGE 88:

Jesus and the Centurion's Servant
(Great Faith!)

Now when he had ended all his sayings in the audience of the people, he entered into Capernaum.

And a certain centurion's servant, who was dear unto him, was sick, and ready to die.

And when he heard of Jesus, he sent unto him the elders of the Jews, beseeching him that he would come and heal his servant.

And when they came to Jesus, they besought him instantly, saying, that he was worthy for whom he should do this:

For he loveth our nation, and he hath built us a synagogue.

Then Jesus went with them. And when he was now not far from the house, the centurion sent friends to him, saying unto him, Lord, trouble not thyself: for I am not worthy that thou shouldest enter under my roof:

Wherefore neither thought I myself worthy to come unto thee: but say in a word, and my servant shall be healed.

For I also am a man set under authority, having under me soldiers, and I say unto one, Go, and he goeth; and to another, Come, and he cometh; and to my servant, Do this, and he doeth it.

When Jesus heard these things, he marvelled at him, and turned him about, and said unto the people that followed him, I say unto you, I HAVE NOT FOUND SO GREAT FAITH, NO, NOT IN ISRAEL.

And they that were sent, returning to the house, found the servant whole that had been sick.

Luke 7:1-10

1. This centurion was worthy of a miracle. Tonight you deserve a miracle!

And when they came to Jesus, they besought him instantly, saying, that HE WAS WORTHY for whom he should do this: For he loveth our nation, and he hath built us a synagogue.

Luke 7:4-5

2. The centurion realized that for healing to take place Jesus did not have to go to his servant, to see him or even lay hands on him to be healed.

Then Jesus went with them. And when he was now not far from the house, the centurion sent friends to him, saying unto him, LORD, TROUBLE NOT THYSELF: for I am not worthy that thou shouldest enter under my roof:

Luke 7:6

3. The centurion knew that Jesus could stand in one place and speak a word and his servant would be healed even though he was far away.

Wherefore neither thought I myself worthy to come unto thee: but SAY IN A WORD, and my servant shall be healed.

Luke 7:7

4. **Today, wherever you are, even if you are far away, the power of God will come to you! If Jesus says to demons, 'Go' they must go!**

For I also am a man set under authority, having under me soldiers, and I SAY UNTO ONE, GO, and he goeth; and to another, Come, and he cometh; and to my servant, Do this, and he doeth it.

Luke 7:8

5. **There is no concept of distance in the spirit. A command spoken from miles away can correct a situation powerfully. In the spirit realm, distance does not reduce the amount of power available.**

And they that were sent, returning to the house, found the servant whole that had been sick.

Luke 7:10

6. **The miracle healing of the centurion's servant demonstrates the love of God, the compassion of Jesus Christ, the greatness of Jesus Christ and the power of the Holy Spirit.**

… For this purpose the Son of God was manifested, that he might destroy the works of the devil.

1 John 3:8

For God so loved the world, that he gave his only begotten Son, that whosoever believeth in him should not perish, but have everlasting life.

John 3:16

7. **Jesus was impressed with the great faith of the centurion.**

When Jesus heard these things, he marvelled at him, and turned him about, and said unto the people that followed him, I say unto you, I HAVE NOT FOUND SO GREAT FAITH, NO, NOT IN ISRAEL.

Luke 7:9

8. **You must have faith in Jesus Christ in order to be saved. Without faith it is impossible to please God. We are saved by faith! Believe in your heart today, confess with your mouth and you shall be saved.**

That if thou shalt confess with thy mouth the Lord Jesus, and shalt believe in thine heart that God hath raised him from the dead, thou shalt be saved.

For with the heart man believeth unto righteousness; and with the mouth confession is made unto salvation.

Romans 10:9-10

SALVATION MESSAGE 89:

Jesus and the Man Full of Leprosy
(I Will, Be Thou Clean)

And it came to pass, when he was in a certain city, behold a man full of leprosy: who seeing Jesus fell on his face, and besought him, saying, Lord, IF THOU WILT, THOU CANST make me clean.

And he put forth his hand, and touched him, saying, I WILL: BE THOU CLEAN. And immediately the leprosy departed from him.

And he charged him to tell no man: but go, and shew thyself to the priest, and offer for thy cleansing, according as Moses commanded, for a testimony unto them.

Luke 5:12-14

1. **This man had a serious problem, a serious case of the disease, leprosy. He was full of leprosy. That means he was covered from head to toe with leprous skin.**

And it came to pass, when he was in a certain city, behold a man FULL OF LEPROSY: who seeing Jesus fell on his face, and besought him, saying, Lord, if thou wilt, thou canst make me clean.

Luke 5:12

2. **This man knew that if Jesus wanted to heal him, He could.**

And it came to pass, when he was in a certain city, behold a man full of leprosy: who seeing Jesus fell on his face, and besought him, saying, Lord, IF THOU WILT, THOU CANST make me clean.

Luke 5:12

3. **This man found out for all of us whether it was the will of God for us to be healed. Jesus revealed that it is the will of God for you to be healed when He said, "I will, be thou clean."**

And he put forth his hand, and touched him, saying, I WILL: BE THOU CLEAN. And immediately the leprosy departed from him.

Luke 5:13

4. **Jesus was not afraid to touch the leper even though he had a terrible contagious skin disease.**

And HE PUT FORTH HIS HAND, AND TOUCHED HIM, saying, I will: be thou clean. And immediately the leprosy departed from him.

Luke 5:13

5. **Through the touch, Jesus did not get leprosy. The man rather got healing. Do not be afraid that you will contract the disease or the problem of the person you are laying hands on. The power of God is greater than the power of darkness. When hands are laid on you,**

your disease will not enter the man of God. Rather, the power of God will enter you and drive out the disease.

And he put forth his hand, and TOUCHED HIM, saying, I will: be thou clean. And immediately the leprosy departed from him.

Luke 5:13

6. **Jesus told the man not to tell anyone, but to show himself to the priest. Jesus is not trying to impress anyone. That is why He says, "Do not tell anyone." Jesus Christ does not need to impress us.**

And he charged him to TELL NO MAN: but GO, AND SHEW THYSELF TO THE PRIEST, and offer for thy cleansing, according as Moses commanded, for a testimony unto them.

Luke 5:14

7. **The miracle healing of the leper demonstrates the love of God, the compassion of Jesus Christ, the greatness of Jesus Christ and the power of the Holy Spirit.**

… For this purpose the Son of God was manifested, that he might destroy the works of the devil.

1 John 3:8

For God so loved the world, that he gave his only begotten Son, that whosoever believeth in him should not perish, but have everlasting life.

John 3:16

8. **"I will, be thou clean." It is the will of God for you to be healed, delivered and saved. It is not the will of God that you should die and go to hell. It is the will of God that you be saved and washed with the blood of Jesus. Open your heart and receive the blood of Jesus today.**

The Lord is not slack concerning his promise, as some men count slackness; but is longsuffering to us-ward, NOT WILLING THAT ANY SHOULD PERISH, but that all should come to repentance.

2 Peter 3:9

SALVATION MESSAGE 90:

Jesus and the Man By the Pool of Bethesda
(Rise and Be Healed!)

Now there is at Jerusalem by the sheep market a pool, which is called in the Hebrew tongue Bethesda, having five porches.

In these lay a great multitude of impotent folk, of blind, halt, withered, waiting for the moving of the water.

For an angel went down at a certain season into the pool, and troubled the water: whosoever then first after the troubling of the water stepped in was made whole of whatsoever disease he had. And a certain man was there, which had an infirmity thirty and eight years.

When Jesus saw him lie, and knew that he had been now a long time in that case, he saith unto him, Wilt thou be made whole?

The impotent man answered him, Sir, I have no man, when the water is troubled, to put me into the pool: but while I am coming, another steppeth down before me.

Jesus saith unto him, RISE, TAKE UP THY BED, AND WALK. And immediately the man was made whole, and took up his bed, and walked: and on the same day was the Sabbath.

John 5:2-9

1.   **Jesus visited a place where there were a lot of sick people but He healed only one person. It is a mystery why Jesus heals some and leaves others.**

Now there is at Jerusalem by the sheep market a pool, which is called in the Hebrew tongue Bethesda, having five porches. In these lay A GREAT MULTITUDE of impotent folk, of blind, halt, withered, waiting for the moving of the water.

John 5:2-3

2.   **Jesus explained why He healed only one person, even though there was a multitude of sick people. Do not be discouraged when a few people are healed out of a multitude. Jesus explained that He could only do what He saw His father doing.**

Jesus explained why he healed only one person when he said "My father works and I work. I only do what I see my father do. Jesus only ministered to people who were being touched by the Father.

Jesus gave them this answer: "Very truly I tell you, the Son can do nothing by himself; HE CAN DO ONLY WHAT HE SEES HIS FATHER DOING, because whatever the Father does the Son also does.

John 5:19 (NIV)

3.   **An angel from the Lord was involved in the healing of the sick people by the pool of Bethesda. Today, angels are involved in the ministration of the power of God and the ministry of healing. Accept the ministry of angels and you will be healed.**

For AN ANGEL went down at a certain season into the pool, and troubled the water: whosoever then first after the troubling of the water stepped in was made whole of whatsoever disease he had.

John 5:4

4. **Jesus is able to heal problems that have been there for a long time. This miracle demonstrates that Jesus is able to heal problems that are almost forty years old.**

And a certain man was there, which had an infirmity THIRTY AND EIGHT YEARS.

John 5:5

5. **Jesus asked the man, "Do you want to be made whole?" God delivers you from your enemies and not from your friends. That is why Jesus asked this question.**

When Jesus saw him lie, and knew that he had been now a long time in that case, he saith unto him, WILT THOU BE MADE WHOLE?

John 5:6

6. **The impotent man did not have anyone to help him. He said, "I have no man to help me." Jesus is the One who will help you when no one is available to help you. When there is no one to help you financially or socially, Jesus will be there to help you.**

The impotent man answered him, Sir, I HAVE NO MAN, when the water is troubled, to put me into the pool: but while I am coming, another steppeth down before me.

John 5:7

7. **Jesus ministered to him by telling him what to do. You receive the power of God when you receive instructions on what to do. "Rise, take up your bed and walk" was a clear instruction from the Lord. May you be healed when you follow the word of the Lord as it comes to you.**

Jesus saith unto him, RISE, TAKE UP THY BED, AND WALK. And immediately the man was made whole, and

465

took up his bed, and walked: and on the same day was the Sabbath.

John 5:8-9

8.   The miracle healing of the impotent man demonstrates the love of God, the compassion of Jesus Christ, the greatness of Jesus Christ and the power of the Holy Spirit.

… For this purpose the Son of God was manifested, that he might destroy the works of the devil.

1 John 3:8

For God so loved the world, that he gave his only begotten Son, that whosoever believeth in him should not perish, but have everlasting life.

John 3:16

9.   "Rise, take up thy bed, and walk."

Jesus told the man to do what he could not do before. As he obeyed he became well. As you begin to do what you cannot do, the healing power will come into your body.

The legalistic Pharisees were concerned with the technicalities and legalities of the man carrying his bed on a Sabbath day, rather than the powerful result of the man being healed after thirty-eight years.

Jesus warned the man not to sin again, lest more diseases with more complications came to him.

10.   Rise out of your sins and be healed and be saved by accepting Jesus as your Saviour and being washed by the Blood of Jesus!

Jesus and the Blind Man Healed at the Pool of Siloam
(The Works of God)

And as Jesus passed by, he saw a man which was blind from his birth.

And his disciples asked him, saying, Master, who did sin, this man, or his parents, that he was born blind?

Jesus answered, Neither hath this man sinned, nor his parents: but that the works of God should be made manifest in him.

I must work the works of him that sent me, while it is day: the night cometh, when no man can work.

As long as I am in the world, I am the light of the world.

When he had thus spoken, he spat on the ground, and made clay of the spittle, and he anointed the eyes of the blind man with the clay,

And said unto him, Go, wash in the pool of Siloam, (which is by interpretation, Sent.) He went his way therefore, and washed, and came seeing. The neighbours therefore, and they which before had seen him that he was blind, said, Is not this he that sat and begged?

Some said, This is he: others said, He is like him: but he said, I am he. Therefore said they unto him, How were thine eyes opened? He answered and said, A man that is called Jesus made clay, and anointed mine eyes, and said unto me, Go to the pool of Siloam, and wash: and I went and washed, and I received sight. Then said they unto him, Where is he? He said, I know not. They brought to the Pharisees him that aforetime was blind.

John 9:1-13

1. Some people are sick because they sinned.

And as Jesus passed by, he saw a man which was blind from his birth. And his disciples asked him, saying, Master, WHO DID SIN, this man, or his parents, that he was born blind?

John 9:1-2

2. Some people are sick because their parents sinned.

And his disciples asked him, saying, Master, who did sin, this man, or his parents, that he was born blind?

Jesus answered, Neither hath this man sinned, NOR HIS PARENTS: but that the works of God should be made manifest in him.

John 9:2-3

3. Some people are sick so that the works of God can be manifested.

Jesus answered, Neither hath this man sinned, nor his parents: but THAT THE WORKS OF GOD SHOULD BE MADE MANIFEST in him.

John 9:3

4. The works of God are healing, salvation and deliverance from evil spirits.

I must work the works of him that sent me, while it is day: the night cometh, when no man can work. As long as I am in the world, I am the light of the world.

John 9:4-5

5. **Jesus used an unusual method of healing to minister to this man. Jesus anointed the man's eyes with a mixture of saliva and clay and asked him to go and wash in the pool of Siloam.**

When he had thus spoken, he spat on the ground, and made clay of the spittle, and he anointed the eyes of the blind man with the clay,

And said unto him, Go, wash in the pool of Siloam, (which is by interpretation, Sent) He went his way therefore, and washed, and came seeing.

John 9:6-7

6. **The neighbours and people in the community recognized that a miracle had happened.**

The neighbours therefore, and they which before had seen him that he was blind, said, Is not this he that sat and begged?

Some said, This is he: others said, He is like him: but he said, I am he.

John 9:8-9

7. **The Jews and the Pharisees were so hard-hearted that they could not accept that such a great and obvious miracle had taken place.**

Therefore said they unto him, How were thine eyes opened?

He answered and said, A man that is called Jesus made clay, and anointed mine eyes, and said unto me, Go to the pool of Siloam, and wash: and I went and washed, and I received sight.

Then said they unto him, Where is he? He said, I know not.

They brought to the Pharisees him that aforetime was blind.

But the Jews did not believe concerning him, that he had been blind, and received his sight until they called the parents of him that had received his sight.

John 9:10-13,18

8. **The miracle healing of the man born blind demonstrates the love of God, the compassion of Jesus Christ, the greatness of Jesus Christ and the power of the Holy Spirit.**

… For this purpose the Son of God was manifested, that he might destroy the works of the devil.

1 John 3:8

For God so loved the world, that he gave his only begotten Son, that whosoever believeth in him should not perish, but have everlasting life.

John 3:16

9. **Open your heart to the Word of God and the Blood of Jesus that you might be saved.**

Jesus and Lazarus
(Lazarus, Come Forth!)

Now a certain man was sick, named Lazarus, of Bethany, the town of Mary and her sister Martha.

(It was that Mary which anointed the Lord with ointment, and wiped his feet with her hair, whose brother Lazarus was sick.)

Therefore his sisters sent unto him, saying, Lord, behold, he whom thou lovest is sick.

When Jesus heard that, he said, This sickness is not unto death, but for the glory of God, that the Son of God might be glorified thereby.

John 11:1-4

Jesus answered, Are there not twelve hours in the day? If any man walk in the day, he stumbleth not, because he seeth the light of this world. But if a man walk in the night, he stumbleth, because there is no light in him.

These things said he: and after that he saith unto them, Our friend Lazarus sleepeth; but I go, that I may awake him out of sleep.

Then said his disciples, Lord, if he sleep, he shall do well.

Howbeit Jesus spake of his death: but they thought that he had spoken of taking of rest in sleep.

Then said Jesus unto them plainly, Lazarus is dead.

And I am glad for your sakes that I was not there, to the intent ye may believe; nevertheless let us go unto him.

Then said Thomas, which is called Didymus, unto his fellow disciples, Let us also go, that we may die with him.

Then when Jesus came, he found that he had lain in the grave four days already.

Now Bethany was nigh unto Jerusalem, about fifteen furlongs off:

And many of the Jews came to Martha and Mary, to comfort them concerning their brother.

Then Martha, as soon as she heard that Jesus was coming, went and met him: but Mary sat still in the house.

Then said Martha unto Jesus, Lord, if thou hadst been here, my brother had not died.

But I know, that even now, whatsoever thou wilt ask of God, God will give it thee.

Jesus saith unto her, Thy brother shall rise again.

Martha saith unto him, I know that he shall rise again in the resurrection at the last day.

Jesus said unto her, I am the resurrection, and the life: he that believeth in me, though he were dead, yet shall he live:

And whosoever liveth and believeth in me shall never die. Believest thou this?

She saith unto him, Yea, Lord:I believe that thou art the Christ, the Son of God, which should come into the world.

And when she had so said, she went her way, and called Mary her sister secretly, saying, The Master is come, and calleth for thee.

As soon as she heard that, she arose quickly, and came unto him. Now Jesus was not yet come into the town, but was in that place where Martha met him.

The Jews then which were with her in the house, and comforted her, when they saw Mary, that she rose up hastily and went out, followed her, saying, She goeth unto the grave to weep there.

Then when Mary was come where Jesus was, and saw him, she fell down at his feet, saying unto him, Lord, if thou hadst been here, my brother had not died.

When Jesus therefore saw her weeping, and the Jews also weeping which came with her, he groaned in the spirit, and was troubled,

And said, Where have ye laid him? They said unto him, Lord, come and see.

Jesus wept.

Then said the Jews, Behold how he loved him!

And some of them said, Could not this man, which opened the eyes of the blind, have caused that even this man should not have died?

Jesus therefore again groaning in himself cometh to the grave. It was a cave, and a stone lay upon it.

Jesus said, Take ye away the stone. Martha, the sister of him that was dead, saith unto him, Lord, by this time he stinketh: for he hath been dead four days.

Jesus saith unto her, Said I not unto thee, that, if thou wouldest believe, thou shouldest see the glory of God?

Then they took away the stone from the place where the dead was laid. And Jesus lifted up his eyes, and said, Father, I thank thee that thou hast heard me.

And I knew that thou hearest me always: but because of the people which stand by I said it, that they may believe that thou hast sent me.

And when he thus had spoken, he cried with a loud voice, Lazarus, come forth.

And he that was dead came forth, bound hand and foot with graveclothes: and his face was bound about with a napkin. Jesus saith unto them, Loose him, and let him go

John 11:9-44

1. Your relationships and your friendships will connect you to the power of God.

Lazarus was connected to the power of God because of his sisters who were close to Jesus. Jesus Himself was interested and moved to help Lazarus because of His relationship with his sisters.

Now a certain man was sick, named Lazarus, of Bethany, the town of Mary and her sister Martha.

(It was that Mary which anointed the Lord with ointment, and wiped his feet with her hair, whose brother Lazarus was sick.)

Therefore HIS SISTERS SENT UNTO HIM, saying, Lord, behold, he whom thou lovest is sick.

John 11:1-3

2. Some problems come for the glory of God. Through that problem, the glory of God is revealed.

When Jesus heard that, he said, This sickness is not unto death, but FOR THE GLORY OF GOD, that the Son of God might be glorified thereby . . .

John 11:4

3. Jesus is never in a hurry. Do not worry if Jesus does not seem alarmed about your problem. He is well able to solve your problem in due time.

Jesus answered, ARE THERE NOT TWELVE HOURS in the day? If any man walk in the day, he stumbleth not, because he seeth the light of this world.

John 11:9

4. The miracle of raising someone from the dead is the most fantastic of all the miracles Jesus ever did because it combined 3 fantastic miracles in one.

Then they took away the stone from the place where the dead was laid. And Jesus lifted up his eyes, and said, Father, I thank thee that thou hast heard me.

And I knew that thou hearest me always: but because of the people which stand by I said it, that they may believe that thou hast sent me.

And when he thus had spoken, he cried with a loud voice, Lazarus, come forth.

And he that was dead came forth, bound hand and foot with graveclothes: and his face was bound about with a napkin. Jesus saith unto them, Loose him, and let him go

John 11:41-44

i. The first miracle was the calling of the spirit of Lazarus from heaven or hell.

ii. The second miracle was the restoration of a decomposed body to normalcy.

iii. The third miracle was the healing of Lazarus' body of the disease from which he died. If he were not healed of the disease he died from, he would have immediately died again when his spirit returned to his body.

iv. Through this ultimate miracle, Jesus Christ demonstrated His supremacy over death, sickness and all the tragedies of mankind.

5.   The miracle raising of Lazarus from the dead demonstrates the love of God, the compassion of Jesus Christ, the greatness of Jesus Christ and the power of the Holy Spirit.

… For this purpose the Son of God was manifested, that he might destroy the works of the devil.

1 John 3:8

For God so loved the world, that he gave his only begotten Son, that whosoever believeth in him should not perish, but have everlasting life.

John 3:16

6.   "Lazarus come forth" - Jesus is calling you to come forth from physical death and spiritual death.

7.   Open your heart to the call of the Lord as He summons you to come forth out of death.

SALVATION MESSAGE 93:

Jesus and the Widow of Nain
("I Say Unto Thee, Arise")

And it came to pass the day after, that he went into a city called Nain; and many of his disciples went with him, and much people.

Now when he came nigh to the gate of the city, behold, there was a dead man carried out, the only son of his mother, and she was a widow: and much people of the city was with her.

And when the Lord saw her, he had compassion on her, and said unto her, weep not.

And he came and touched the bier: and they that bare him stood still. And he said, Young man, I SAY UNTO THEE, ARISE.

And he that was dead sat up, and began to speak. And he delivered him to his mother.

And there came a fear on all: and they glorified God, saying, that a great prophet is risen up among us; and, That God hath visited his people.

Luke 7:11-16

1.   **Jesus has great compassion on the sorrowful and tragic circumstances of people's lives. That is why He was moved by this widow's plight as she buried her only son.**

Now when he came nigh to the gate of the city, behold, there was a dead man carried out, the only son of his mother, and she was a widow: and much people of the city was with her. And when the Lord saw her, HE HAD COMPASSION ON HER, and said unto her, weep not.

Luke 7:12-13

2.   **Jesus is able to raise the dead even when they are on the way to the cemetery for burial.**

Now when he came nigh to the gate of the city, behold, there was A DEAD MAN CARRIED OUT, the only son of his mother, and she was a widow: and much people of the city was with her.

Luke 7:12

3.   **Jesus is saying to you, "Arise from your sins and difficulties!"**

And he came and touched the bier: and they that bare him stood still. And he said, Young man, I SAY UNTO THEE, ARISE.

Luke 7:14

4.   **Through the power of God, fear comes on people and they respect the power of God. This is why miracles and healing are important today.**

And there came A FEAR ON ALL: and they glorified God, saying, That a great prophet is risen up among us; and, That God hath visited his people.

Luke 7:16

5. **The miracle healing of the widow of Nain's son demonstrates the love of God, the compassion of Jesus Christ, the greatness of Jesus Christ and the power of the Holy Spirit.**

    … For this purpose the Son of God was manifested, that he might destroy the works of the devil.

    1 John 3:8

    For God so loved the world, that he gave his only begotten Son, that whosoever believeth in him should not perish, but have everlasting life.

    John 3:16

6. **Jesus raised three people from the dead: Jairus' daughter, the widow of Nain's son and Lazarus. Every time Jesus raised somebody from the dead, He demonstrated the greatest kind of power because the raising of the dead is three miracles in one:**

    i.   The first miracle was the calling of the spirit of the widow of Nain's son from heaven or hell.

    ii. The second miracle was the restoration of a decomposed body to normalcy.

    iii. The third miracle was the healing of the body of the widow of Nain's son of the disease from which he died. If he were not healed of the disease he died from, he would have immediately died again when his spirit returned to his body.

7. **Today, Jesus is telling you to rise out of your sins by receiving the Blood of Jesus and being born again.**

SALVATION MESSAGE 94:

Jesus and the Nobleman's Son
(Go Thy Way, Thy Son Liveth)

So Jesus came again into Cana of Galilee, where he made the water wine. And there was a certain nobleman, whose son was sick at Capernaum.

When he heard that Jesus was come out of Judaea into Galilee, he went unto him, and besought him that he would come down, and heal his son: for he was at the point of death.

Then said Jesus unto him, except ye see signs and wonders, ye will not believe.

The nobleman saith unto him, Sir, come down ere my child die.

Jesus saith unto him, Go thy way; thy son liveth. And the man believed the word that Jesus had spoken unto him, and he went his way.

And as he was now going down, his servants met him, and told him, saying, Thy son liveth.

Then inquired he of them the hour when he began to amend. And they said unto him, Yesterday at the seventh hour the fever left him. So the father knew that it was at the same hour, in the which Jesus said unto him, THY SON LIVETH: AND HIMSELF BELIEVED, AND HIS WHOLE HOUSE.

John 4:46-53

1. The nobleman had a son who was suffering from an illness.

So Jesus came again into Cana of Galilee, where he made the water wine. And there was a certain nobleman, whose son was sick at Capernaum.

John 4:46

2. The nobleman wanted Jesus to come to his house, unlike the centurion who knew that Jesus Christ did not actually have to come to the house for his son to be healed.

When he heard that Jesus was come out of Judaea into Galilee, he went unto him, and BESOUGHT HIM THAT HE WOULD COME down, and heal his son: for he was at the point of death.

John 4:47

3. Jesus knows that some people would not believe except they see signs and wonders.

Then said Jesus unto him, EXCEPT YE SEE SIGNS and wonders, ye will not believe.

John 4:48

4. The nobleman was concerned about his son's miracle and he believed that Jesus was the solution that would prevent his son from dying.

The nobleman saith unto him, Sir, come down ere my child die.

John 4:49

5. **Even though the man insisted that Jesus should come, Jesus did not go but rather spoke a word and the nobleman's son was healed where he was.**

Jesus saith unto him, Go thy way; thy son liveth. And the man believed the word that Jesus had spoken unto him, and he went his way.

John 4:50

6. **The time at which the nobleman's son was healed was the exact moment that Jesus spoke the Word. It means that the moment at which the Word is spoken is the holy and special moment when a miracle occurs.**

And as he was now going down, his servants met him, and told him, saying, Thy son liveth.

Then inquired he of them the hour when he began to amend. And they said unto him, YESTERDAY AT THE SEVENTH HOUR THE FEVER LEFT HIM.

John 4:51-52

7. **You can expect your miracle at the moment in which the Word is spoken.**

And as he was now going down, his servants met him, and told him, saying, Thy son liveth.

Then inquired he of them the hour when he began to amend. And they said unto him, Yesterday AT THE SEVENTH HOUR THE FEVER LEFT HIM.

John 4:51-52

8. **The miracle healing of the nobleman's son demonstrates the love of God, the compassion of Jesus Christ, the greatness of Jesus Christ and the power of the Holy Spirit.**

… For this purpose the Son of God was manifested, that he might destroy the works of the devil.

1 John 3:8

For God so loved the world, that he gave his only begotten Son, that whosoever believeth in him should not perish, but have everlasting life.

John 3:16

9.   **"Go thy way, thy son liveth". When you receive the Word of God, life will come into your household instead of death. By receiving the Word of Jesus, the nobleman had life instead of holding a funeral.**

10. **Open your heart to Jesus and you will receive everlasting life.**

He that hath the Son hath life; and he that hath not the Son of God hath not life.

1 John 5:12

Jesus and the Syrophoenician Woman's Daughter
(The Devil is Gone Out of Thy Daughter)

And from thence he arose, and went into the borders of Tyre and Sidon, and entered into an house, and would have no man know it: but he could not be hid.

For a certain woman, whose young daughter had an unclean spirit, heard of him, and came and fell at his feet:

The woman was a Greek, a Syrophenician by nation; and she besought him that he would cast forth the devil out of her daughter.

But Jesus said unto her, Let the children first be filled: for it is not meet to take the children's bread, and to cast it unto the dogs. And she answered and said unto him, Yes, Lord: yet the dogs under the table eat of the children's crumbs.

And he said unto her, For this saying go thy way; the devil is gone out of thy daughter.

And when she was come to her house, she found the devil gone out, and her daughter laid upon the bed.

Mark 7:24-30

1.　　**The further you travel away from home, the more miracles you will see. A prophet is not accepted in his own home. Jesus travelled towards the borders of Tyre and Sidon and saw great miracles there.**

And from thence he arose, and went into the borders of Tyre and Sidon, and entered into an house, and would have no man know it: but he could not be hid.

Mark 7:24

2.　　**Some people are not open and honest about their families and their problems. This woman admitted that her daughter had a demon. Instead of covering up your family problems, open up and accept you need help for your family.**

For a certain woman, whose young daughter had an unclean spirit, heard of him, and came and fell at his feet:

Mark 7:25

3.　　**Every man of God is anointed and sent to particular people. When a person is anointed for you, you can expect your miracle to happen easily.**

The woman was a Greek, a Syrophenician by nation; and she besought him that he would cast forth the devil out of her daughter.

Mark 7:26

4.　　**Jesus explained the scope of His calling by saying that He could not give the children's bread to dogs. Even though the Syrophoenician woman was outside the scope of His calling, He ministered to her because she had a lot of faith.**

But Jesus said unto her, Let the children first be filled: for it is not meet to take the children's bread, and to cast it unto the DOGS.

Mark 7:27

5. **Humility will open you up to the healing power of God. Many people would have been offended saying, "Jesus called me a dog." But this woman was not offended because she was humble. Her response was simple, "I accept that I am a dog, but I need your healing." Jesus was so impressed with the lady that He said, "Because of these words you will experience your healing."**

And she answered and said unto him, YES, LORD: YET THE DOGS under the table eat of the children's crumbs.

Mark 7:28

6. **What you say is an expression of your faith. The woman with the issue of blood said within herself, if I touch him I will be made whole. This woman also said, every dog can have some crumbs. Watch out for the things you say because your confessions and your words are causing miracles to happen.**

And he said unto her, FOR THIS SAYING go thy way; the devil is gone out of thy daughter. And when she was come to her house, she found the devil gone out, and her daughter laid upon the bed.

Mark 7:29-30

7. **The miracle healing of the Syrophoenician woman's daughter demonstrates the love of God, the compassion of Jesus Christ, the greatness of Jesus Christ and the power of the Holy Spirit.**

… For this purpose the Son of God was manifested, that he might destroy the works of the devil.

1 John 3:8

For God so loved the world, that he gave his only begotten Son, that whosoever believeth in him should not perish, but have everlasting life.

John 3:16

8. **"Go thy way; the devil is gone out of thy daughter". When you believe the words of Jesus, the devil will leave you and the power of the devil over your life will be destroyed.**

9. **Humble yourself like the Syrophoenician woman and believe the words of the Lord Jesus Christ and the devil will lose access to and control over your life. By believing in Jesus, you cause the devil to permanently lose control over your life and you will go to Heaven for eternity.**

10. **Humble yourself and receive Jesus Christ as your Saviour and be washed by the Blood of Jesus.**

Jesus and the Man with the Dropsy
(Is It Lawful To Heal on the Sabbath Day?)

And it came to pass, as he went into the house of one of the chief Pharisees to eat bread on the sabbath day, that they watched him.

And, behold, there was a certain man before him which had the dropsy.

And Jesus answering spake unto the lawyers and Pharisees, saying, IS IT LAWFUL TO HEAL ON THE SABBATH DAY?

And they held their peace. And he took him, and healed him, and let him go;

And answered them, saying, which of you shall have an ass or an ox fallen into a pit, and will not straightway pull him out on the Sabbath day?

And they could not answer him again to these things.

Luke 14:1-6

1. **Miracles can happen even when you are having a meal. Jesus had gone to have lunch in somebody's house. The power of God was present and He was able to minister great miraculous power of the Holy Spirit.**

And it came to pass, as he went into the house of one of the chief Pharisees TO EAT BREAD on the sabbath day, that they watched him.

Luke 14:1

2. **This man was suffering from dropsy, which is oedema or swelling. This swelling could have been caused by a kidney disease, liver disease or even a blood disease. Jesus has power over all complex diseases.**

And, behold, there was a certain man before him which had THE DROPSY.

Luke 14:2

3. **Jesus likened the healing of this man to the rescuing of an ass or an ox from a pit into which it has fallen. When you have certain diseases, you are like an ass or an ox that has fallen into a pit.** The power of God is available to rescue you and set you free from every plague, curse and complex disease.

And answered them, saying, which of you shall have AN ASS OR AN OX FALLEN INTO A PIT, and will not straightway pull him out on the Sabbath day? And they could not answer him again to these things.

Luke 14:5-6

4. **As far as God is concerned, you must be rescued and set free from the curse of sickness.**

And answered them, saying, which of you shall have AN ASS OR AN OX FALLEN INTO A PIT, and will not straightway pull him out on the Sabbath day? And they could not answer him again to these things.

Luke 14:5-6

5. **The miracle healing of the man with dropsy (oedema) demonstrates the love of God, the compassion of Jesus Christ, the greatness of Jesus Christ and the power of the Holy Spirit.**

... For this purpose the Son of God was manifested, that he might destroy the works of the devil.

1 John 3:8

For God so loved the world, that he gave his only begotten Son, that whosoever believeth in him should not perish, but have everlasting life.

John 3:16

6. **"Is it lawful to heal on the Sabbath day" were the words of Jesus to reassure and to fight for the man who had oedema to receive his salvation and healing.**

Legalistic, religious and self-righteous people concern themselves with regulations, rules and technicalities rather than focusing on the great and good work that is done. As far as Jesus is concerned, technicalities must be set aside for you to receive your healing.

7. **Since you can be healed on any day, it means you can be saved on any day. You must be saved today! Open your heart to Jesus and receive your salvation today.**

. . . TO DAY if ye will hear his voice, harden not your heart, as in the provocation, and as in the day of temptation in the wilderness:

Psalm 95:7-8

SALVATION MESSAGE 97:

Jesus and the Man with the Impediment in His Speech
(Be Opened!)

And they bring unto him one that was deaf, and had an impediment in his speech; and they beseech him to put his hand upon him. And he took him aside from the multitude, and put his fingers into his ears, and he spit, and touched his tongue; And looking up to heaven, he sighed, and saith unto him, EPHPHATHA, that is, BE OPENED. And straightway his ears were opened, and the string of his tongue was loosed, and he spake plain. And he charged them that they should tell no man: but the more he charged them, so much the more a great deal they published it; And were beyond measure astonished, saying, He hath done all things well: he maketh both the deaf to hear, and the dumb to speak.

Mark 7:32-37

1. **Jesus healed the man who was both deaf and dumb. Even today, medical science is not able to do much for people who are deaf and dumb.**

And they bring unto him one that was deaf, and had an IMPEDIMENT IN HIS SPEECH; and they beseech him to put his hand upon him.

Mark 7:32

491

2.   **It was necessary for Jesus to take the man aside because it is not easy to perform a miracle in the presence of faithless and sceptical people.**

And HE TOOK HIM ASIDE from the multitude, and put his fingers into his ears, and he spit, and touched his tongue;

Mark 7:33

3.   **Jesus needed a substance with which to minister to the man. In the absence of oil, He used His saliva.**

And he took him aside from the multitude, and put his fingers into his ears, and HE SPIT, and touched his tongue;

Mark 7:33

4.   **Jesus did not even look at the man when He said, "Be opened" and yet a miracle took place instantly.**

And LOOKING UP TO HEAVEN, he sighed, and saith unto him, Ephphatha, that is, Be opened.

Mark 7:34

5.   **The miracle happened immediately and the evidence was his plain speech.**

And STRAIGHTWAY HIS EARS WERE OPENED, and the string of his tongue was loosed, and he spake plain.

Mark 7:35

6.   **Many of the greatest miracles of our Lord were done in private and not in public**

And he charged them that they should TELL NO MAN: but the more he charged them, so much the more a great deal they published it;

Mark 7:36

7. **Miracles cause astonishment and raise the faith of people.**

And were beyond measure ASTONISHED, saying, He hath done all things well: he maketh both the deaf to hear, and the dumb to speak.

Mark 7:37

8. **The miracle healing of the man with the impediment in his speech demonstrates the love of God, the compassion of Jesus Christ, the greatness of Jesus Christ and the power of the Holy Spirit.**

… For this purpose the Son of God was manifested, that he might destroy the works of the devil.

1 John 3:8

For God so loved the world, that he gave his only begotten Son, that whosoever believeth in him should not perish, but have everlasting life.

John 3:16

9. **"Be opened". The command of the Lord will cause a healing to take place.**

a. God is opening the eyes of the blind.

b. God is also opening your eyes to the reality of Heaven and hell.

c. Be open in your heart as well so that you can receive salvation and total deliverance.

10. **Open your heart to receive the Word of God and the Love of Jesus Christ. If you do not open your heart you will be sent to hell.**

Jesus and the Two Blind Men

(Be it unto You According to Your Faith)

And when Jesus came into the ruler's house, and saw the minstrels and the people making a noise,

He said unto them, Give place: for the maid is not dead, but sleepeth. And they laughed him to scorn.

But when the people were put forth, he went in, and took her by the hand, and the maid arose.

And the fame hereof went abroad into all that land.

And when Jesus departed thence, two blind men followed him, crying, and saying, Thou Son of David, have mercy on us.

And when he was come into the house, the blind men came to him: and Jesus saith unto them, Believe ye that I am able to do this? They said unto him, Yea, Lord.

Then touched he their eyes, saying, ACCORDING TO YOUR FAITH BE IT UNTO YOU.

And their eyes were opened; and Jesus straitly charged them, saying, See that no man know it.

But they, when they were departed, spread abroad his fame in all that country.

Matthew 9:23-31

1. **From the time Jesus left Jairus' house, till he got to His own abode, two blind men followed him. Jesus ignored these blind men until they proved that they were serious about receiving their healing.**

And WHEN JESUS DEPARTED THENCE, TWO BLIND MEN FOLLOWED HIM, crying, and saying, Thou Son of David, have mercy on us.

And when he was come into the house, the blind men came to him: and Jesus saith unto them, Believe ye that I am able to do this? They said unto him, Yea, Lord.

Matthew 9:27-28

2. **Jesus ignored the two blind men until they had shown enough humility by crying and following Him all the way from Jairus' house to His own house. Jesus ignored these two blind men until He was sure that they believed in His ability to heal.**

And when HE WAS COME INTO THE HOUSE, the blind men came to him: and Jesus saith unto them, Believe ye that I am able to do this? They said unto him, Yea, Lord.

Matthew 9:28

3. **Jesus ignored these two men until they demonstrated faith.**

Then touched he their eyes, saying, ACCORDING TO YOUR FAITH BE IT UNTO YOU.

Matthew 9:29

4. **Jesus was not concerned about showing people His great healing power.**

And their eyes were opened; and Jesus straitly charged them, saying, SEE THAT NO MAN KNOW IT.

Matthew 9:30

5. **The news of one miracle can make a man of God famous.**

But they, when they were departed, SPREAD ABROAD HIS FAME in all that country.

Matthew 9:31

6. **The miracle healing of the man born blind demonstrates the love of God, the compassion of Jesus Christ, the greatness of Jesus Christ and the power of the Holy Spirit.**

… For this purpose the Son of God was manifested, that he might destroy the works of the devil.

1 John 3:8

For God so loved the world, that he gave his only begotten Son, that whosoever believeth in him should not perish, but have everlasting life.

John 3:16

7. **"According to your faith be it unto you."**

   a. According to your faith, you receive healing

   b. According to your faith you can also receive salvation

8. **Have faith in the Word of God and receive your salvation and a new life through Jesus Christ.**

But as many as received him, to them gave he the right to become children of God, even TO THOSE WHO BELIEVE IN HIS NAME,

John 1:12 (NASB)

Jesus and the Ten Lepers
(Give Glory to God)

And it came to pass, as he went to Jerusalem, that he passed through the midst of Samaria and Galilee.

And as he entered into a certain village, there met him ten men that were lepers, which stood afar off:

And they lifted up their voices, and said, Jesus, Master, have mercy on us.

And when he saw them, he said unto them, Go shew yourselves unto the priests. And it came to pass, that, as they went, they were cleansed.

And one of them, when he saw that he was healed, turned back, and with a loud voice glorified God,

And fell down on his face at his feet, giving him thanks: and he was a Samaritan. And Jesus answering said, Were there not ten cleansed? but where are the nine? There are not found that returned to give glory to God, save this stranger. And he said unto him, Arise, go thy way: THY FAITH HATH MADE THEE WHOLE.

Luke 17:11-19

1. **Jesus healed ten lepers in one stroke. The power of Jesus Christ is available for many people. God can do ten miracles of the same kind in one day because His power is awesome. The power of God can cure incurable diseases. In those days, leprosy was an incurable and insurmountable disease.**

    And it came to pass, as he went to Jerusalem, that he passed through the midst of Samaria and Galilee.

    And as he entered into a certain village, there met him TEN MEN that were lepers, which stood afar off:

    Luke 17:11-12

2. **Incurable diseases are death sentences. That is why mercy from God must be sought. The ten lepers were wise to seek for mercy and nothing else.**

    And they lifted up their voices, and said, Jesus, Master, HAVE MERCY on us.

    Luke 17:13

3. **The miracle happened to the ten lepers as they obeyed the commandment of the Lord. It was only as they went to see the priests that they realized that they were healed. As you obey the instruction of the man of God to stand, to open your eyes or to walk, you will discover that the power of God has healed you.**

    And when he saw them, he said unto them, Go shew yourselves unto the priests. And IT CAME TO PASS, THAT, AS THEY WENT, THEY WERE CLEANSED.

    Luke 17:14

4. **It's sad to say, only one person came back to say thank you for what God had done. Many people do not realise that it is God who healed them. Many people do not thank God for healing them.**

And ONE OF THEM, when he saw that he was healed, turned back, and with a loud voice GLORIFIED GOD,

Luke 17:15

5. **When the one Samaritan came back to say thank you, a greater miracle occurred in his life and Jesus declared him to be whole. So the nine were cleansed but this one was made whole.**

And fell down on his face at his feet, giving him thanks: and he was a Samaritan.

And Jesus answering said, were there not ten CLEANSED? but where are the nine?

There are not found that returned to give glory to God, save this stranger.

And he said unto him, Arise, go thy way: thy faith hath made thee WHOLE.

Luke 17: 16-19

6. **The miracle healing of the ten lepers demonstrates the love of God, the compassion of Jesus Christ, the greatness of Jesus Christ and the power of the Holy Spirit.**

… For this purpose the Son of God was manifested, that he might destroy the works of the devil.

1 John 3:8

For God so loved the world, that he gave his only begotten Son, that whosoever believeth in him should not perish, but have everlasting life.

John 3:16

7. **Show your appreciation to God for what He has done for you in sending His Son Jesus Christ to die on a cross for you. Say "Thank you" to God by opening your heart and receiving Jesus Christ as your Lord and personal Saviour.**

How shall we escape, if we neglect so great salvation; which at the first began to be spoken by the Lord, and was confirmed unto us by them that heard him;

Hebrews 2:3

SALVATION MESSAGE 100:

Jesus and the Madman of Gadara

(Come out of the Man, Thou Unclean Spirit)

And they came over unto the other side of the sea, into the country of the Gadarenes. And when he was come out of the ship, immediately there met him out of the tombs a man with an unclean spirit, who had his dwelling among the tombs; and no man could bind him, no, not with chains: Because that he had been often bound with fetters and chains, and the chains had been plucked asunder by him, and the fetters broken in pieces: neither could any man tame him.

And always, night and day, he was in the mountains, and in the tombs, crying, and cutting himself with stones.

But when he saw Jesus afar off, he ran and worshipped him, and cried with a loud voice, and said, What have I to do with thee, Jesus, thou Son of the most high God? I adjure thee by God that thou torment me not. For he said unto him, COME OUT OF THE MAN, THOU UNCLEAN SPIRIT.

And he asked him, What is thy name? And he answered, saying, My name is Legion: for we are many.

And he besought him much that he would not send them away out of the country.

Now there was there nigh unto the mountains a great herd of swine feeding. And all the devils besought him, saying, Send us into the swine, that we may enter into them. And forthwith Jesus gave them leave. And the unclean spirits went out, and entered into the swine: and the herd ran violently down a steep place into the sea, (they were about two thousand;) and were choked in the sea.

And they that fed the swine fled, and told it in the city, and in the country. And they went out to see what it was that was done.

And they come to Jesus and see him that was possessed with the devil, and had the legion, sitting, and clothed, and in his right mind: and they were afraid.

Mark 5:1-15

1.   The demons made the mad man live in a cemetery.

And when he was come out of the ship, immediately there met him out of the tombs a man with an unclean spirit, who had his DWELLING AMONG THE TOMBS; and no man could bind him, no, not with chains:

Mark 5:2-3

2.   The demons made the man uncontrollable and untameable and gave him super-human strength.

Because that he had been often bound with fetters and chains, and the chains had been plucked asunder by him, and the fetters broken in pieces: NEITHER COULD ANY MAN TAME HIM.

Mark 5:4

3.   The demons made the mad man injure and harm himself.

And always, night and day, he was in the mountains, and in the tombs, crying, and CUTTING HIMSELF with stones.

Mark 5:5

4. **When the power of God was present, the demons could not prevent the man from worshipping Jesus.**

But WHEN HE SAW JESUS AFAR OFF, HE RAN AND WORSHIPPED him,

And cried with a loud voice, and said, What have I to do with thee, Jesus, thou Son of the most high God? I adjure thee by God that thou torment me not.

For he said unto him, Come out of the man, thou unclean spirit.

Mark 5:6-8

5. **Jesus asked for the name of the demon.** Commanding the demon by its name releases more power and compels the evil spirit to obey.

And he asked him, WHAT IS THY NAME? And he answered, saying, My name is Legion: for we are many.

Mark 5:9

6. **The madman of Gadara was possessed by one devil but had six thousand other demons in him.** The demonic power in the man made him unusually strong.

And he asked him, what is thy name? And he answered, saying, MY NAME IS LEGION: for we are many.

Mark 5:9

7. **The demons were willing to come out of the man but they did not want to leave that part of the world.** Demons are associated with regions and areas, which they dominate. Demons cause certain characteristics to exist in certain places.

And he besought him much that he would not send them away OUT OF THE COUNTRY.

Mark 5:10

8. The evil spirits preferred to occupy the pigs than to remain without a habitation.

Many animals have evil spirits in them. Even the pigs reacted by behaving abnormally when the evil spirits entered into them. Many people react and behave abnormally because of the presence of evil spirits. Abnormal behaviour must always prompt you to think of evil spirits. The pigs preferred to commit suicide than to have the evil spirits live in them.

Now there was there nigh unto the mountains a great herd of swine feeding.

And all the devils besought him, saying, SEND US INTO THE SWINE, that we may enter into them… and the herd ran violently down a steep place into the sea…

Mark 5:11-13

9. Jesus preferred to sacrifice the "pig farm" and to save the man. The life of a man is worth far more than a thousand pigs. You are important to Jesus and He will do great things just to set you free.

And forthwith Jesus gave them leave. And the unclean spirits went out, and entered into the swine: and the herd ran violently down a steep place into the sea, (they were about TWO THOUSAND;) AND WERE CHOKED IN THE SEA.

Mark 5:13

10. Today medical science is not able to easily cure mad men. The power of Jesus Christ did what human beings with all their science and knowledge are still unable to do.

And they that fed the swine fled, and told it in the city, and in the country. And they went out to see what it was that was done.

And they come to Jesus and see him that was possessed with the devil, and had the legion, SITTING, AND CLOTHED, AND IN HIS RIGHT MIND: and they were afraid.

Mark 5:14-15

11. **The miracle healing of the mad man of Gadara demonstrates the love of God, the compassion of Jesus Christ, the greatness of Jesus Christ and the power of the Holy Spirit.**

… For this purpose the Son of God was manifested, that he might destroy the works of the devil.

1 John 3:8

For God so loved the world, that he gave his only begotten Son, that whosoever believeth in him should not perish, but have everlasting life.

John 3:16

12. **Let the goodness of God and His power lead you to salvation.** As you see the greatness of Jesus Christ through his healings and miracles, you must open your heart to his message of salvation so that you will be saved from going to hell. Let the goodness of God lead you to repentance and salvation. The message of Jesus is clear: repent or you will likewise perish!

Or despisest thou the riches of his goodness and forbearance and longsuffering; NOT KNOWING THAT THE GOODNESS OF GOD LEADETH THEE TO REPENTANCE?

Romans 2:4

SALVATION MESSAGE 101:

Jesus and the Man with the Withered Hand
(Stretch Forth Thine Hand)

And when he was departed thence, he went into their synagogue:

And, behold, there was a man which had his hand withered. And they asked him, saying, is it lawful to heal on the Sabbath days: that they might accuse him.

And he said unto them, what man shall there be among you, that shall have one sheep, and if it fall into a pit on the Sabbath day, will he not lay hold on it, and lift it out?

How much then is a man better than a sheep? Wherefore it is lawful to do well on the Sabbath days.

Then saith he to the man, STRETCH FORTH THINE HAND. And he stretched it forth; and it was restored whole, like as the other.

Matthew 12:9-13

1. **The man with the withered hand came to church. That is where Jesus saw him. As you go to church today, you have already been identified by Jesus Christ and you will receive your healing.**

And when he was departed thence, he went into their SYNAGOGUE: and, behold, THERE WAS A MAN which had his hand withered.

Matthew 12:9-10

2.   Unspiritual and self-righteous people are constantly looking at technicalities and passing judgment on things that they do not understand.

...And they asked him, saying, IS IT LAWFUL to heal on the Sabbath days: that they might accuse him.

Matthew 12:10

3.   Church services and crusades are where the presence of God is found.

These are always good places to go to because the power and the presence of God are there. As far as God is concerned, your sickness and your problem have made you like a sheep that has fallen into a pit. Today God will deliver you out of that pit and set you free.

And he said unto them, what man shall there be among you, that shall have one sheep, and if it fall into a pit on the sabbath day, will he not lay hold on it, and lift it out?

Matthew 12:11

4.   Today, you must know that you are better than a sheep and God has decided to heal you.

How much then is a man better than a sheep?...Then saith he to the man, stretch forth thine hand. And he stretched it forth; and it was restored whole, like as the other.

Matthew 12:12,13

5. **The miracle healing on the man with the withered hand demonstrates the love of God, the compassion of Jesus Christ, the greatness of Jesus Christ and the power of the Holy Spirit.**

... For this purpose the Son of God was manifested, that he might destroy the works of the devil.

1 John 3:8

6. **As you see the power of Jesus, which delivered and healed the man with the withered hand, you must open your heart to His saving power so that your sins can be washed away and you will have Eternal Life through Jesus Christ.**

For God so loved the world, that he gave his only begotten Son, that whosoever believeth in him should not perish, but have everlasting life

John 3:16

7. **Let the goodness of God and His power lead you to salvation.**

As you see the greatness of Jesus Christ through his healings and miracles, you must open your heart to His message of salvation so that you will be saved from going to hell.

Let the goodness of God lead you to repentance and salvation. The message of Jesus is clear: repent or you will likewise perish!

Or despisest thou the riches of his goodness and forbearance and longsuffering; NOT KNOWING THAT THE GOODNESS OF GOD LEADETH THEE TO REPENTANCE?

Romans 2:4

SALVATION MESSAGE 102:

Jesus and Peter's Mother-In-Law
(Himself Took Our Infirmities)

And when Jesus was come into Peter's house, he saw his wife's mother laid, and sick of a fever.

And he touched her hand, and the fever left her: and she arose, and ministered unto them.

When the even was come, they brought unto him many that were possessed with devils: and he cast out the spirits with his word, and healed all that were sick:

THAT IT MIGHT BE FULFILLED which was spoken by Esaias the prophet, saying, HIMSELF TOOK OUR INFIRMITIES, and bare our sicknesses.

Matthew 8:14-17

1. **Jesus healed Peter's mother-in-law of fever. Fever is the commonest disease that afflicts all men. Fever is a symptom of infections, inflammations and many other dangerous diseases. Jesus Christ is the master of all fevers.**

And when Jesus was come into Peter's house, he saw his wife's mother laid, and SICK OF A FEVER. And he touched her hand, and the fever left her: and she arose, and ministered unto them.

Matthew 8:14-15

2. **Everyone that is connected to you is important to Jesus. That is why Jesus healed Peter's mother-in-law. Peter's mother-in-law was connected to Peter and therefore Jesus was interested in her.**

And when Jesus was come into Peter's house, HE SAW HIS WIFE'S MOTHER laid, and sick of a fever.

Matthew 8:14

3. **After healing Peter's mother-in-law, Jesus then healed the masses. The fact that Jesus healed the masses does not mean that He cannot heal an individual and the fact that He healed an individual does not mean that He was not interested in the masses.**

When the even was come, they BROUGHT UNTO HIM MANY that were possessed with devils: and he cast out the spirits with his word, and healed all that were sick:

Matthew 8:16

4. **These great things that Jesus did were in fulfillment of the great prophecies of Isaiah that "himself took our infirmities" and bore our diseases.**

THAT IT MIGHT BE FULFILLED which was spoken by Esaias the prophet, saying, HIMSELF TOOK OUR INFIRMITIES, and bare our sicknesses.

Matthew 8:17

5. **The miracle healing of Peter's mother-in-law demonstrates the love of God, the compassion of Jesus Christ, the greatness of Jesus Christ and the power of the Holy Spirit.**

    … For this purpose the Son of God was manifested, that he might destroy the works of the devil.

    1 John 3:8

    For God so loved the world, that he gave his only begotten Son, that whosoever believeth in him should not perish, but have everlasting life.

    John 3:16

6. **Let the goodness of God and His power lead you to salvation. As you see the greatness of Jesus Christ through his healings and miracles, you must open your heart to His message of salvation so that you will be saved from going to hell.**

    Let the goodness of God lead you to repentance and salvation. The message of Jesus is clear: repent or you will likewise perish!

    Or despisest thou the riches of his goodness and forbearance and longsuffering; NOT KNOWING THAT THE GOODNESS OF GOD LEADETH THEE TO REPENTANCE?

    Romans 2:4

SECTION 13:

SALVATION FROM THE OLD TESTAMENT

SALVATION MESSAGE 103:

The Sun of Righteousness

But unto you that fear my name shall THE SUN OF RIGHTEOUSNESS ARISE WITH HEALING IN HIS WINGS; and ye shall go forth, and grow up as calves of the stall.

Malachi 4:2

1.   It was predicted that Jesus Christ would come.

Was there a prophecy or prediction concerning your birth? It is a great and wonderful thing if your birth or your coming is predicted or prophesied about. Notice all the scriptures that predict the coming of Jesus.

And there shall come forth a rod out of the stem of Jesse, and a Branch shall grow out of his roots:

Isaiah 11:1

Therefore the Lord himself shall give you a sign; Behold, a virgin shall conceive, and bear a son, and shall call his name Immanuel.

Isaiah 7:14

For unto us a child is born, unto us a son is given: and the government shall be upon his shoulder: and his name shall be called Wonderful, Counsellor, The mighty God, The everlasting Father, The Prince of Peace.

Of the increase of his government and peace there shall be no end, upon the throne of David, and upon his kingdom, to order it, and to establish it with judgment and with justice from henceforth even for ever. The zeal of the Lord of hosts will perform this.

Isaiah 9:6-7

Behold, the days come, saith the Lord, that I will raise unto David a righteous Branch, and a King shall reign and prosper, and shall execute judgment and justice in the earth.

Jeremiah 23:5

Thus saith the Lord; A voice was heard in Ramah, lamentation, and bitter weeping; Rahel weeping for her children refused to be comforted for her children, because they were not.

Jeremiah 31:15

2. It was predicted that Jesus Christ would have healing in His wings.

The Old Testament prophets did not have healing in their wings. All these Old Testament prophets did not have healing in their ministries:

Abraham	Jehu	Jonah
Isaac	Balaam	Micah
Jacob	Isaiah	Nahum
Aaron	Jeremiah	Habakkuk
Samuel	Ezekiel	Zephaniah

Nathan	Daniel	Haggai
Moses	Hosea	Zechariah
Joshua	Joel	Malachi
Ezra	Amos	
Nehemiah	Obadiah	

Both Elijah and Elisha had healing miracles.
(1 Kings 17:17-24; 2 Kings 5:1-14; 2 Kings 4:32-37).

3. We know that Jesus Christ was the Sun of Righteousness with healing in His wings because of the astounding, dramatic and persistent miracles of healing that marked His ministry.

Then the Pharisees went out, and held a council against him, how they might destroy him.

But when Jesus knew it, he withdrew himself from thence: and great multitudes followed him, and HE HEALED THEM ALL;

And charged them that they should not make him known:

Matthew 12:14-16

4. We know that Jesus Christ was the Sun of Righteousness with healing in His wings because thousands and thousands flocked to see Him because of His miracles.

And Jesus went about all Galilee, teaching in their synagogues, and preaching the gospel of the kingdom, and healing all manner of sickness and all manner of disease among the people.

And his fame went throughout all Syria: and they brought unto him all sick people that were taken with divers diseases and torments, and those which were possessed with devils, and those which were lunatick, and those that had the palsy; and he healed them.

And THERE FOLLOWED HIM GREAT MULTITUDES OF PEOPLE from Galilee, and from Decapolis, and from Jerusalem, and from Judaea, and from beyond Jordan.

Matthew 4:23-25

5. We know that Jesus Christ was the Sun of Righteousness with healing in His wings because He had healing in all the major departments of medicine.

i. Eye Department

And when Jesus departed thence, two blind men followed him, crying, and saying, Thou Son of David, have mercy on us.

And when he was come into the house, the blind men came to him: and Jesus saith unto them, Believe ye that I am able to do this? They said unto him, Yea, Lord.

Then touched he their eyes, saying, According to your faith be it unto you. And THEIR EYES WERE OPENED; and Jesus straitly charged them, saying, See that no man know it.

Matthew 9:27-30

ii. Ear, Nose and Throat (ENT) Department

Jesus said unto him, If thou canst believe, all things are possible to him that believeth.

And straightway the father of the child cried out, and said with tears, Lord, I believe; help thou mine unbelief. When Jesus saw that the people came running together, he rebuked the foul spirit, saying unto him, THOU DUMB AND DEAF SPIRIT, I charge thee, come out of him, and enter no more into him. And the spirit cried, and rent him sore, and came out of him: and he was as one dead; insomuch that many said, He is dead. But Jesus took him by the hand, and lifted him up; and he arose.

Mark 9:23-27

iii. Psychiatry Department

And they came over unto the other side of the sea, into the country of the Gadarenes.

And when he was come out of the ship, immediately there met him out of the tombs a man with an unclean spirit,

Who had his dwelling among the tombs; and no man could bind him, no, not with chains:

Because that he had been often bound with fetters and chains, and the chains had been plucked asunder by him, and the fetters broken in pieces: neither could any man tame him.

And always, night and day, he was in the mountains, and in the tombs, crying, and cutting himself with stones.

But when he saw Jesus afar off, he ran and worshipped him,

And cried with a loud voice, and said, what have I to do with thee, Jesus, thou Son of the most high God? I adjure thee by God, that thou torment me not.

For he said unto him, Come out of the man, thou unclean spirit.

And he asked him, what is thy name? And he answered, saying, my name is Legion: for we are many.

And he besought him much that he would not send them away out of the country. Now there was there nigh unto the mountains a great herd of swine feeding.

And all the devils besought him, saying, send us into the swine, that we may enter into them. And forthwith Jesus gave them leave. And the unclean spirits went out, and entered into the swine: and the herd ran violently down a steep place into the sea, (they were about two thousand;) and were choked in the sea.

And they that fed the swine fled, and told it in the city, and in the country. And they went out to see what it was that was done.

And they come to Jesus, and see him that was possessed with the devil, and had the legion, sitting, and clothed, and in his right mind: and they were afraid.

Mark 5:1-15

iv. Gynaecology Department

And a certain woman, which had an issue of blood twelve years,

And had suffered many things of many physicians, and had spent all that she had, and was nothing bettered, but rather grew worse,

When she had heard of Jesus, came in the press behind, and touched his garment.

For she said, If I may touch but his clothes, I shall be whole.

And straightway THE FOUNTAIN OF HER BLOOD WAS DRIED UP; and she felt in her body that she was healed of that plague.

Mark 5:25-29

v. Orthopaedics Department

Some men came, bringing to him a paralytic, carried by four of them.

Since they could not get him to Jesus because of the crowd they made an opening in the roof above Jesus and, after digging through it, lowered the mat the PARALYZED MAN was lying on.

When Jesus saw their faith, he said to the paralytic, "Son, your sins are forgiven."

Mark 2:3-5 (NIV)

vi. Paediatrics Department

The nobleman saith unto him, Sir, come down ere MY CHILD die.

Jesus saith unto him, Go thy way; thy son liveth. And the man believed the word that Jesus had spoken unto him, and he went his way. And as he was now going down, his servants met him, and told him, saying, Thy son liveth.

John 4:49-51

vii. Dermatology Department

And there came a leper to him, beseeching him, and kneeling down to him, and saying unto him, If thou wilt, thou canst make me clean.

And Jesus, moved with compassion, put forth his hand, and touched him, and saith unto him, I will; be thou clean.

And as soon as he had spoken, immediately the LEPROSY departed from him, and he was cleansed.

Mark 1:40-42

viii. Pathology Department

Then they took away the stone from the place where the dead was laid. And Jesus lifted up his eyes, and said, Father, I thank thee that thou hast heard me.

And I knew that thou hearest me always: but because of the people which stand by I said it, that they may believe that thou hast sent me.

And when he thus had spoken, he cried with a loud voice, Lazarus, come forth.

And HE THAT WAS DEAD CAME FORTH, bound hand and foot with graveclothes: and his face was bound about with a napkin. Jesus saith unto them, Loose him, and let him go.

John 11:41-44

6. You must receive the Sun of Righteousness so that you can be born again and be saved.

Christ died on the cross and shed His blood so we could have forgiveness for all our sins through His blood. Thank God for the blood of Jesus!

> In whom we have redemption THROUGH HIS BLOOD, THE FORGIVENESS of sins, according to the riches of his grace;
>
> Ephesians 1:7

By His Stripes
We Are Healed

Who hath believed our report? And to whom is the arm of the Lord revealed?

For he shall grow up before him as a tender plant, and as a root out of a dry ground: he hath no form nor comeliness; and when we shall see him, there is no beauty that we should desire him.

He is despised and rejected of men; a man of sorrows, and acquainted with grief: and we hid as it were our faces from him; he was despised, and we esteemed him not.

Surely he hath borne our griefs, and carried our sorrows: yet we did esteem him stricken, smitten of God, and afflicted.But he was wounded for our transgressions, he was bruised for our iniquities: the chastisement of our peace was upon him; and with his stripes we are healed.

Isaiah 53:1-5

1. **Who hath believed our report?** How many people will believe in Jesus Christ? Believing in Jesus Christ will bring you salvation and healing.

    Who hath believed our report? And to whom is the arm of the Lord revealed?

    Isaiah 53:1

2. **He hath no form nor comeliness; and when we shall see Him, there is no beauty that we should desire Him. Jesus was ordinary.** Jesus was not special or attractive. He was an ordinary carpenter.

    For he shall grow up before him as a tender plant, and as a root out of a dry ground: he hath no form nor comeliness; and when we shall see him, there is no beauty that we should desire him.

    Isaiah 53:2

3. **He was despised and rejected of men.**

    Jesus was despised and rejected by the Jews when he was exchanged for Barabbas.

    He is despised and rejected of men; a man of sorrows, and acquainted with grief: and we hid as it were our faces from him; he was despised, and we esteemed him not.

    Isaiah 53:3

4. **He was bruised for our iniquities: the chastisement of our peace was upon Him.**

    Jesus was nailed to the cross. He had a crown of thorns and He was beaten because of our sins.

    But he was wounded for our transgressions, he was bruised for our iniquities: the chastisement of our peace was upon him;...

    Isaiah 53:5

5.   With His stripes we are healed.

...with his stripes we are healed

Isaiah 53:5

Jesus received one stripe for every known disease of man:

1. He received a stripe for malaria and all other fevers.

2. He received a stripe for all skin diseases like leprosy.

3. He received a stripe for all eye diseases like blindness.

4. He received a stripe for all ear diseases such as deafness.

5. He received a stripe for all lung diseases like tuberculosis and pneumonia.

6. He received a stripe for all bone diseases such as arthritis.

7. He received a stripe for all pancreatic diseases like diabetes.

8. He received a stripe for all abdominal diseases like ulcer, worms, stomach pains, constipation and diarrhoea.

9. He received a stripe for all diseases in the breast.

10. He received a stripe for all diseases of the womb like bleeding and fibroids.

11. He received a stripe for all injuries.

12. He received a stripe for all neurological diseases like trembling, Parkinson's disease.

13. He received a stripe for all poisonous bites such as snakebites.

14. He received a stripe for all psychiatric diseases such as epilepsy and madness.

15. He received a stripe for all liver diseases such as hepatitis.

16. He received a stripe for all diseases of the hair such as baldness or alopecia.

17. He received a stripe for all diseases of the testes such as low sperm count.

18. He received a stripe for all diseases of the penis such as impotence, double penis and epispadis.

19. He received a stripe for all dental problems.

20. He received a stripe for all diseases of the heart.

21. He received a stripe for all diseases of the blood like leukaemia.

22. He received a stripe for all sexually transmitted diseases like gonorrhoea and syphilis.

23. He received a stripe for all urinary diseases such as cystitis.

24. He received a stripe for all ovarian diseases such as ovarian cysts.

25. He received a stripe for all types of bodily pains.

26. He received a stripe for all diseases of the brain such as headaches, brain tumours and Alzheimer's.

27. He received a stripe for all diseases of the kidney.

28. He received a stripe for all diseases of the muscles such as tumours of the muscles and general weakness.

29. He received a stripe for all diseases of the immune system such as allergies.

30. He received a stripe for all diseases related to weight such as obesity.

31. He received a stripe for all diseases of the blood vessels like hypertension and aneurysms.

32. He received a stripe for all diseases of the nose such as colds and sinusitis.

33. He received a stripe for all diseases of the throat such as sore throat, cancer, goitre and tonsillitis.

34. He received a stripe for all diseases caused by bacteria such as appendicitis, cystitis, and pneumonitis.

35. He received a stripe for all fungal diseases such as Candidiasis and ringworm infections.

36. He received a stripe for all viral diseases such as small pox, Ebola virus and Zika virus.

37. He received a stripe for all parasitic diseases such as schistosomiasis, onchocerciasis, and elephantiasis.

38. He received a stripe for all cancers.

39. He received a stripe for all diseases not diagnosable by man.

40. He received a stripe for all new diseases like HIV.

Seek Ye the Lord While He May Be Found

Seek ye the Lord while he may be found, call ye upon him while he is near:

Let the wicked forsake his way, and the unrighteous man his thoughts: and let him return unto the Lord, and he will have mercy upon him; and to our God, for he will abundantly pardon.

For my thoughts are not your thoughts, neither are your ways my ways, saith the Lord. For as the heavens are higher than the earth, so are my ways higher than your ways, and my thoughts than your thoughts.

Isaiah 55:6-9

1. Seek ye the Lord when He may be found. You will find the Lord in your youth. After the rich man went to hell, he could no longer find God. God could not be found at that time.

Remember now thy Creator in the days of thy youth, while the evil days come not, nor the years draw nigh, when thou shalt say, I have no pleasure in them;

Ecclesiastes 12:1

2.   Seek ye the Lord at the time when He may be found, before you become hardened by life's experiences.

Remember now thy Creator in the days of thy youth, WHILE THE EVIL DAYS COME NOT, nor the years draw nigh, when thou shalt say, I have no pleasure in them;

Ecclesiastes 12:1

3.   Seek ye the Lord when He may be found, before it is too late, before you die.

But Abraham said, Son, REMEMBER that thou in thy lifetime receivedst thy good things, and likewise Lazarus evil things: but now he is comforted, and thou art tormented.

Luke 16:25

4.   It is time to turn away from sin, repent, make a U-turn and come to the Lord.

Let the wicked FORSAKE HIS WAY, and the unrighteous man his thoughts: and let him return unto the Lord, and he will have mercy upon him; and to our God, for he will abundantly pardon.

Isaiah 55:7

5.   This is the time that God is showing mercy.

Let the wicked forsake his way, and the unrighteous man his thoughts: and let him return unto the Lord, and HE WILL HAVE MERCY upon him; and to our God, for he will abundantly pardon.

Isaiah 55:7

6.   Because His ways are so different and His thoughts are so different, it is important to believe and receive the preaching when you hear it, even if it sounds improbable.

For my thoughts are not your thoughts, neither are your ways my ways, saith the Lord.

For as the heavens are higher than the earth, so are my ways higher than your ways, and my thoughts than your thoughts.

Isaiah 55:8-9

There is a hell to be shunned and a punishment so severe that you cannot possibly imagine it actually exists. So seek the Lord when He may be found.

SALVATION MESSAGE 106:

Unto Us a Child is Born

For unto us a child is born, unto us a son is given: and the government shall be upon his shoulder: and his name shall be called Wonderful, Counsellor, The mighty God, The everlasting Father, The Prince of Peace.

Isaiah 9:6

1.   "The government shall be upon his shoulder".

This prophecy was given 800 years before Jesus was born. The prophecy said that the government would be upon His shoulder. This means that Jesus shall take over the ruling and the governing of this world. This is Good News because all over the world, people are wondering what is happening to their governments. Every country should be crying for Jesus to come and take over the ruling of this world.

2.   He will be called "Wonderful". Why would this child be called "Wonderful"?

It was predicted that Jesus would be full of wonders. That is why He was called "Wonderful". Jesus did many wonderful things! He walked on water! Have you seen anyone walking on water before?

Jesus was called "Wonderful" because He healed the sick. Jesus healed those who could not hear. He healed a woman who had been bleeding for 12 years. A woman should bleed for 3 to 5 days but this one had been bleeding for 12 years. Jesus met a mad man living in the cemetery and healed him.

3. He shall be called Counsellor.

Jesus spoke with great wisdom. He spoke the words of a great Counsellor. He said amazing things no one could say. "I am the way, the truth, and the life". "You can only come to the Father by me". "I am the bread of life."

4. He shall be called Mighty God.

He did what only God could do. Lazarus was dead for four days and he was resurrected. All the miracles of Jesus prove that He was a mighty God in our midst.

5. He shall be called Everlasting Father.

Tonight if you will come to Him He will be your Father.

Come, Let Us
Reason Together

Come now, and let us reason together, saith the Lord: though your sins be as scarlet, they shall be as white as snow; though they be red like crimson, they shall be as wool.

Isaiah 1:18

Think about the wonderful creation we are a part of! Think of the galaxies!

Imagine that such a mighty God, who created all things, is inviting you to have a discussion with Him.

The Man Who Went to Heaven

One day a man fell from a height on a construction site. They thought he was dead but he was not. He was taken to the hospital and was in a coma for some days. His pastor was called and the pastor went to the hospital and prayed for him and he recovered. One day he came to church and gave this testimony.

He said that when he fell from the height, he died and went to Heaven. He said Heaven is very nice and no one who goes there wants to come back. He was so happy to see Jesus. Jesus told him, he had to go back to earth, but he did not like the idea.

So Jesus took him to a curtain and pulled it aside. The dead man heard his pastor's voice. The pastor was praying for him in the hospital. In the prayer, the pastor explained to God why the man should not die yet. The pastor told God that the man was important to him and his church. He explained to the Lord that it was unreasonable for God to take him from earth at that time. Jesus explained to the dead man that his pastor was reasoning with Him and He would have to let him go back to the earth.

Tonight, God is asking you to come and reason with Him like the pastor was doing!

1.   Come let us reason with God: Let's think about the future.

Where will you be in 70 years? Where will you be in a 100 years? Have you thought about that? We must be wiser than chickens that do not know that they are about to be slaughtered.

The Short-Sighted Chickens

There were once some chickens that lived on a farm. Their owner used to feed them daily and would sometimes even bring in a vet to care for them. One day, one of the chickens went to town and saw restaurants like KFC, Chicken Lickin' and Chicken Supreme. The chicken ran back to tell its friends that their body parts were for sale in town. The chicken was frightened and started fretting about what would happen to them. However the other chickens would not listen to this chicken that had been to town. These other chickens were simply happy to have food, water, shelter and medicine.

Indeed, we human beings must be wiser than that. Where will you go when you die? Where will you be after this life? That is why God is asking to reason with you. Where are your fathers, your friends and all those who have died already? Where did they go? They are at a place where they cannot contact us physically.

2. Come let us reason with God: You are a dirty sinner and you need salvation.

How many of you have told lies before? How many of you have stolen something before? How many of you have committed fornication before?

3. Come let us reason together: It is a miracle to be forgiven.

God says that though your sins are red like crimson, He will clean your sins and make you white. It is a reasonable offer.

Only Christianity promises you the washing away of your sins.

4. Come let us reason together: What are your options if you say "no" to Jesus?

If you say "no" to God, how will you get rid of your sins? What will you do when you stand before Him after you die? What are your options if you say "no" to Jesus? Whilst you were in sin, Christ loved you and died for you. Remember, you can escape from men but not from God. You may murder someone and escape from the police, but you cannot escape from God when you sin.

5. Come let us reason together: God commended His love to us when we were still filthy sinners.

What will happen if you reject such great love?

6. Come let us reason together: Without the shedding of blood there is no remission of sins. Only the blood of Jesus can wash away your terrible sins.

And almost all things are by the law purged with blood; and without shedding of blood is no remission.

Hebrews 9:22

For the life of the flesh is in the blood: and I have given it to you upon the altar to make an atonement for your souls: for it is the blood that maketh an atonement for the soul.

Leviticus 17:11

7. **Come let us reason together: The best thing to do is to receive Jesus Christ today. God sent Jesus to die on the cross for us. The blood of Jesus has washed our sins away.**

Yet to all who did receive him, to those who believed in his name, he gave the right to become children of God –

John 1:12 (NIV)

Behold, the Lord's Hand Is Not Shortened

Behold, the Lord's hand is not so short that it cannot save; nor is His ear so dull that it cannot hear.

But your iniquities have made a separation between you and your God, and your sins have hidden His face from you so that He does not hear.

Isaiah 59:1-2 (NASB)

1.   **Our God is not a stone! Our God is not a tree! Our God is not a river! Our God is alive!**

The Insecticide Man

In some places, there are several temples for different gods. People worship gods of wood, gods of silver and gods of stone.

One day, I met a businessman who was in the business of manufacturing insecticides. His factory made insecticides for wall geckos. He had become prosperous from this business.

One day, a lady came to his factory to buy some of the insecticides that killed wall geckos. This lady was the cleaner and keeper at a shrine for one of the gods in the country.

The lady needed medicine to kill wall geckos because the gods of silver, gold and wood were not answering prayer. She suspected that a wall gecko had gone into the ears of the gods, making them not hear and answer the prayers that were offered to them.

Your God is not a piece of wood! Your God is not an idol! Your God can hear! His ears are neither heavy nor blocked by wall geckos!

2. Why are our prayers not answered sometimes?

Our prayers are not answered because our iniquities have separated God from us. Our sins have hidden His Face from us! Our God is affected by our sins. The sins of our hands, the sins of our tongues and the sins of our mouths separate us from God.

3. What did Jesus come to earth for?

When Jesus was born, a lot of questions were asked; for example - what is He coming to do? The Bible says of Jesus:

And she shall bring forth a son, and thou shalt call his name Jesus: for HE SHALL SAVE HIS PEOPLE FROM THEIR SINS.

Matthew 1:21

4. Our sins are our greatest problems.

God told Adam and Eve,

But of the tree of the knowledge of good and evil, thou shalt not eat of it: for in the day that thou eatest thereof thou shalt surely die.

Genesis 2:17

Every time you sin, you draw evil spirits into your life. When Miriam criticised Moses, she developed leprosy (Numbers 12:1-10).

5.   **Every time you sin, you draw death towards yourself.** When Adam and Eve sinned, they drew death to themselves.

But of the tree of the knowledge of good and evil, thou shalt not eat of it: for in the day that thou eatest thereof thou shalt surely die.

Genesis 2:17

6.   **Thank God for the Good News – the Gospel.** Turn away from your sins and you will discover that God's hand is not shortened. Your prayers will be answered when you turn away from your sins.

And she shall bring forth a son, and thou shalt call his name Jesus: for HE SHALL SAVE HIS PEOPLE FROM THEIR SINS.

Matthew 1:21

Jesus did not come to give us electricity, democracy, running water or to build universities – He came to save us from our sins.

7.   **Come to Jesus tonight. Don't wait till it is too late!**

There is a Way that Seems Right to a Man

There is a way which seemeth right unto a man, but the end thereof are the ways of death.

Proverbs 14:12

1. Amassing wealth may seem to be the right way but the end thereof is the way of death. It is not the way to Heaven or to God.

Do not weary yourself to gain wealth, Cease from your consideration of it. When you set your eyes on it, it is gone. For wealth certainly makes itself wings, like an eagle that flies toward the heavens.

Proverbs 23:4-5 (NASB)

He that hasteth to be rich hath an evil eye, and considereth not that poverty shall come upon him.

Proverbs 28:22

RICHES PROFIT NOT IN THE DAY OF WRATH: but righteousness delivereth from death. The righteousness of the perfect shall direct his way: but the wicked shall fall by his own wickedness.

Proverbs 11:4-5

By thy great wisdom and by thy traffick hast thou increased thy riches, AND THINE HEART IS LIFTED UP BECAUSE OF THY RICHES:

Therefore thus saith the Lord GOD; because thou hast set thine heart as the heart of God;

Behold, therefore I will bring strangers upon thee, the terrible of the nations: and they shall draw their swords against the beauty of thy wisdom, and they shall defile thy brightness.

They shall bring thee down to the pit, and thou shalt die the deaths of them that are slain in the midst of the seas.

Ezekiel 28:5-8

2.   **"Eat and drink, for tomorrow we die" may seem to be the right way but the end thereof is death. A life of eating and drinking with the mind that "tomorrow we will die anyway" is not the way to Heaven or to God.**

And behold joy and gladness, slaying oxen, and killing sheep, eating flesh, and drinking wine: LET US EAT AND DRINK; FOR TO MORROW WE SHALL DIE.

And it was revealed in mine ears by the LORD of hosts, Surely this iniquity shall not be purged from you till ye die, saith the Lord GOD of hosts.

Isaiah 22:13-14

3.   **Becoming proud because of your achievements may seem to be the right way. But it is not the right way. The end thereof is the way of death.**

Their land also is full of silver and gold, neither is there any end of their treasures; their land is also full of horses, neither is there any end of their chariots:

Their land also is full of idols; THEY WORSHIP THE WORK OF THEIR OWN HANDS, that which their own fingers have made:

Isaiah 2:7-8

4. **Giving lip service to God may seem to be the right way. The end thereof is the way of death. Being religious is not the way to Heaven.** Following traditions and singing hymns without knowing God is not the way to Heaven.

He answered and said unto them, Well hath Esaias prophesied of you hypocrites, as it is written, This people honoureth me with their lips, but their heart is far from me.

Howbeit in vain do they worship me, teaching for doctrines the commandments of men.

Mark 7:6-7

Not every one that saith unto me, Lord, Lord, shall enter into the kingdom of heaven; but he that doeth the will of my Father which is in heaven.

Many will say to me in that day, Lord, Lord, have we not prophesied in thy name? And in thy name have we cast out devils? And in thy name done many wonderful works?

Matthew 7:21-22

5. **Following other religions may seem to be the right way, but the end thereof is the way of death! Following any other religion apart from Christianity is not the way to Heaven.** False religions offer many other ways that are not true.

For there is one God, and one mediator between God and men, the man Christ Jesus;

1 Timothy 2:5

Neither is there salvation in any other: for there is none other name under heaven given among men, whereby we must be saved.

Acts 4:12

And to Jesus the mediator of the new covenant, and to the blood of sprinkling, that speaketh better things than that of Abel.

Hebrews 12:24

6.   Doing good works may seem to be the right way but the end thereof is the way of death. Being a good person and doing good works is not the way to Heaven.

Good works will not take you to Heaven. The only way is through the Blood of Jesus! There is a life that seems to be the life, but Jesus Christ is *the* Life – He gives abundant life.

But we are all as an unclean thing, and all our righteousnesses are as filthy rags; and we all do fade as a leaf; and our iniquities, like the wind, have taken us away.

Isaiah 64:6

As it is written, There is none righteous, no, not one:

Romans 3:10

7.   No one, including you, can come to the Father except through Jesus. "No one" means presidents, your mother, your friends, your brothers, and your teachers.

Come to Jesus today, come to the cross, and come to the blood, if you want to get to the Father!

541

Jesus saith unto him, I am the way, the truth, and the life: no man cometh unto the Father, but by me.

John 14:6

For there is one God, and one mediator between God and men, the man Christ Jesus; who gave himself a ransom for all, to be testified in due time.

1 Timothy 2:5-6

Neither is there salvation in any other: for there is none other name under heaven given among men, whereby we must be saved.

Acts 4:12

Belshazzar and the Great Feast

BELSHAZZAR THE KING MADE A GREAT FEAST TO A THOUSAND OF HIS LORDS, AND DRANK WINE before the thousand. Belshazzar, whiles he tasted the wine, commanded to bring the golden and silver vessels which his father Nebuchadnezzar had taken out of the temple which was in Jerusalem; that the king, and his princes, his wives, and his concubines, might drink therein. Then they brought the golden vessels that were taken out of the temple of the house of God which was at Jerusalem; and the king, and his princes, his wives, and his concubines, drank in them. They drank wine, and praised the gods of gold, and of silver, of brass, of iron, of wood, and of stone. In the same hour came forth fingers of a man's hand, and wrote over against the candlestick upon the plaister of the wall of the king's palace: and the king saw the part of the hand that wrote.

Daniel 5:1-5

1. **Judgment day is coming for the men of the world who have gone astray and given themselves to all forms of pleasure and partying.** Belshazzar made a great feast. He wasted his life away by feasting and playing the fool.

Belshazzar the king made a great feast to a thousand of his lords, and DRANK WINE BEFORE THE THOUSAND.

Daniel 5:1

2. **Judgment day is coming for the men of the world who have gone astray and given themselves to alcoholism and drugs.** Belshazzar gave himself to drinking in public. The Holy Bible warns us about the dangers of drinking alcohol.

Wine is a mocker, strong drink is raging: and whosoever is deceived thereby is not wise.

Proverbs 20:1

Who hath woe? Who hath sorrow? Who hath contentions? Who hath babbling? Who hath wounds without cause? Who hath redness of eyes? They that tarry long at the wine; they that go to seek mixed wine.

Proverbs 23:29-30

Woe unto him that giveth his neighbour drink, that puttest thy bottle to him, and makest him drunken also, that thou mayest look on their nakedness!

Habakkuk 2:15

3. **Judgment day is coming for the men of the world who have given themselves to blaspheme God and His house.**

Some people are not content just to practice immorality and loose living. They want to make fun of God and God's people. Belshazzar decided to drink from the vessels in the temple. He could have drunk from his cup but wanted to ridicule sacred things. Be careful as you make fun of God, the Holy Spirit and the church.

> Belshazzar, whiles he tasted the wine, COMMANDED TO BRING THE GOLDEN AND SILVER VESSELS WHICH HIS FATHER NEBUCHADNEZZAR HAD TAKEN OUT OF THE TEMPLE which was in Jerusalem; that the king, and his princes, his wives, and his concubines, might drink therein.

> Then they brought the golden vessels that were taken out of the temple of the house of God which was at Jerusalem; and the king, and his princes, his wives, and his concubines, drank in them.

> They drank wine, and praised the gods of gold, and of silver, of brass, of iron, of wood, and of stone.

> Daniel 5:2-4

I once witnessed to an unbeliever. I told him that he needed Jesus. He got so angry with me for talking to him about God. "Who do you think you are?" he asked. "Do you think you are better than me? What makes you think that I don't know God?"

I apologised, but he would not be appeased and threatened to beat me up physically for talking to him that way. Some months later, as he lay dying on a hospital bed, he called for me to pray for him.

People are not afraid of God and bring railing accusations against God's servants. To some people, every pastor is a thief and every minister is a crook. It is sad that ministers of the gospel are denigrated in this way.

One day, I visited a large church in a certain country. This church had very little parking space on their premises, so the church members would park on the street in front of neighbouring houses.

One Sunday morning an irate neighbour charged out of his front door to confront a church member who had parked in front of his house. After shouting and railing insults, he drove them away from the front of his house. But as he walked towards his house, his heart stopped beating and he dropped dead to the ground outside his house whilst I was preaching in the main service.

By that evening there were canopies in front of his house, to receive mourners who had heard of his sudden death.

Men who insult the church and do not have any respect for God or His people must watch out because judgment day is coming.

4. **Judgment day is coming for men of the world who have gone astray and have given themselves to idol worship.**

"They... praised the gods of gold, and of silver ... and of stone". God warns against idolatry.

They drank wine, and PRAISED THE GODS OF GOLD, AND OF SILVER, OF BRASS, OF IRON, OF WOOD, AND OF STONE.

Daniel 5:4

Thou shalt not make unto thee any graven image, or any likeness of any thing that is in heaven above, or that is in the earth beneath, or that is in the water under the earth:

Thou shalt not bow down thyself to them, nor serve them: for I the LORD thy God am a jealous God, visiting the iniquity of the fathers upon the children unto the third and fourth generation of them that hate me;

Exodus 20:4-5

They shall be turned back, they shall be greatly ashamed, that trust in graven images, that say to the molten images, ye are our gods.

Isaiah 42:17

He that sacrificeth unto any god, save unto the LORD only, he shall be utterly destroyed.

Exodus 22:20

5. **You can escape the judgment day by repenting and turning away from your sinful life.**

For God so loved the world, that he gave his only begotten Son, that whosoever believeth in him should not perish, but have everlasting life. ⁷For God sent not his Son into the world to condemn the world; but that the world through him might be saved.

John 3:16-17

References

1-1. Death, Sentenced. "Sentenced To Death". *Theinfobasket.blogspot. com.* N.p., 2017. Web. 25 Jan. 2017 retrieved from https://theinfobasket.blogspot.com/2014/05/sentenced-to-death.html

2-2. "Sermon: Branded By Whom?". *Epreacher.org.* Web. 25 Jan. 2017 retrieved from http://epreacher.org/sermons/06-05-05am.html

3-3. "You Cannot Escape Judgement..." - The Apostolic Church - Ghana | Facebook". *Facebook.com.* N.p., 2017. Web. 25 Jan. 2017 retrieved from https://www.facebook.com/asiakwadistrict/posts/563569733675839

4-4. Ibid,. 288-289

5-5. "Parable Of The River". *Donaldsona.tripod.com.* N.p., 2017. Web. 25 Jan. 2017 retrieved from http://donaldsona.tripod.com/Drama14.html

6-6. Hudson, Trevor and Dallas Willard. *Invitations To Abundant Life.* 1st ed. Cape Town: New Holland Pub., 2010. Print.